RETHINKING FRANK LLOYD WRIGHT

HISTORY, RECEPTION, PRESERVATION

RETHINKING FRANK LLOYD WRIGHT

EDITED BY **NEIL LEVINE**
& RICHARD LONGSTRETH

University of Virginia Press | CHARLOTTESVILLE AND LONDON

University of Virginia Press
© 2023 by the Rector and Visitors of the University of Virginia
All rights reserved
Printed in the United States of America on acid-free paper

First published 2023

9 8 7 6 5 4 3 2 1

Library of Congress Cataloging-in-Publication Data

Names: Levine, Neil, editor. | Longstreth, Richard W., editor.
Title: Rethinking Frank Lloyd Wright : history, reception, preservation / edited by
    Neil Levine and Richard Longstreth.
Description: Charlottesville : University of Virginia Press, 2022. | Includes
    bibliographical references and index.
Identifiers: LCCN 2022036160 (print) | LCCN 2022036161 (ebook) | ISBN
    9780813947693 (hardcover) | ISBN 9780813947709 (ebook)
Subjects: LCSH: Wright, Frank Lloyd, 1867–1959—Appreciation. | Wright, Frank Lloyd,
    1867–1959—Influence. | Architecture—Conservation and restoration.
Classification: LCC NA737.W7 R48 2022 (print) | LCC NA737.W7 (ebook) |
    DDC 720.92—dc23/eng/20220902
LC record available at https://lccn.loc.gov/2022036160
LC ebook record available at https://lccn.loc.gov/2022036161

Cover art: Wright in his studio at Talisien, 1938. (AP photo)

For Roland Reiseley, Tom Schmidt, the late
Susan Jacobs Lockhart, and the late John Thorpe,
who have contributed enormously, and in many ways,
to the Frank Lloyd Wright Building Conservancy's mission
to preserve the architect's work and advance knowledge
of its significance

CONTENTS

The idea for this book came from the need to counter the marginalization of Frank Lloyd Wright scholarship and return it to the mainstream of modern architectural history, where it belongs. The intellectual questions involved in this inquiry are treated at some length in the first chapter and, again, in the afterword, although they underlie in different ways all the essays in the book. Falling under the three general categories of historiography, critical reception, and preservation, the essays variously contemplate how and on what bases can we reassess the meaning of Wright's architecture and its broad impact over the past century and a quarter? How broad was that impact, in effect, and in what ways did it manifest itself? How have our perceptions of Wright's work changed and evolved over time, and how have these affected the ways we talk about his buildings, his theoretical concerns, and why and how we choose to preserve and restore his buildings? Finally, how have the issues raised by the preservation of Wright's work intersected with the preservation movement as a whole?

The ten authors initially came together in a symposium titled "Rethinking Frank Lloyd Wright at 150" that was organized by the Frank Lloyd Wright Building Conservancy on the occasion of Wright's sesquicentennial. It took place at the Museum of Modern Art in New York in the fall of 2017 to coincide with the exhibition "Unpacking the Archive: Frank Lloyd Wright at 150," which was designed to celebrate the transfer of the architect's archives from Taliesin West in Scottsdale, Arizona, to the Avery Fine Arts & Architectural Library at Columbia University and the Museum of Modern Art in New York.

Four of the contributors (Bergdoll, Levine, Longstreth, and Quinan) are or have been members of the conservancy's board of directors. However, all the views expressed in this book are those of their respective authors and should not in any way be construed as reflecting an official view of the conservancy's leadership or membership more generally. The conservancy encourages responsible inquiry about the work of Wright and related subjects. Discussion of and debate on differing viewpoints are a part of that process, and the conservancy welcomes such exchanges in the name of the advancement of knowledge. While the conservancy's board has been kept apprised of this book, it has neither reviewed nor sanctioned its content. The project has been an entirely independent undertaking.

We want to thank Janet Halsted and Barbara Gordon for the support the Building Conservancy gave to the symposium. Joel Hoglund's role was critical for its success. His contributions ranged from the most time-consuming and complex details of logistics and organization to the stunning graphic design of the poster and brochure. At the Museum of Modern Art, we thank Barry Bergdoll and Peter Reed along with Nadine Dosa, Arièle Dionne-Krosnick, Carson Parish, and Hunter Webb. Janet Parks and Jennifer Gray of the Avery Library were, as ever, generous with their time and advice.

Our deepest appreciation goes to Tony Maddalena, a longtime and enthusiastic member of the Frank Lloyd Wright Building Conservancy, whose Maddalena Group at Morgan Stanley generously supported both the symposium out of which this book evolved and the illustration costs of the book itself. We cannot thank him enough.

Finally, we are grateful to Boyd Zenner; her successor, Mark Mones; and others at the University of Virginia Press for the careful attention they have paid to the production of this volume at every stage. They have made what could have been an arduous task a pleasure.

RETHINKING FRANK LLOYD WRIGHT

NEIL LEVINE

Introduction

Thoughts on Rethinking Frank Lloyd Wright

To anyone interested in Modern architecture as a cultural phenomenon—and despite all that has been written about him—Frank Lloyd Wright remains a profound enigma. It is not that his work has been unstudied or that his life and career have gone undocumented. On the contrary. There have probably been more books and articles about Wright than about any other twentieth-century architect, not to speak of several television and radio documentaries, an opera, and even a notorious roman à clef and Hollywood film based on it produced during his lifetime (*The Fountainhead,* 1943/1949).

The problem lies elsewhere. At the heart of the enigma is a paradox of critical reception unique in the history of Modern art and architecture. It is impossible to think of another figure in these spheres who possesses Wright's acknowledged stature as celebrated in the popular realm but is so largely ignored or dismissed by the academic and professional elite. For the so-called lay audience, Wright is as close to the "greatest architect of all time" as he himself told Henry-Russell Hitchcock he would be.[1] No museum exhibitions of architecture attain his attendance figures, and few buildings can match the public interest in his Fallingwater or Guggenheim Museum. It is commonly said that more visitors come to see that museum's building than the exhibitions installed in it. No other modern architect or artist has spawned a similar industry of branded tchotchkes, ranging from coffee mugs and house numbers to neckties, bookmarks, and birdhouses, produced and yearly updated by the Frank Lloyd Wright Foundation's licensing program.

By contrast, in the leading schools of architecture, professional meetings, and journals of theory and criticism, Wright is nearly invisible. Toward the end of his life and in the years immediately after his death in 1959, his late work was often devastatingly criticized. This was even more true of that of his successor firm, Taliesin Associated Architects. Following a line of criticism already established by the likes of Sigfried Giedion and Nikolaus Pevsner in the 1920s and 1930s, and especially taken up by the important cadre of British architects and critics who came to prominence in the late 1950s and

1960s, nothing Wright did after 1910 was considered of much value, and what he did up until then was essentially regarded as but a prelude to or anticipation of the so-called Modern Movement. Whether his post-1910 work was dismissed as decorative, out of touch with the times, or, even worse, pure kitsch, it was held to be irrelevant to contemporary purposes and ideas.

In his seminal 1980 *Modern Architecture: A Critical History,* which has served as a primary text for architecture students around the world, Kenneth Frampton wrote of the "folly" of Fallingwater's cantilevers, the "ultra-kitsch" of the Marin County Civic Center, and the "science-fiction architecture" for "some extraterrestrial species" of Wright's later projects in general.[2] By 2002 the notion of Wright's irrelevancy, not to speak of his toxicity, led to his virtual exclusion from the next important history of modern architecture by another Britisher, Alan Colquhoun, a leading theorist, critic, and distinguished professor in Princeton University's School of Architecture. In his *Modern Architecture,* published in the prestigious Oxford History of Art series, Wright was given only two and a quarter pages of text. Astoundingly, neither the Larkin Building or Unity Temple, nor Fallingwater, Johnson Wax, or the Guggenheim Museum was even mentioned. The brief discussion of Wright as an Arts and Crafts "regional Mid-western domestic architect of rural innocence" stops in 1909, and he and his work play no role whatsoever in the ensuing history of twentieth-century architecture.[3]

Why this critical dismissal, and why the paradox of Wright's divergent reception? The group of distinguished architectural historians whose essays follow will provide important answers and ways to rethink Wright. The authors were mainly chosen not because of their previous work on Wright—of which there is in most cases none, or at least none primarily on Wright—but because of their profound engagement with the issues of twentieth-century architecture in which, as they reveal, Wright played an important and instrumental role. They were initially gathered together to take part in a symposium organized by the Frank Lloyd Wright Building Conservancy held at the Museum of Modern Art in New York in the fall of 2017 on the occasion of the museum's exhibition celebrating the 150th anniversary of Wright's birth. In order to open the discourse as widely as possible, it was decided that none of the featured symposium speakers should have contributed to the show and its catalog.

The exhibition, "Unpacking the Archive: Frank Lloyd Wright at 150," more specifically celebrated, as its title suggests, the transfer of the architect's archive from its home in Wright's winter headquarters at Taliesin West in Scottsdale, Arizona, to the Avery Architectural and Fine Arts Library at Columbia University and the Museum of Modern Art. The intention there, as with the symposium and this book, was to turn a page in the discourse around

Wright facilitated by the move of the primary research materials from a relatively closed and isolated environment laden with enormous historic baggage to more "neutral," world-renowned institutions easily accessible to a wider group of students, scholars, and others. The hope, as here, is that the concerns of both an elite and lay audience can find common cause and produce new synergies.

By way of introduction, I would like to offer some of my own thoughts on what I have characterized as Wright's enigmatic and paradoxical status. The general critical dismissal of his work after 1910 as a significant force in the evolution of Modern architecture had few naysayers until the later 1930s, and even then only a handful. There are many reasons for this. The so-called International Style revealed a very different, more austere, more abstract, and more socially oriented form of architecture than Wright's was thought to be, one that could be related in principle to his earlier work but that appeared to have so transformed it that any relationship now seemed strained and distant. Furthermore, by the 1920s, when the purist, iconic forms of buildings by Oud, Le Corbusier, Mies, and others began to be seen and published, Wright's own work, as inconsiderable as it was at that time, had taken on a highly decorative, sometimes historicizing, and extremely romantic cast that removed it entirely from the avant-garde horizon established by the younger European modernists. There is the famous story, apparently apocryphal, of Philip Johnson telling Henry-Russell Hitchcock in 1931 that there was no reason even to consider Wright for inclusion in the "Modern Architecture: International Exhibition" to be held at the Museum of Modern Art in the following year since Wright was "dead"—as he certainly was, at least in the figurative sense of the word, in most critics' minds.

Wright had been outspokenly critical of his younger European peers for some time, but it was his reaction to the 1932 MoMA show—immediately before, during, and after it closed—that really set the stage for his self-imposed isolation from the mainstream of Modern architecture. His criticism of the European work and its defenders was acerbic, unrelenting, and often mean-spirited. It could even stoop to vulgarity, as when he insinuated that the architectural preferences of Hitchcock and Johnson had to do with their sexual preferences.[4] For Wright, the followers of the International Style were, as he often wrote, mere two-dimensional picture makers who lacked the sense of depth, both physical and emotional, that he and his work had. As his polemic continued on this track from the later 1930s into the 1950s, he opposed his brand of "organic architecture" to "modern architecture," thus extricating himself from the latter and thereby acknowledging his own distance from the contemporary scene.

Making all this worse was the animus Wright publicly expressed toward any and all in elite critical and professional circles who countered him or tried, objectively, to assess his place in current events. He could take no criticism and made that acutely evident to anyone who tried. This made his presence in the academic world almost a nonstarter since the academy is ultimately based on a type of intellectual give-and-take, discussion and revision, that Wright would not countenance. To an audience gathered to hear his counsel at the San Rafael High School in the late 1950s, he declared: "You learn nothing about architecture really worth knowing in school."[5] And to his own apprentices in the Taliesin Fellowship, whom he would never call students or consider to be learning architecture in a traditional, academic way, Wright warned: "When you go to be educated, you go up against a pile of rubbish, and you paw around in that scrap heap . . . and come out with nothing." The "educated man," he added in a populist slur, "is a menace to society."[6]

While Wright's anti-intellectualism and anti-elitism could superficially be seen as broadly participating in the populist context defined at the time by Richard Hofstadter in his *Anti-Intellectualism in American Life* (1966), it was never precisely assimilable to such easy categorization. Its particularity, coming from such a deeply admired artistic figure, made it sting that much more. As Philip Johnson noted, with a certain degree of sadness and perhaps even pity, toward the very end of Wright's life:

> Mr. Wright has been annoying me for some time. . . .
> He can have his opinions. . . .
> [But] I find annoying . . . his contempt . . . for all architecture that preceded him. Was he born full-blown from the head of Zeus that he could be the only architect that ever lived or ever will? . . .
> Then almost worse is the contempt for the people who are going to come after him—and this is where it hurts us most, we slightly younger, older architects. He is determined that there shall not be any architect after him.[7]

Wright protected himself from the outside world by creating his own intentionally self-sufficient community of architectural apprentices, the Taliesin Fellowship, way out in rural Wisconsin and the Arizona desert. Thus insulated from ideas and images of nonorganic architecture, Wright assumed the so-called principles of his designs could flourish in their own native soil, uncontaminated by nefarious outside (meaning academic and, especially, European) influence. But they didn't, and really couldn't. After the master's death, the self-reflexiveness of the endeavor at what Vincent Scully called "Wright's own inbred Taliesins" soon showed the signs of weakness and impoverishment endemic to such isolationist projects.[8] This universally perceived devolution of the Wright legacy led one critic, cited anonymously

NEIL LEVINE

in an early article by Michael Kimmelman of 1984, to ironize as following: "If it weren't for [the] Taliesin [Fellowship], Wright might well have been recognized as the greatest artist of this century."[9] The marketing of Wright-inspired products by the foundation continues to devalue the legacy further and undermine the artistic seriousness of their model with examples of kitsch that substantiate one of the most persistent criticisms of the architect's own later work.

Despite the short-lived critical respite Wright's work enjoyed from the 1940s into the early 1960s, based in part on the extraordinary conception and resolution of such buildings as Fallingwater, Johnson Wax, and the Guggenheim, the main lines of architectural discourse shifted inevitably and ineluctably away from Wright. While museum exhibitions still take place, Wright-branded products still sell, and books about his scandals and love life are still consumed, he has not yet made deep incursions in the historical and critical discourse of the twenty-first century. It is hoped that the move of the archives from Scottsdale to New York will generate the all-important seminars and Ph.D. dissertations that have kept thinking about the other major figures of Modern architecture relevant to a contemporary generation. The essays in this book represent a significant step in the much-needed effort to rethink Frank Lloyd Wright outside the insular framework he established for himself and his legacy, and in the broad context of the architectural culture he helped shape.

It is certainly not unusual for a protean figure such as Wright to demand to be judged on his own—sui generis, without reference to others, a singular genius. One need only think of Michelangelo or, in Wright's own century, Le Corbusier. Historians usually take the bait. It is not difficult since, as in these cases, there is so much significant work by the artist that one can easily disregard anything else. Also, the work is so seemingly self-generated, so independent, so integral, and so comprehensive that any reference to that of others may pale by comparison. And with Wright there was the even more powerful inhibiting factor of his own defensive personality and self-protective independence.

Once Wright established himself as an artist-architect with high ambitions, which is to say, by the late 1890s, he refused categorically to enter competitions; later, he refused just as categorically to be interviewed for jobs—both time-honored methods for architects to gain commissions by comparative means. He also generally refused to allow his work to be included in group exhibitions; when on the rare occasions he did, he made exorbitant demands on the curators to preserve his exclusivity, while often railing against their best-intentioned efforts. In one way or another the publications about Wright and exhibitions of his work during his lifetime reflect their subject's controlling hand. Those after his death reflect that of his defender and near-ventriloquist, Bruce Pfeiffer, who maintained the Frank Lloyd Wright Archives in Arizona until the recent move to New York. From that distant outpost, Pfeiffer churned out book after book embodying "His [Wright's] Living Voice," aiming to preserve his mentor as a living presence outside of and beyond the natural, historical course of events.[10] But the quasi-religious fervor of those who "touched the hem of his garment" could only last a human lifetime.

The nine essays that follow emerge from a new historical condition. Their purpose is neither to celebrate, to proselytize, nor to denigrate their protean subject. They were not construed to prove Wright's "relevance" to contemporary practice nor to deny that either. Aiming at some objective form of reality, they deal, broadly speaking, with historiography, critical reception, influence, intentionality, preservation, and cultural significance. While only one of the authors, Jack Quinan, is known primarily for his work on Wright, all have been deeply invested in charting and explaining the evolution of Modern architecture in which Wright played such an enormous role. The first two essays take up in highly original ways one of the most problematized issues in Wright scholarship. Wright's critical reception in Europe, especially between the two world wars, has always been a major axle on which discussions of his architecture's significance has turned. The information, analyses, and conclusions of Dietrich Neumann and Jean-Louis Cohen add significantly to this discourse and will undoubtedly remain points of reference in the future.

Dietrich Neumann, who has devoted much of his scholarly research and writing to the interwar period in Europe, focuses in the opening essay on events in Holland and Germany, the two European countries where Wright found his earliest recognition and support, before detailing in a rich and subtle exegesis some of the ways in which that discourse later played out in the United States. The very different aspects of the Dutch and German contexts are revealed through deft comparisons of the writings and personalities of such prominent figures as Hendrik Petrus Berlage, J. J. P. Oud, Hendrik Theodore Wijdeveld, Werner Hegemann, Heinrich de Fries, Erich Mendelsohn, and Henry-Russell Hitchcock, all of whom offered different takes on the American architect's meaning for contemporary theory and practice.

The work of Mies van der Rohe dominates the final part of the essay, as well it should, given Mies's significance both as a major modernist figure in his own right and as one of the most, if not the most, important exemplars of the dialogue Wright entertained with his European peers. Neumann situates the first instance of this meeting of minds on Mies's part in the year 1923. He shows how his radical projects culminating in the Barcelona Pavilion at the end of the decade grew out of a new expression of movement, flowing space, and time that are connected to the writings of the art historians Heinrich Wölfflin and August Schmarsow and the relativity theory of Albert Einstein, all the while weaving an intricate web in which Wright's spatial innovations are convincingly bound. This argument serves as the basis for giving new meaning to the oft-noted cross-fertilization between Mies's designs and Wright's later Usonian houses and other works.

No stranger to Wright, having published among other things the introduction to the French edition of the 1910 Wasmuth portfolio, Jean-Louis Cohen focuses on the lesser-studied developments in France, Russia/USSR, and Italy. His essay offers a conspectus of the ways in which Wright's architecture and philosophy were characterized and integrated into the complex political and social conditions obtaining in the three countries in question, how that reception changed over time, and, in the process, how interest in Wright was instrumentalized for specific political and cultural purposes. In the French context, we are provided with new and important revelations regarding Wright's varied impact on well-studied figures such as Le Corbusier and virtually unknown ones such as Jean Prévost. We learn that in the postwar period Wright's champions generally used him for their conservative purposes, while he inspired a new group of more independent followers (Hervé Balay, Edmond Lay, Dominique Zimbacca, and Jean-François Zevaco) all virtually unknown to the American audience.

Shifting scenes, Cohen introduces us to the roles played by Moisei Ginzburg and, especially, David Arkin, in introducing Wright to Russia and the Soviet Union in the 1910s and 1920s. In the ensuing years, Wright's reception is related to the changing dynamics of Soviet politics as Wright's work was "instrumentalized," to use Cohen's term, in the debates over communism versus capitalism. In this regard, he points out that after a cooling off of interest, Wright's books began to appear in translation in the later 1950s to be followed by the first Russian monograph on his work in 1973.

The impact of politics becomes explicit in postwar Italy, where the appreciation of Wright belatedly evolved into arguably its most consequential manifestation in Europe—and the only European country where the architect received a design commission (a topic addressed in the later essay in this volume by Alice Thomine-Berrada). The key figure in the Italian context was Bruno Zevi, whose celebration of Wright's organic architecture as the only appropriate democratic response to the recent history of fascism under Mussolini is tellingly delineated and analyzed. The significant and often quite imitative body of work produced by architects under the spell of Wright (and Zevi), such as Carlo Scarpa and Marcello d'Olivo, leads Cohen to advance one of his most important, and provocative, points regarding the general reception of Wright. While Wright may initially have been seen merely as a precursor of the Modern Movement and later used in some countries as a political tool, his influence through the imitation of his outward style came to be viewed as a form of modern "mannerism" that had to be critiqued and avoided.

The next two essays, by Cammie McAtee and Timothy M. Rohan, complement those of Neumann and Cohen in bringing the discussion of Wright's critical reception fully into the postwar period and into the context of the United States. McAtee, whose previous publications had been mainly devoted to Mies van der Rohe, developed an interest in Wright's critical significance in the 1950s and 1960s through her study of Eero Saarinen and what was then known as the New Formalism in American postwar architecture. Unlike the "mannerist" pitfalls noted by Cohen in Italy, the renewed impact of Wright's work in the United States took an entirely different, less explicitly imitative turn. Here Wright became, finally on his own home grounds so to speak, a recognized leader of contemporary architecture rather than a superannuated precursor or "pioneer."

Organized around the 1959 exhibition "Form Givers at Mid-Century," held in Washington, D.C., and New York, highlighting America's cultural ascendancy in the Cold War atmosphere of the period, McAtee's groundbreaking essay reveals how Wright had become by that time the leading figure in the new triumvirate of "starchitects," including Le Corbusier and Mies in second and third places, that dominated contemporary architectural theory and practice. Key to this renewed perception of Wright's primacy in the hierarchy was the importance given to the idea of form in architectural design. While Saarinen and Matthew Nowicki had revised Louis Sullivan's dictum that "form ever follows function" to read "form follows form," it was Wright's work, especially that of the 1930s, 1940s, and early 1950s, that was considered to embody the idea at its highest artistic level. Even earlier, less than enthusiastic critics of Wright such as Sigfried Giedion, as McAtee shows in a trenchant rereading of his work, now came around to praise the emotional and at times primordial power of Wright's latest creations. The promotion of Wright's work to its preeminent place in the Wright–Le Corbusier–Mies triad, and the consequent demotion of Walter Gropius to a second tier, resulted among other things in the several exhibitions at the Museum of Modern Art, curated by Philip Johnson and his successor Arthur Drexler, that prominently featured Wright's work—and, it should be added, laid the groundwork for a new generation of architectural-historical research.

In his essay tantalizingly titled "The Meaning of an Anecdote," Timothy M. Rohan develops the critical framework laid out by McAtee to reveal, in a fascinating take on Gombrichian art-historical writing, how the story later told by Paul Rudolph, about whom Rohan has written the major monograph, of a visit to Philip Johnson's Glass House in 1956 that was dramatically interrupted by the unannounced appearance of Wright, can be read as a revelatory event, not only for Rudolph and Johnson but also, surprisingly, for Wright himself. Wright's public animus toward the Glass House was and is well known, yet his numerous visits to it clearly indicate that he was deeply intrigued by Johnson's Miesian effort. Johnson's and Rudolph's education at Gropius's Harvard, where Wright was always a no-no, is also well known. But in the visit recounted by Rudolph, often embellished as he retold it, an epiphany occurs to all three architects as they are enthralled by a series of events, generated by Wright's physical reactions to Johnson's architecture, in which light, both natural and artificial, acts in concert with the Glass House to bring it alive and give it dramatic and psychological resonance.

To this event and its retelling Rohan directly relates Rudolph's turn away from the neutrality of the International Style of corporate modernism to a more emotionally charged form indebted to Wright and, especially, to the manipulation of light effected in Wright buildings such as Florida Southern College, which Rudolph had visited as a student. In a similar way, he interprets Johnson's appreciation for the mythopoeic character of Wright's Taliesin West informed by a dramatic use of the desert light and of a "processional" path of movement. But more surprisingly, as already noted, he emphasizes the positive aspect of Wright's response to the emotional and psychological experience of the Glass House. The event at the Glass House thus becomes a metaphor for the new creative dialogue between Wright and a younger generation of architects that was grounded in a sense of architecture as a phenomenological experience based on the elements of form.

Architecture understood in terms of phenomenology is the theme of Jack Quinan's contribution. A leading scholar of Wright's work, Quinan has published seminal books on the Larkin Building and Martin house complex in Buffalo, as well as being the founding force behind the Frank Lloyd Wright Building Conservancy. In this essay, he moves beyond the issue of the architect-client relationship that has often directed his approach to Wright's work to focus on how to explain—and describe—the special experience of a Wright building. Edmund Husserl's philosophy of phenomenology, which was developed into a phenomenology of perception by Maurice Merleau-Ponty that became extremely important in critical writing on art in the decades following World War II, serves as the foundation for Quinan's quest to understand the essential character of the embodied experience of a Wright space.

The argument, developed through numerous case studies, is that Wright buildings engage their occupants in a multisensory experience generated by the physical qualities of his use of materials, orchestration of movement through varied types of spaces, provision of wide vistas and landscape-like interior spaces, use of water for its qualities of light refraction and sound, and attention to acoustical effects and their interrelation with optical ones in his unusual theater designs. Through intense formal analysis, Quinan shows how all this plays out in examples ranging from residential works such as the Barton house in Buffalo, the Laurent house in Rockford, Illinois, and Fallingwater, to the two Taliesins and the Kalita Humphreys Theater in Dallas. The explanation of the design of the late Cabaret Theater at Taliesin West serves as a compelling conclusion in its synthesis of how Wright marshaled sight and sound together with the senses of touch and taste and smell to create the kind of multisensory experience that so impressed architects like Johnson, Rudolph, and others at that time.

The next three essays provide a change of direction. Grouped around the issue of preservation, they move the focus from the reception of Wright's work as such to how it would be understood and treated in its afterlife. None of these essays deals exclusively with the saving of a Wright masterpiece, so to speak, but rather with the social, economic, cultural, and political contexts in which the preservation effort was embroiled. In this way, we come to see how the several works by Wright in question not only were significant subjects in the nascent movement of preserving twentieth-century architectural heritage but also often became positive agents of change in the field itself.

The group begins with the essay by Richard Longstreth, a major figure in preservation studies and former president of the Society of Architectural Historians and the Frank Lloyd Wright Building Conservancy, who offers a remarkably coherent, at times dramatic, and insightful overview of the numerous cases in which Wright's buildings have been involved. Placing them in the larger context of American preservation history, he begins his study with the former Larkin Building in Buffalo and Robie house in Chicago (the subject of Daniel Bluestone's extended study), and includes Fallingwater; the Pope-Leighey house in Falls Church, Virginia; the former Imperial Hotel in Tokyo; the Storer house in Los Angeles; Wright's own house and studio in Oak Park; and the Village of Oak Park itself.

Despite Wright's lack of interest in preservation and in sharp contrast to the way he rebuilt and reconfigured his own works over time, Longstreth shows how a growing public concern for the conservation of his legacy helped lead in a number of cases to landmark changes in preservation laws and practices that served as catalyst: in the effort to preserve twentieth-century architecture in general as well as expand the scope of conservation thinking. The saving of the Robie house proved a catalyst for preservationists to consider modernist works as an important part of the nation's historic legacy; while that of the Pope-Leighey house laid the foundation for a major review component of the National Historic Preservation Act of 1966. Fallingwater was an early and influential example of integrating building and natural site into a larger context of land conservation; while the concept that twentieth-century heritage should be protected through the designation of historic districts, not just individual landmarks, coalesced in the early 1970s around Wright's contribution to the Village of Oak Park. In that context, the restoration of Wright's house and studio set a precedent for taking into account the multiple temporal layers of a building while at the same time establishing a new model for the joint venture of private and public funding. The picture Longstreth paints is not entirely rosy, however. Just as the Imperial Hotel and Adler & Sullivan's Stock Exchange in Chicago were lost to financial considerations, challenges of a similar sort continue to plague the unusually large body of Wright's remaining domestic architecture, the most recent example threatened being the David and Gladys Wright house, built for Wright's son and daughter-in-law in Phoenix, near the headquarters of the Frank Lloyd Wright Foundation at Taliesin West.

The demolition of the Larkin Building and the threat to raze the Robie house were the first two instances of such in the afterlife of Wright's architecture. The Larkin Building raised barely a peep from the public, but the same was hardly the case for the Robie house, which aroused a national and international outcry. It was the only known instance in which Wright himself entered the fray on behalf of the preservation of one of his buildings. But, as Daniel Bluestone shows in his richly documented, critically calibrated retelling of the complex story, Wright's voice was an important but hardly a deciding factor in the eventual save.

Bluestone is an architectural historian specializing in the study of preservation who has written much about Chicago. He uses his extensive knowledge of the city, its institutions, its urban history, and its archival resources, to draw a multilayered picture of the events surrounding the decision by the Chicago Theological Seminary to replace the Wright building with a student dormitory and the various efforts culminating in the developer William Zeckendorf's purchase and eventual donation of the Robie house to the seminary's neighbor, the University of Chicago. The battleground for the fight was, as Bluestone documents, the urban renewal of the Hyde Park neighborhood. Zeckendorf came to the rescue in part to serve his own interests in becoming a significant player in this process. In outlining the various motives and actions by the different parties involved, Bluestone raises several important points regarding the preservation field, ranging from the role of private ownership and stewardship to that of institutional responsibility. In the end, he concludes, rather contentiously, that while the saving of the

Robie house represented a victory for the preservationist cause, the campaign was instrumental in instituting a narrow emphasis on the iconic landmark at the expense of broader urban and community concerns that would last for years to come.

An opposite effect is revealed in Alice Thomine-Berrada's essay on Wright's Masieri Memorial project for Venice, where she astutely shows that while the project would have involved the destruction of an existing piece of relatively insignificant urban fabric and was nevertheless rejected by the municipal authorities in part for this reason, the design opened the way for Modern architecture to be accepted in the historically venerated city precisely because it gave evidence of how a modern building could be respectful of its urban context and even give new life to vernacular traditions.

Thomine-Berrada, an architectural historian who has published important studies of nineteenth-century architecture in Europe, takes a subject that has generally been approached in terms of its architectural design and its failure to get built to craft a case, quite novel and unexpected, for the larger issues of preservation, especially regarding Modern architecture, that the failure raised. Thomine-Berrada outlines how Venice came to be considered a place where such different theoretical positions as those of John Ruskin, Camillo Sitte, Le Corbusier, and Lewis Mumford could all converge on the assumption of its being an untouchable museum-city. Wright's conception of organic architecture, she shows, disputed this idea in its belief that growth and change are inevitable. That the Masieri Memorial manifested this change without upsetting or denying the historical conditions out of which it grew had an impact on the faculty at the Venice architecture school influenced by Bruno Zevi. The most well known, Carlo Scarpa, was, as Thomine-Berrada illustrates, profoundly influenced by the project, while Egle Renata Trincanato soon applied Wright's suggestion of the idea of culling for dealing with what to preserve and what not to preserve. Within less than a decade, at the 1962 conference on "The Problem of Venice" leading to the Venice Charter drawn up two years later, the city councilor in charge of urbanism specifically cited Wright's rejected design as providing a solid basis for permitting Modern architecture to be built in the city.

An afterword by Barry Bergdoll, the historian of nineteenth- and twentieth-century architecture who, as curator of architecture and design at the Museum of Modern Art, was instrumental in effecting the transfer of the Wright archives to New York and organized the "Unpacking the Archive" exhibition around which the conservancy's symposium evolved, provides a lively, highly intelligent, sometimes even tender, and fitting closure to this volume. It neatly bookends this introduction in picking up on the theme of Wright's divergent reception by the popular and the academic audiences.

He optimistically views the new home of the archives, not only through its location in New York but, even more, through the courses offered at Columbia University using the archive, as a certain inspiration for new research and publications at the high level the material deserves. I totally agree with him, and his future role in this as a Columbia faculty member will certainly continue to be a significant factor. He also raises the very knotty question of whether architectural practice will equally take part in this renewed research. It is one to which the answer, I think he agrees, is not yet clear.

This book, as I have already said, stands as a first step in the effort to move Wright out of the margins and fully back into the mainstream where, as we see in many of the essays, he dwelt for so long—and with such a significant presence. Blind devotion, celebration of genius, assertions of relevance, these will no longer help. Nor, in my view, will it help to see Wright's work, at every instance a new concern arises, such as affordable housing or sustainability, as a precedent, even road map for a solution. Certainly, the need for everyone at both Taliesins to own a car to get wherever they have to go should give the lie to such a presupposition.

I think we should content ourselves for the moment with serious thinking and writing that will re-place Wright at the forefront of architectural education, as *a* leader in the twentieth-century creation of modernism, not *the* leader. The essays in this book offer just a suggestion of topics for further exploration. The Wright archives in New York, now fully accessible to any qualified student or researcher, provide an incredible amount of primary documentary material for the monographs on Wright buildings still to be done. No scholarly book yet exists on the Willits house, the two Jacobs houses, the Imperial Hotel, Marin County Civic Center, or, hard to believe, the Broadacre City project. Despite being bandied about in all discussions of Wright, no critical work exists on his concept of organic architecture or on that of his conception of architectural space. Neumann says in his essay that Wright first used the word "space" as late as 1928, but one would not know this from all that has been written about his supposed "breaking the box." Less obvious to many, though just as crucial for understanding Wright's place in twentieth-century American architecture and urbanism, in particular, would be a serious study of the multifold relations between his work and that of his traditionalist, sometimes Beaux-Arts educated peers. And finally, one still awaits a major study of Wright's design process that can help clear up the mystery the Dutch modernist Oud attributed to his work in 1925, no doubt based on the fact that Wright, rare among his profession, left almost no paper trail of preliminary sketches: "Whereas it is a peculiarity of our day that even the work of the cleverest [architect] nearly always betrays how it grew to be such as it is, with Wright everything is, without being at all perceptible [that it took] any mental exertions to produce. Where others are admired for the talent with which we see them master their material, I revere Wright because the process . . . remains . . . a perfect mystery."[11]

With this at the back of your minds, you are now invited to turn to the nine essays that follow and see what thoughts, and questions, and ideas they evoke.

NOTES

1. Quoted in Frederick Gutheim, ed., *Frank Lloyd Wright on Architecture: Selected Writings, 1894–1940* (New York: Duell, Sloan & Pearce, 1941), 136.
2. Kenneth Frampton, *Modern Architecture: A Critical History* (New York: Oxford University Press, 1980), 189.
3. Alan Colquhoun, *Modern Architecture* (New York: Oxford University Press, 2002), 55.
4. Frank Lloyd Wright, "Of Thee I Sing," *Shelter* 2 (April 1932): 10–12.
5. Quoted in Patrick J. Meehan, ed., *Truth against the World: Frank Lloyd Wright Speaks for an Organic Architecture* (New York: John Wiley, 1987), 389.
6. Frank Lloyd Wright, "Civilization and Culture," 18 January 1953, reprinted in Bruce Brooks Pfeiffer, ed., *Frank Lloyd Wright: His Living Voice* (Fresno: Press at California State University, 1987), 105.
7. Philip Johnson, "100 Years, Frank Lloyd Wright and Us," *Pacific Architect and Builder* (March 1957), reprinted in Philip Johnson, *Writings* (New York: Oxford University Press, 1979), 193–94.
8. Vincent Scully, "The Heritage of Wright," *Zodiac* 8 (1961): 12.
9. Michael Kimmelman, "The Frank Lloyd Wright Estate Controversy," *Art News,* April 1984, 102.
10. I have reference here to Pfeiffer's *Frank Lloyd Wright: His Living Voice,* published twenty years after his subject's death..
11. J[acobus] J[ohannes] P[ieter] Oud, "The Influence of Frank Lloyd Wright on the Architecture of Europe," *Wendingen* 7 (July 1925): 85–86.

DIETRICH NEUMANN

Wright, Mies, and the German and Dutch Contexts

"Frank Lloyd Wright belongs entirely to the Germans. . . . His fame is truly a product made in Germany . . . !" one of Berlin's premiere intellectual journals, *Die Weltbühne,* declared in June 1929. The author, architect, and city planner Werner Hegemann claimed that while the two famous Wasmuth publications of 1910 and 1911 had quickly sold out in Germany eighteen years earlier, the three hundred copies that Wright took home with him "are still lying around in his attic" because "the Americans are not interested in him."[1] Hegemann, whose depiction of Wright had recently caused somewhat of a scandal (more on which below), took some poetic license here in making an important point: Wright had seen few commissions and scant recognition at home since 1911 while being the subject of extraordinary adulation and impassioned debates in Europe—a puzzling and much noted contradiction.

Wright's reception played an important part in the evolving modernist discourse, especially in Germany and Holland. This was somewhat complicated by the fact that much of his recent work stood in striking contrast to the ideological and aesthetic goals of the Modern movement in these countries. Questions of national or continental cultural identities played a prominent role in the debates, which unfolded in Germany against the backdrop of its *Amerikanismus*—that curious phenomenon of both attraction and revulsion—with the United States being seen in so many clichéd expressions as the land "of the future" or of "unlimited possibilities," where things tended to be stronger, faster, higher, but also less cultured, less refined, louder, more ostentatious. Of course, the decisive impact of the United States' late entry into World War I in 1917, which sped up Germany's defeat, and subsequent economic help through the Dawes and Young plans of 1924 and 1927, respectively, had complicated the picture even more.

After a trip to Europe in the summer of 1927, the young architectural historian Henry-Russell Hitchcock noted that in order to comprehend "the formation of contemporary architecture and the ideology behind it," it was crucial to understand the European admiration for Wright. After all, "The

American in Europe finds himself a little embarrassed by the excessive adulation for Frank Lloyd Wright on the part of the leading contemporary architects." Hitchcock found it "paradoxical . . . that on the desks of these same European architects for whom Wright is Mohammed, Sweet's catalogue of architectural and engineering details lies as a Koran, describing in detail the joys of the American paradise where almost all fixtures may be had in standard and mechanical forms. Yet the prophet who has been much read in Holland and Germany—and much written about—. . . has not shown in his work indication of that practical allurement to the modern aesthetic. . . . The American anxious to understand and if possible to join in the admiration of Wright . . . turns to Europe, as he could not in America, to a set of elaborate publications in German and Dutch," but "he still fails to understand completely the European point of view even though he can hardly longer be uncertain of Wright's genius and his unique position in America."[2]

This essay briefly surveys Wright's German and Dutch reception in the 1920s and then focuses on his complex relationship with Ludwig Mies van der Rohe, whose early work was firmly rooted in the architectural culture of those two countries and continued in the United States after 1938.[3] Comparisons between Wright and Mies became particularly pertinent for discussions of national or continental cultural identities in the years following World War II, as a set of new critical tools emerged in the process.

Frank Lloyd Wright's European reception began in Berlin on 16 February 1910. He had arrived in the city five months earlier and negotiated with the publisher Ernst Wasmuth the printing of a lithograph edition of his drawings, which appeared in late 1910, and a separate, cheaper volume with an overview of his work, issued in 1911.[4] By February 1910, Wright had moved on to Fiesole, outside Florence, where he worked on additional drawings and wrote the introduction, but enough material had remained with the publisher for editor and architect Bruno Möhring to organize a lecture at the local architects' association. Möhring was a prominent and influential figure, whose engineering structures, urban plans, and publications helped pave the way for Modern architecture in Germany. That winter evening at the *Architektenhaus* in Berlin's elegant government quarter, Möhring showed several plates of Wright's drawings, presumably exhibited on easels around the room. The Neo-Renaissance interiors of the 1875 building by Ende & Boeckmann where the architects gathered could hardly have provided a starker contrast to Wright's delicate renderings. Möhring had seen some of Wright's work in the United States when he traveled to the 1904 Louisiana Purchase Exposition in St. Louis. He praised the "poetic power" of that work and described Wright

DIETRICH NEUMANN

as a "non-academic" and a typical American "self-made man."[5] Of course, it is tempting to speculate who was in the audience that night: Peter Behrens and his collaborator Walter Gropius were members of the association and might have attended. Le Corbusier was in Berlin in 1910 on two occasions, but not on the evening of the presentation, as Anthony Alofsin has shown.[6] Mies van der Rohe was probably in Berlin, but not a member of the group.

The critic Walter Curt Behrendt's 1913 review of the Wasmuth publications presented Wright's work as the logical product of a "country not burdened by the richness of traditions of the old world." The author even suggested that Americans in general were predestined to become architects, due to their "natural talent for organization." Many important contributions, he claimed, were to be expected from them for the development and regeneration of architecture.[7]

Wright's influence would be noticeable in Gropius's work a few years later, but at the time of Möhring's lecture Gropius was focused on a different kind of American architecture.[8] Working with Adolph Meyer on his first major commission, the Fagus shoe last factory in Alfeld (1911–12), Gropius acquainted himself with its financial backer, the American United Shoe Machinery Corporation, whose main factory in Beverly, Massachusetts (1903–6), was designed by the engineer and pioneer in reinforced-concrete construction, Ernest Ransome, as a simple post-and-beam structure with floor-to-ceiling glazing. For Gropius the plant suggested the raw beauty of American industrial architecture. He also acquired images of concrete grain elevators, coaling bunkers, and factories, showing them at his first public lecture, in January 1911.[9] American "builders," he declared, had "retained a natural feeling for large compact forms" just like the "ancient Egyptians"; and he saw a causal connection between their "primitive culture and the highest, purest . . . art form." The most essential American architecture, he suggested, was anonymous, unornamented, monumental—in many ways the opposite of Wright's idiosyncratic, delicate renderings.

Dutch architect Hendrik Petrus Berlage was traveling in the United States that same year and published his impressions afterward in a Swiss magazine.[10] He praised Wright's Unity Temple (1905–8) and Larkin Company Administration Building (1902–6) and was particularly taken with the beauty of the floor plans and interior organization of Wright's houses. "Americans like to keep the actual living rooms open towards each other," he observed, resulting in "the most beautiful views among the individual rooms and from the rooms towards the staircase, into the hallways, etc." Paralleling Behrendt, Berlage considered Wright's architecture "originally American, as nothing similar could be found in Europe," and predicted that Wright's residential work would become paradigmatic for the American suburban house.[11]

Instead, Wright's architecture became a rather ubiquitous model in Dutch architecture, and none of the major artistic circles emerging in the following years could fully escape his influence. In particular the modernist De Stijl group around Gerrit Rietveld, Theo van Doesburg, and J. J. P. Oud and the Expressionist Amsterdam School of Michel de Klerk and Piet Kramer used Wright to help define their differences.

After World War I, the Germans and the Dutch found themselves in vastly different positions. While the Netherlands had stayed neutral during the conflict and continued to build, most notably ambitious social housing projects, Germany had tumbled into the horrors of war and experienced five years of economic crisis afterward. Little was built, and architectural debates were somewhat muted. Nevertheless, debates about Wright continued in astonishing simultaneity in both countries.

The members of De Stijl, who favored unornamented, simple geometries, had initially embraced Wright and, just like their modernist German colleagues shortly afterward, avoided commenting on the lavish ornamentation of Wright's Prairie style by focusing attention on his floor plans and their functionality. In 1918 Oud praised Wright's Robie house (1908–10) as "a new departure from architectural design as we have previously known it," since the "practical function of the house—its purpose—is the basis of the plan."[12] His colleague Jan Wils concurred: "In the ground plan lies the true modernity of Wright's architecture"—a result of America's democracy and self-respect.[13]

The German architect Ludwig Hilberseimer, who later became Mies van der Rohe's close friend and collaborator, commented on Wright and American architecture right after World War 1, when European architecture urgently needed inspiration to reinvent itself. He described Wright's large, open living spaces without fully enclosing walls as prophetic of a new way of life, with a pathos of sobriety and objectivity and delight in natural materials, in striking contrast to common American Beaux-Arts interiors.[14] He also noted that while American architects in general tended to build vertically, Wright preferred horizontal lines and cubic forms combining Japanese delicacy and Egyptian roughness. Similarly, in 1923, modernist critic Adolph Behne praised Wright, "to whom the American public could never relate," as the creator of the "first truly modern floor plans."[15] Just like Hilberseimer and his Dutch colleagues, Behne avoided the question of Wright's love for ornamentation, but instead concentrated on layout and spatial connections. He was working on his book *The Functional Building,* which would appear three years later, where he conceded that Wright's houses would not necessarily qualify as "functional buildings," despite the fact that their floor plans were liberated "from formalist rigidity by returning to the functional element."[16]

After a currency reform ended Germany's postwar economic crisis, traveling became easier, and contacts with the United States intensified. In 1924, Werner Moser from Zurich had started working for Wright, and later that year Richard Neutra accepted Wright's offer of employment. Neutra arranged for the visit of Erich Mendelsohn, for whom he had worked in Berlin, in early November. Mendelsohn had long been fascinated with Wright. Stationed on the eastern front near Riga during the war, he had a copy of the 1911 Wasmuth publication delivered to him in the trenches.[17]

Mendelsohn's letters from America to his wife, Luise, in November 1924 reveal how deeply emotional the encounter with Wright was for him. Despite their twenty-year age difference and a considerable language barrier, Mendelsohn felt an immediate kinship, both men "enchanted in space, joining hands . . . the same path, the same goal, the same life." Mendelsohn delivered "greetings of the entire young movement of Europe to Wright, to the father and fighter." Wright complimented Mendelsohn's work as "original, powerful—future." While Mendelsohn mentioned the international group of architects surrounding Wright that evening—"Kanada, Switzerland, Japan, Austria and Armenia"—Wright pointedly emphasized his regional roots. For a walk after lunch, he made Mendelsohn change into something "vaguely native American," a button-less frock and raffia shoes and handed him a long walking stick, gloves and a tomahawk to carry along.[18] Apparently, Wright was at work, as he put it later, "quietly Americanizing Europe while American architects Europeanized America."[19] Before Mendelsohn left, he confessed to Wright that he looked forward to telling his friends in Europe: "I have seen him, I was with him." Wright responded diplomatically that he felt just the same about Mendelsohn. While one could hardly imagine a greater contrast than that between Mendelsohn's urbane, streamlined additions to the Rudolf Mosse publishing house in Berlin (1920–22) or his expressionistic Einstein Tower in Potsdam (1920–22) and Wright's Prairie style, the current work in Wright's studio, such as the dynamic Gordon Strong Automobile Objective and Planetarium, planned for Dickerson, Maryland (1924–25), or the reinforced concrete skyscraper for the National Life Insurance Company in Chicago (1923–25) had more affinity to Mendelsohn's work.

Thanks to massive American investments through the Dawes Plan, Germany began to recover from the war and its devastating economic crisis. The time around 1925 saw a flood of new publications, several of them discussing Wright.[20] Gropius published the first of his Bauhaus Books, about his famous 1923 exhibition "Internationale Architectur" in Weimar, and demonstrated that an "essential approach to building is evolving simultaneously in all civilized countries." Wright was represented twice, firmly embedded into Gropius's narrative of the modernity of American industrial buildings and the internationalism of Modern architecture: a photograph of the Larkin Building was paired with the corn silo of the Washburn Crosby Company in Minneapolis, the Robie house faced the model of Mies's Concrete Country House project (1923).[21] The Swiss magazine *Werk* published a special number on American architecture in May 1925. Werner Moser, still at Taliesin, told its readers: "The work of the architect Frank Lloyd Wright has little in common with that of the other American architects." In contrast to the materialism and historicism in U.S. architecture, Wright was presented as a genuine seeker for honest, natural forms in response to materials and functions. Moser stressed the connection between exterior and interior in Wright's houses and their spatial continuity and recommended his principles as a model to follow. [22]

Heinrich de Fries, a pupil of Peter Behrens and a moderately modern architect and critic, became one of Wright's most important advocates in Germany. He was an editor at Wasmuth, Wright's former publisher in Berlin. Early on, he had noted Wright's increasing influence in Europe.[23] De Fries decided to publish a book on Wright and contacted J. J. P. Oud in the spring of 1923 regarding photographs of Wright's work.[24] He was completing a large book on international residential architecture at the time, *Moderne Villen und Landhäuser,* which appeared in 1924. De Fries included some American examples but left out Wright entirely. He probably did not want to steal the thunder of his own planned publication, but teasingly mentioned Wright in his introduction as "the greatest living architect of our time."[25]

After leaving Wasmuth later that year, de Fries became the editor of the journal *Baugilde* and intensified his search for material on Wright, contacting him in the fall of 1924. Neutra facilitated the interaction and translated. A package from Wright arrived in late December 1924, containing color drawings of his latest California projects—the Doheny Ranch in Beverly Hills (1923), the Lake Tahoe Resort (1923–24), and the Millard house in Pasadena (1923–24), as well as texts and photographs, and de Fries began working on his book. Just as the discovery of Wright had unfolded simultaneously in Germany and the Netherlands around 1911, now the production of the first monographs on his work proceeded at the same time in both countries. We can only imagine de Fries's disappointment when the most elegant and luxurious architecture journal of its time, the Dutch *Wendingen,* announced an ambitious publishing project on Wright in October 1925.[26] The next seven numbers of the magazine (twenty-four pages each) would be devoted to Wright and published as a bound volume afterward. The project was led by former editor Hendricus Theodorus Wijdeveld, who wrote the introduction and included "many articles by famous European Architects and American writers" (there were essays by Wright, Mendelsohn, Oud, Berlage, Robert Mallet-Stevens, Louis Sullivan, and Lewis Mumford).

Wendingen was generally aligned with the more conservative Expressionists of the Amsterdam School (and financed through the architect's group Architectura et Amicitia), but it also embraced other views. The essay by Oud, "The Influence of Frank Lloyd Wright on the Architecture of Europe," which appeared in February 1926, became the only piece that did not join the laudatory choir Wijdeveld had assembled. After his initial enthusiasm for Wright, Oud had gotten worried about the extent to which Wright-inspired buildings were springing up all over the Netherlands and warned his colleagues about Wright's "pernicious" influence. While Wright was clearly "one of the very greatest," Dutch architects were just imitating aspects of his personal style such as "the shifting of planes, the projecting penthouse-roofs, the repeatedly interrupted and again continued masses, the predominantly horizontal development," without the reasoning behind them. What European architecture needed instead of American "luxurious growth," "plastic exuberance," and "sensuous abundance" was the opposite, namely "abstraction," "puritanic asceticism and mental abstinence": in other words, the Cubism of De Stijl. "Imitating a modern master," according to Oud, was worse than designing historicizing architecture.[27]

Mumford's essay tackled the often-asked question of Wright's cultural identity head-on: "Finally, to what extent is Mr. Wright's architecture 'American'? Those in Europe who admire Mr. Wright's work are particularly distressed by the fact that it has scarcely achieved a wide recognition in our own country."[28] Not surprisingly, Mumford found an explanation in the notion of regionalism that had occupied him for a number of years. Wright had "created a true regional form," he noted, as his "low-lying houses, with their flat roofs, which seem about to dissolve into the landscape are an expression of the prairie." This, he added in a surprising sleight-of-hand (while undermining the concept of regionalism) conditioned their acceptance elsewhere: "it is no accident that these forms have been so readily appreciated in the Netherlands and on the plains of Prussia."[29]

The hardcover book edition finally appeared during the early fall of 1926 in *Wendingen*'s large square format (13″ × 13″) on heavier, folded paper stock. Its 164 pages contained Wright's best-known work—including the Larkin Building, Unity Temple, and the Willits house (1902–03)—in excellent, often full-page, black-and-white photographs and large reproductions of his plans,

FIG. I. Frank Lloyd Wright, Coonley house, Riverside, Illinois, 1906–9, as depicted in *Wendingen,* November 1925, 22–23.

all framed by Wijdeveld's elaborate border designs. To this day, the volume is one of the most luxurious books on Wright ever published (fig. 1).

The production of de Fries's book on Wright also dragged on, until September 1926, long delayed by his search for an appropriate printer for color reproductions—still a rarity at that time. The young publisher Ernst Pollak, having produced only one book so far, finally took on the task of printing three thousand copies (after de Fries invested considerable funds of his own). De Fries's publication was markedly smaller than Wijdeveld's, with a format of 9″ × 11½″ and only eighty pages. Furthermore, the book suffered from a rather slapdash layout that was no match to the careful composition of its Dutch counterpart. What set the volume apart were the nine color plates of the three recent California projects: the Doheny Ranch, Lake Tahoe Resort, and the Millard house. In addition, there were well-known photographs of the Larkin Building, Unity Temple, the Imperial Hotel in Tokyo (1913–23), and the Dana (1902–04) and Martin (1903–04) houses in Springfield, Illinois, and Buffalo, respectively. The book also contained a number of amateur photographs of concrete-block houses under construction, of the Robie and Barnsdall (1918–21) houses and Taliesin (begun 1911). Some came from the *Schweizerische Bauzeitung,* others from the Swiss architect Max Haefeli, de Fries's father-in-law, who had recently traveled to the United States.[30] As if to demonstrate Wright's modernity and contemporary relevance, the

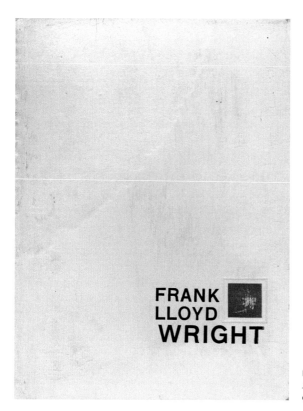

FIG. 2. Heinrich de Fries, *Frank Lloyd Wright,* 1926, cover.

book's cover simply carried Wright's name in a sans serif font and his trademark red square on an unadorned lemon yellow background, making it one of the most resolutely minimalist designs of its genre produced in the Weimar Republic (fig. 2).

De Fries noted in his introduction that the "culturally immature Americans" still preferred historicizing modes of expression, and thus "Wright appears to us as the most un-American imaginable." Instead he was an internationalist, who "has lived for many years in China [*sic*]," and "among his collaborators and students are Europeans, Americans and Asians."[31] De Fries had apparently mixed up Wright's recent sojourns to Japan with an extended stay in China, whose "old architectural and cultural landscape" was Wright's "spiritual home," he declared.[32]

Neutra contributed to de Fries's book an essay about concrete-block houses in Los Angeles. Wright's new essay on the "Third Dimension," as part of his revived "In the Cause of Architecture" series, appeared in both the *Wendingen* edition and de Fries's book. Berlage's essay of 1911 was also reprinted. In a separate chapter, de Fries analyzed the evolution of Wright's open floor plans. Studying plans, he said, had long been his favorite pastime, and Wright's floor plans were among the greatest achievements in the history of architecture. With eight examples from Wright's residential work, he demonstrated how rooms increasingly reached beyond an initial rectangular container to bring the inhabitants into closer contact with nature and define each space individually.[33]

In the end, both Wijdeveld and de Fries expressed disappointment about their respective publications to Wright. De Fries mentioned several times how much of his personal funds he had invested, while apparently the *Wendingen* volume had enjoyed some support from Wright. Thanks to his financial sacrifice, de Fries wrote, his book ended up being affordable and was going to "make your work truly available to the European architects," while the luxurious Dutch edition, which cost four times as much, would only be acquired by wealthy architects who, he maintained, were usually mere businessmen rather than creative artists and surely not the type Wright tried to reach.[34] Wijdeveld, on the other hand, bemoaned the fact that his publication was not the exclusive and complete first book on Wright that he had hoped: "I heard that you gave a set of the latest designs to a commercial publisher in Germany. . . . I can't help being disappointed about the publication which de Fries made in Germany. Now, nothing can be done anymore."[35] While Wright expressed his delight with Wijdeveld's sumptuous *Wendingen* edition, he never once thanked de Fries for his parallel efforts on the more affordable German publication.[36]

Ultimately, though, the two volumes were complementary rather than competitive. Both contained letters by Wright to his European colleagues. In Wijdeveld's case, the text, which appeared in the final number of the *Wendingen* series, in April 1926, was titled "To My European Co-Workers." Addressing an audience of likeminded architects, such as Wijdeveld and his fellow Expressionists of the Amsterdam School ("we all seem to desire much the same thing"), Wright presented a rhapsodic praise of the creative process.[37] In de Fries's book, an essay by Wright in German was called "An die europäischen Kollegen." This title, sounding very similar to the one in the Dutch edition, led later scholars to assume that it was simply a translation of the *Wendingen* piece.[38] In reality, the text in de Fries's publication is completely different and far more interesting. Yet it has been widely overlooked and never been translated into English.[39] It contains Wright's first direct response to modernist tendencies and stylistic preferences in Europe— seven years before his better-known reaction to the "Modern Architecture" exhibition at the Museum of Modern Art in New York.[40]

Wright wrote that he felt misunderstood by his European critics, claiming that they had missed the most valuable elements of his work. Distracted by his rich ornaments, they overlooked the straight lines of mechanical production underneath. In his early works (Wright was likely thinking of the Larkin Building and Unity Temple), such straight lines and flat surfaces of machine-made materials had been a concession to the mechanistic method or the machine as a tool, he explained. But Wright found that the human element was missing. Mankind had a right to "poetics of form," which lends "eloquence and emotion" to the raw, straight delineation. This, he said, "is the art of architecture, different from the scientific aspect of an achievement in engineering. But both are not separate spheres, they hang together in the production of the whole." Wright mocked the "affectation of simplicity" among European modernists as just "another form of old-fashioned artistic pretentiousness" and "a new kind of showing off," which had just "as little right to be considered architecture as copying the forms of antiquity." In addition, executing this simplicity needed even more effort and falsehood than imitating the classical orders, "since the architect still starts from the outside and tries to work his way to the interior."[41] The essay, dated 3 January 1925, was thus written shortly after de Fries had contacted Wright for the first time. It was also prepared long before the *Wendingen* series began, and hence before Oud's critical essay on Wright appeared in February 1926, to which it otherwise seemed a perfect response.

An interesting counterpart to de Fries's book in Germany was a massive portfolio about American architecture and urban planning, *Amerikanische Architektur,* by Werner Hegemann. Appearing earlier, in 1925, it seemed to reflect some expectations of *Amerikanismus.* The book was oversized, richly illustrated, and celebrated the historicizing, Beaux-Arts architecture in the United States—its skyscrapers, universities, railroad stations, civic centers, and suburban houses. It contained much work by McKim, Mead & White, whom Hegemann greatly admired and found vastly superior to anything comparable produced in Europe. Trained as an art historian and economist, Hegemann had organized a large and influential city planning exhibition in Berlin in 1910 and then spent ten years in the United States, where he worked as an urban planner and historian. Together with Elbert Peets he published a survey of American urbanism, *The American Vitruvius* (1922), which formed a basis for *Amerikanische Architektur.*[42] He returned to Berlin in 1920 and became editor of the well-established conservative architecture journal *Wasmuths Monatshefte für Baukunst,* and his book *Stony Berlin: History of the Largest Tenement City in the World* was a national success in 1930. Hegemann was perhaps the most clear-eyed and reasonable among Germany's critics. He delighted in humorously exposing architectural pretentiousness, ideologies, and fashions. Hegemann had no problem criticizing the Bauhaus for its serious and grandiloquent rhetoric, or the blind devotion of his fellow architects to Wright: "the inability to differentiate between religion and architecture is quite common among architecture professors."[43] A few years later, Hegemann applied the same skepticism to the hollow proclamations of the rising Nazi Party, mocking it in a book called *Entlarvte Geschichte* (*Debunked History*).[44]

Benignly reviewed in the general press, Hegemann's 1925 volume on American architecture received a furious response in de Fries's journal *Baugilde*. (Hegemann had taken over de Fries's editorial responsibilities at the Wasmuth publishing house, and their relationship had become rather acrimonious.)[45] Adolf Rading, a modernist architect, professor in Breslau, and apparently somewhat of a hothead, found Hegemann's book "pompous . . . sloppily produced" and a "deception," since Hegemann had ignored "the reality of truly modern architecture in the USA." By this he meant its utilitarian architecture, the new residential and office buildings with their "utmost objectivity" and "new beauty," and, in particular, the work of Frank Lloyd Wright. This clearly indicated that Hegemann was, according to Rading, "a pathetic creature," ignorant of God and the world and "hostile to life." Such a "dangerous" book should be "publicly burned."[46] This comment was darkly prophetic; both Rading and Hegemann had to leave Germany when the Nazis assumed power. Among the books famously burned by the Nazis in front of Berlin's University Library on 10 May 1933 was indeed one of Hegemann's, though not *Amerikanische Architektur*.[47]

Hegemann responded graciously to Rading's fiery critique. While he noted the "noticeable wind force of this comical storm," Hegemann made clear that he could take neither his attacker nor Wright all that seriously. Years earlier he had mocked Wright's Prairie designs, whose "strangely deep and flat cantilevered roofs," which were clearly inspired by a study trip to Japan, now supposedly "reflect[ed] the spirit of the prairies from which Chicago has grown."[48] Only horizontally growing plants should be allowed in its gardens, he joked.[49] Hegemann defended his approach by quoting de Fries, who had, after all, pointed out that Wright was the most "un-American of architects." Why then should he include him in a book on American architecture? That unconditional love for Wright in Germany was already grotesque enough, he said; everyone talked about *him,* but no one knew anything about McKim, Mead & White, the real champions of American architecture. This went so far, he recounted, that an esteemed colleague, whom he wanted to tell about the work of McKim, Mead & White, interrupted him with a superior air and informed him politely that the name was correctly pronounced Frank Lloyd Wright.[50]

Hegemann's exchange with Rading became a cause célèbre—making waves beyond Germany's borders. *Das Werk* scolded Rading for insulting

Hegemann, while sharing Rading's concern about the absence of Wright in his book, which otherwise it found informative and richly illustrated. When he prepared the second edition of *Amerikanische Architektur* in 1927, Hegemann included a few Wright buildings and adopted de Fries's false claim that Wright had lived for many years in China. He used this supposed source of influence, then, "to demonstrate that Wright's architecture was not very good in the first place."[51] He compared houses in China's Shensi province, which happened to have two vertical pylons in front, with the Larkin Building and the Martin house, to show that they were inferior to their models.[52] For good measure he threw in an image of the Seidenhaus Weichmann in Gleiwitz (1922) by Erich Mendelsohn, whose admiration for Wright was well known, to complete his depictions of the pitfalls of imitation (fig. 3).

During Henry-Russell Hitchcock's travels in Germany and France, between his graduation from Harvard and his first teaching job at Vassar, he took notes for a future book. He might very well have picked up on the quarrel between Hegemann, Rading, and de Fries about Wright when he declared Wright's reception in Europe was central to an understanding of Modern architecture. Hitchcock was just as interested in the question of national identity in architecture as were Wright's European admirers, but he considered it from the opposite perspective, writing that "in a wide sense all truly Modern architecture in Europe is American."[53] Since Berlage, for example, had been influenced by Henry Hobson Richardson and greatly admired Wright, Hitchcock suggested calling the "architecture of the first quarter of the twentieth century 'American' despite the triumphs of the Dutch." He identified the "principle of the new architecture" as "aesthetically conscious engineering. . . . I need hardly remark how American this program is." At the 1927 Weissenhof Exhibition in Stuttgart, he had witnessed the structural experiments and found that "we do that better in America." In short, Modern architecture is "waiting for American genius to achieve its masterpieces."[54]

Hitchcock's concept for his book evolved in the next few months. He presented his key ideas of the "New Tradition" and the "New Pioneers" via a *tour d'horizon* of recent European architecture in two essays in *Architectural Record* in the spring of 1928. While Wright was mentioned only briefly as a member of the "New Tradition," with Behrens, Josef Hoffmann, and Berlage, he was still lauded as a "complete 'modernist'" and as no "follower of European fashions," but rather as "the founder of a tradition much followed in Europe" and a "far greater architect than even Auguste Perret."[55]

Later that year, however, in a slim book on Wright published by the magazine *Cahiers d'Art* in Paris, Hitchcock's tone had markedly changed (fig. 4). He advanced cocky proclamations, which were clearly influenced by the misgivings that some European modernists, in particular Oud, had voiced.

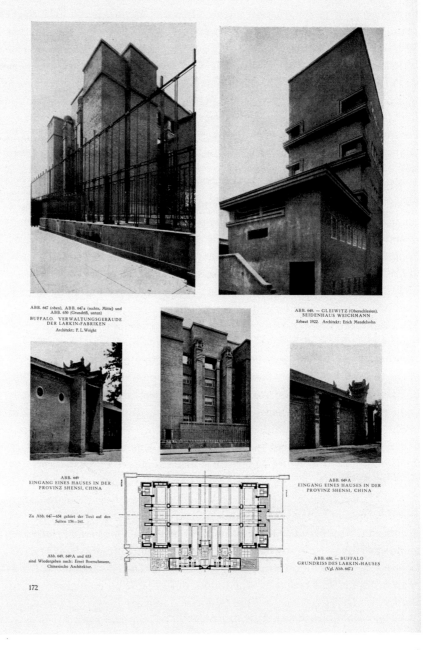

ABB. 647 (oben), ABB. 647a (rechts, Mitte) und
ABB. 650 (Grundriß, unten)
BUFFALO. VERWALTUNGSGEBÄUDE
DER LARKIN-FABRIKEN
Architekt: F. L. Wright

ABB. 648. — GLEIWITZ (Oberschlesien).
SEIDENHAUS WEICHMANN
Erbaut 1922. Architekt: Erich Mendelsohn

ABB. 649
EINGANG EINES HAUSES IN DER
PROVINZ SHENSI, CHINA

ABB. 649A
EINGANG EINES HAUSES IN DER
PROVINZ SHENSI, CHINA

Zu Abb. 647–654 gehört der Text auf den
Seiten 159–161.

Abb. 649, 649A und 653
sind Wiedergaben nach: Ernst Boerschmann,
Chinesische Architektur.

ABB. 650. — BUFFALO
GRUNDRISS DES LARKIN-HAUSES
(Vgl. Abb. 647.)

172

FIG. 3. Frank Lloyd Wright, Larkin Company Administration Building, Buffalo, 1902–6, and several Wright houses compared with contemporary European and traditional Chinese examples in Werner Hegemann, *Amerikanische Architektur und Stadtbaukunst,* 1925, 172–73.

Die Abbildungen 647 A, 652 und 652 A zeigen, wie F. L. Wright asiatische (Abb. 649, 649 A und 653) „Motive" übernommen und vergröbert hat. (Vgl. Text Seite 158—161.)

Abbildung 648 zeigt den Anschluß, den moderne deutsche Architekten an das von F. L. Wright gegebene Vorbild ver= suchen.

ABB. 651. — TALIENSIN. F. L. WRIGHT'S EIGENES HAUS

ZU ABB. 647—654 GEHÖRT DER TEXT AUF DEN SEITEN 158—161

ABB. 652.
BUFFALO. WOHNHAUS MARTIN
Architekt: F. L. Wright

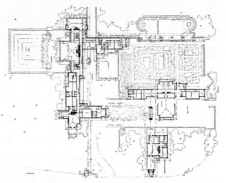

Mitte und unten: ABB. 654 und 654 A. — CHICAGO RIVERSIDE, COONLEY-HAUS
Grundriß und Ansicht, Architekt: F. L. Wright

ABB. 653. — EINGANG EINES HAUSES
IN DER PROVINZ SHENSI, CHINA

ABB. 652a.
BUFFALO. WOHNHAUS HEATH
Architekt: F. L. Wright

173

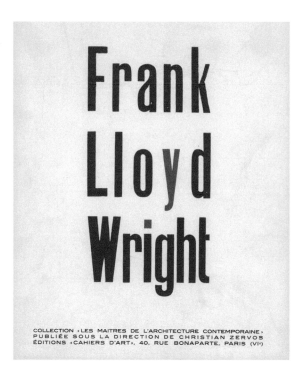

FIG. 4. Henry-Russell Hitchcock, *Frank Lloyd Wright,* 1928, cover.

While he praised the Larkin Building and Unity Temple for their clear lines and lack of ornamentation, he had little patience with the Prairie style and Wright's interiors, which "had never been really good" and had since become worse. The outsized ornaments were sometimes interesting, but even then they destroyed, at least in part, those qualities of pure architecture in which he had shown an unequal mastery." After scolding Wright for his "anti-architectural . . . picturesqueness," he turned his sights to the Imperial Hotel in Tokyo: "No conventional architecture has ever produced reception halls that are more mediocre. . . . And those who think highly of Wright's work regret that this monument, thanks to the engineering talent of its creator, was spared by various earthquakes."[56]

Hitchcock's book *Modern Architecture: Romanticism and Reintegration* finally appeared in 1929 and presented Wright as a member of the "New Tradition" just like Berlage, Behrens, and Otto Wagner, as opposed to the "New Pioneers"—notably Mies, Le Corbusier, Gropius, and Oud. Continuing the approach he had put forth in his French publication of the previous year, the twenty-five-year-old historian delivered a series of rather cranky verdicts. Wright owed "a great deal" to architects before him, he pointed out, in particular to Richardson, who "was surely as great an architect as Wright," and Sullivan, who had more talent than Wright for the design of ornament.[57] A case in point was the Coonley house in Riverside, Illinois (1906–9), the ornamentation of which was "out of keeping with the dignity of the whole." Midway Gardens in Chicago (1913–14), while "one of his greatest works," did not fare much better: "regrettably the interior was not up to the exterior and the ornament in detail was of a peculiarly awkward and ill-understood Cubism." In general, Hitchcock declared Wright's "house interiors . . . never worthy of his exteriors. . . . His rooms were dark, uncomfortable and generally at once cluttered and monotonous. His efforts to make them light and playful only increased their self-conscious fussiness and their self-righteous stodginess." The design of the Imperial Hotel was "redundant, overburdened with skillfully exotic ornament, and . . . vastly ineffective." The Barnsdall house was "one of his least successful buildings." Wright's ideas were "curiously incomplete and even in part contradictory." After all this, Hitchcock's final note, while sounding conciliatory, was a rather damning judgment on recent American architecture: Wright was "the greatest American architect of the first quarter of the twentieth century."[58]

In 1931, a long expected exhibition about Wright was shown in Amsterdam and then in Berlin. Not surprisingly, Wijdeveld was deeply involved in the organization in the Netherlands, as de Fries was in Germany. In his review, the well-known and respected art historian, writer, and journalist Max Osborn probably expressed the opinion of many modernists when he singled out Wright's work before 1910 (his early houses, the Luxfer Prism building [1895], and the Larkin Building), which he considered "the first, already admiringly sure and self-confident appearance of modern architecture." But he then harshly dismissed what came afterward, "as if Wright had suffered a relapse into American conventions." Perhaps it was some "modern confection which lured him into its dangerous embrace with the help of Japanese, English, Scottisch [sic] ingredients, in the style of Mackintosh, but weaker, oriental, exotic elements were mixed in, sometimes one thinks of Vienna, also of Art Nouveau . . . a big mess—in short it became horrible. . . . Wright lost his way. . . . American Luxury, Hollywood taste drove this superbly talented man all the way into kitsch." But Osborn saw a recent turn around, the Steel Cathedral project of 1925 and that for St. Mark's-in-the-Bowerie Tower in New York of 1928–30. He "sighed with relief" that the genial architect was again developing ideas and experiments in the spirit of his time. Wright's twenty years of "splashing around in shallow waters" should be forgotten, Osborn opined.[59] Progressive critic Paul F. Schmidt argued similarly in an essay on "Greatness and Decline of a Groundbreaking Modern Architect."[60] Wright responded to the many reviews of his exhibition with yet another letter to his European colleagues, or rather: "To my critics in the Land of the

Danube and the Rhine," where he repeated the argument that he had first laid out in his essay for de Fries's book.[61]

When Wright, Hitchcock, and Philip Johnson quarreled about Wright's participation in the "Modern Architecture" exhibition at MoMA, Wright referred to the question of his national identity, which so many of his European admirers had addressed by declaring him decidedly un-American. "I find myself rather a man without a country, architecturally speaking, at the present time. If I keep on working another five years, I shall be at home again, I feel sure," he added somewhat prophetically.[62] The 1932 show became the crucial moment of matching Wright and the avant-garde Europeans. Mies van der Rohe, whose work was prominently presented in the show and the catalog, played a key role.

WRIGHT, MIES, AND A NEW VOCABULARY

Mies had seen Wright's Wasmuth portfolio for the first time when Behrens brought it into the office in 1911 or 1912, much later recalling, "It was a revelation."[63] But if Wright's work left an impression on him at that time, it certainly did not have any impact on his residential designs of the following ten years, which were just as conventional as anything in Berlin's suburbs at that time.[64] In 1922, while still producing such villas and seemingly out of the blue, Mies joined several avant-garde groups, created his artist name via the "van der Rohe" suffix, which further underlined his German-Dutch identity, and designed five visionary projects that immediately put him on the map. Werner Hegemann's humorous mockery did not spare him either. Mies had "awoken one morning as the Dutch nobleman van der Rohe," he wrote, and "newly baptized," realized "that as a German, one can build very decent houses with sloping roofs without attracting much attention, while with a Dutch name one only needs to design one very impractical, Dutch-style high-rise to gain . . . the enthusiasm of the young. "[65]

Hegemann was referring to Mies glass skyscraper projects of 1922, which were followed in 1923 by the design for a concrete office building and a concrete country house with a pinwheel plan that reached out into the landscape (a device often associated with Wright by German critics). In December 1923, Mies wrote to Berlage, asking for material on Wright, a few months after de Fries had written to Oud with a similar request.[66] Apparently, Mies wanted to publish Berlage's essay on Wright in the magazine *Der Neubau* (edited by his fellow Werkbund member Walter Curt Behrendt), to make it better known in Germany. He also asked for Berlage's own recent work for future publications. Mies's interest in Wright in late 1923 is significant.

His idea of contemporary architecture at that moment was more inclusive and less radical than that of many of his peers who harbored reservations about Wright's recent architecture. While Mies had shown his own glass skyscraper and concrete country house designs at Gropius's Bauhaus exhibition in Weimar earlier that same year, he confessed in private that he disapproved of the exhibit's "wild constructivist formalism" and its "artistic fog."[67] He began, without telling Gropius, in conversations with Adolf Behne and Hugo Häring, to reimagine the exhibition in an enlarged format for a new showing in Berlin and elsewhere, which would have included Behrens, Henry van de Velde, Berlage (all of whom Mies had contacted already), Häring, and Hans Scharoun, among others. Wright perfectly fit into this context. When Gropius found out about Mies's plan, he was livid, and nothing came of it. Instead, the Bauhaus exhibition was shown in a reduced version (without the models) at the Provinzialmuseum Hannover.[68] Shortly afterward, in the early months of 1924, Mies began work on his Brick Country House project— clearly inspired by Wright's layouts and open spatial connections, which he would present at the "Great Berlin Art Exhibition" the following summer to great acclaim (fig. 5).

The architect Barry Byrne and sculptor Alfonso Iannelli, both of whom had worked for Wright, visited Mies in Berlin in early June 1924 and were

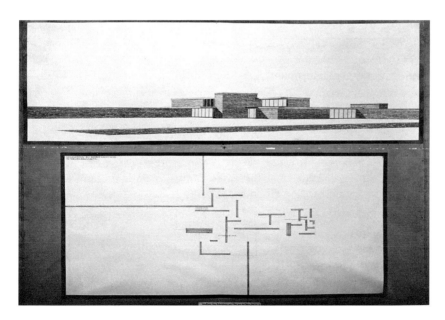

FIG. 5. Ludwig Mies van der Rohe, Brick Country House, schematic project, 1924. (Kunsthalle Mannheim)

impressed by this "powerful and reposeful person." They "got on famously" with him and, one would assume, discussed Wright's work, but probably not in any depth, given the fact that Mies "spoke no English."[69] Byrne would publish a critical evaluation of Wright in a German journal two years later, an important contribution to the local debates. Like his European colleagues before him, he praised Wright's floor plans as "absolute perfection" but accused him of "design for design's sake" and diagnosed a disconnect between structure and form, which he called "a danger for architecture." Despite their occasional exoticisms, he found Wright's houses more convincing than the Larkin Building and Unity Temple, both of which had been developed when Byrne was working for Wright between 1902 and 1907.[70] At the end of their visit, Mies talked Byrne and Iannelli into visiting the Netherlands, which they had not originally planned, and gave them a letter to his friend Oud, asking him to show them his work.[71]

The most exciting new tropes in architectural criticism in central Europe were movement, space, and, eventually, time. "Dynamics," "penetration," "breaking through walls"—such notions had assumed a central position in deliberations about Modern architecture by the early 1920s. The ground had been prepared for this new way of reading architecture in the late nineteenth century through art historians such as Heinrich Wölfflin, who had identified the key difference between the static Renaissance and the vibrant Baroque as the difference between "linear and voluminous," "flat and spatial," "calm and moving." Italian Baroque architecture suggested "the impression of continuous movement" and "spatial infinity."[72] Wölfflin's cohort, August Schmarsow, emphasized the central importance of space in architecture and of the "kinesthetic sensations" of our spatial experience; in other words, the need for the viewer to move in and around a building in order to comprehend it.[73] In the Netherlands, Berlage picked up on this new vocabulary, declaring in 1908: "The art of architecture lies in the creation of spaces, not in the design of façades."[74] Wölfflin's student Paul Frankl, in his *Principles of Architectural History* (1914), developed these ideas further when he noted that on occasion a building can contain such "a great flood of movement that [it] urges us round and through."[75] Similar to his teacher, he observed a "smooth flow of space" in Baroque architecture in contrast to the compartmentalization of the Renaissance.[76]

Wright seems to have been the first contemporary whose work was analyzed with this new focus on movement and the primacy of space. Oud claimed in 1918 that Wright had created a new "plastic" architecture by "achieving movement of the planes. . . . his masses slide back and forth and left and right; there are plastic effects in all directions. This movement, which one finds in his work, opens up entirely new aesthetic possibilities for architecture."[77] In 1923, Adolf Behne followed suit. Wright's "rooms are not inserted next to one another but set in motion—as asymmetrically as life itself." The aesthetic composition of Wright's houses, he continued, stems "from the basic elements of accelerated horizontal movement, subtly and strikingly stopped verticals, and textured walls that never appear as supporting but always as supported parts. All visible parts are completely conveyed as function: the precise relationship of open and closed areas produces the 'building.'"[78]

This new vocabulary received additional legitimacy from an unexpected source: Albert Einstein's *Special and General Theories of Relativity* of 1905 and 1915 burst into public consciousness when British astronomers found proof of the impact of gravity on the movement of light in 1919, and Einstein received the Nobel Prize in Physics in 1922.[79] While the details of Einstein's work were hardly accessible to the general public, time was now generally accepted as a "fourth dimension," expanding the three-dimensional space of Euclidian geometry.[80]

The recent observation by architectural theorists that spatial sequences reveal themselves in motion could seem to a naive observer a demonstration of Einstein's theorem of an indelible connection of space and time. After all, as several architects pointed out, movement through space needed time. Hamburg's chief planning director Fritz Schumacher, for instance, observed: "As a result of our movement the notion of space is joined by the notion of time. . . . The essence of architectural impact reaches into the fourth dimension, now commonplace thanks to the theory of relativity, which draws its scientific conclusions from the fact that all observations and events are bound by time."[81] Dutch architect Theo van Doesburg similarly declared: "The new architecture calculates not only with space but also with time as an architectural value. The unity of space and time will give architectural form a new and completely plastic aspect, that is, a four-dimensional, plastic space-time aspect."[82] He titled several of his colorful axonometrics "Space-Time Constructions."[83]

Apparently, Wright followed these discussions attentively and skeptically. Even though his designs had been positively analyzed within this framework, he pointedly avoided any use of the terms that had become *en vogue* in Europe, such as "movement," flowing "space," or the element of "time" in architecture.[84] He did not see the need for a new dimension: "We have heard of the fourth dimension frequently, of late, to meet this need. Why a fourth dimension, when we so little understand the possibilities of what we already use as the three dimensions?"[85] Wright explained that the third dimension, which, in his eyes, simply stood for structural depth and expansion, was perfectly sufficient to include "the new conception of architecture as interior space, finding utilization and enclosure" as part of the "*integral* concept of building for which I have pleaded."[86] Space (Wright used the term here for the first time in 1928), thus, was an integral part of his deliberate, three-dimensional planning of the building's fabric, rather than an end in itself.

Mies's Brick Country House project created a sensation at the "Great Berlin Art Exhibition" of 1924 and provoked his most sustained critical response yet. It comes as no surprise that writers applied to it the same new vocabulary that had been recently been used to characterize Wright's architecture. The project was praised as a "spatial fugue," "mathematics filled with music," and a new "continuous dwelling complex." According to Behrendt, its spaces flowed "towards each other as their perimeters have been almost entirely dissolved."[87]

The design's most direct successor was Mies's German Pavilion at the world's fair in Barcelona five years later, a functionless building with an open sequence of interior and exterior spaces, framed by marble walls, chromium-clad columns, and two water basins (fig. 6). Again, Wright's influence played a major role. According to Mies's collaborator, Sergius Ruegenberg, Mies had an issue of *Wendingen* on his desk when designing the pavilion, open to the pages of Wright's Coonley house.[88] We can see similarities, including the relationship between the flat, protruding roofs, the open spaces, and the water basin. When the pavilion opened, critics hailed it as the "most beautiful building at the entire exhibition," a victory for "a rebirth of the art of building," "a spatial work of art," "the manifestation of a higher spirit," even as "metaphysical architecture."[89] Frequently, critics employed the vocabulary used for the earlier Brick Country House project and, before that, for Wright's plans. Justus Bier, another Wölfflin student, noted that the walls seemed "as if simply slid into place."[90] Critic Gustav Adolf Platz declared the pavilion's "abstract space" the most "noble, the most cultivated form for our time," noting: "This 'empty'—flowing as it were—space, created from precious, partially transparent surfaces, is the result of the new art of building."[91]

Philip Johnson picked up the baton in 1932 on the occasion of the "Modern Architecture: International Exhibition" show at MoMA, linking Mies's "system of steel posts and the simple rectangular roof slab" in Barcelona to the earlier design of the Brick Country House. "Space flows around this rigid system," he asserted.[92] In the same catalog, Henry-Russell Hitchcock used similar language for the description of Wright's rooms: "By 1900 Wright had . . . completely reorganized and reformulated the theory of the individual

FIG. 6. Ludwig Mies van der Rohe, German Pavilion, International Exposition, Barcelona, 1929, reconstructed 1981–86. (Photograph © Hassan Bagheri, 2012)

house . . . as an instrument for the new possibilities of expansive modern life. Room flowed into room."[93]

Wright had also been invited to be part of the "Modern Architecture" exhibition and was just as difficult to deal with as he had promised, on three different occasions threatening to withdraw his participation. He was certainly bothered by the amount of attention given to the European modernists and their American followers, as well as his own sidelining as a romantic individualist and only a forerunner of the Modern movement. Wright had promised a new design and model for the show, which did not come until the last minute—Johnson held an empty spot in the exhibition and a space in the catalog. When it finally arrived, the House on the Mesa turned out to be magnificent—a large, expansive residential structure of concrete block shell walls with reinforced concrete slabs, which bore a certain resemblance to Mies's Concrete Country House (fig. 7).

Wright's accompanying letter contained a stab at Mies's Barcelona Pavilion—the rare case where he commented on a specific aspect of a colleague's work: "Someday let's persuade Mies to get rid of those damned little steel posts that look so dangerous and interfering in his lovely designs. He really doesn't need them as much as he thinks he does."[94] Brilliantly, Wright had picked up—he was the first to do so—on a conceptual problem that would

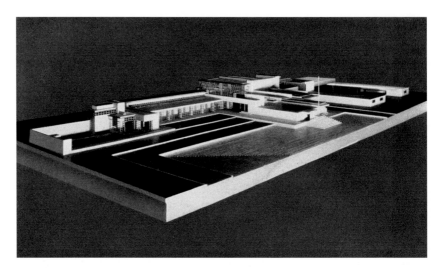

FIG. 7. Frank Lloyd Wright, House on the Mesa, 1932, project (*Modern Architecture: International Exhibition,* 1932, 55).

be confounding critics for decades to come. What was the problem with those columns? At the entrance of the pavilion there was a wall right next to them, and any architect would assume that the walls carried the roof. The thin, reflective columns appear as immaterial as possible; the walls signal mass and weight. Besides Wright, a number of critics, architects, and historians, including Arthur Drexler, Colin Rowe, Kenneth Frampton, William Jordy, and Peter Eisenman, believed that the columns were structurally unnecessary and instead a rhetorical device to, for example, "introduce an objective order,"[95] "allow the eye to measure the space,"[96] demonstrate the distinction "between functions of support and enclosure,"[97] signify the "absent presences"[98] of the corners, or smuggle in "a metaphor for a classical belvedere,"[99] or "the specter of a classical temple."[100]

Wright himself had never used thin, freestanding columns in the middle of a space. Not only did the columns in the German Pavilion interfere with Mies's design in Wright's eyes, but a column where none was needed was contrary to a core tenet of organic architecture. Wright could not know that Mies himself had not wanted those columns either; his early sketches and a floor plan are without them. But when financial constraints delayed construction, the fastest way forward in the remaining six weeks was a separate steel frame for the roof, rather than resting it on the irregularly spaced, hollow marble walls. Mies wanted the columns as invisible as possible, which explains their reflective veneer. Wright presented his house on the Mesa as a better alternative of "organic simplicity," "where style arises from the nature of construction," and "machine age luxury might compare with that of the Greeks or Goths."[101] Wright's project was a magnificent answer to the European challenge and to Mies's designs.

In 1937, Mies visited Wright at Taliesin. The two men got along so well that the intended afternoon visit stretched to four days. Wright took Mies to the construction site of his Johnson Wax Building in Racine, Wisconsin (1936–39), where, for the first time, he used freestanding columns in an interior. At the same time, his first Jacobs (1936–37) and Rosenbaum (1939–40; see fig. 2 on p. 122) houses in Madison, Wisconsin, and Florence, Alabama, respectively, emulated the Barcelona Pavilion, translating Mies's marble walls into brick and wood.

Behrendt, who had been the first to review Wright's Wasmuth publications in 1913 and the first one to use the term "spatial flow" for Mies's country house designs, emigrated to the United States at that same moment.[102] In his book *Modern Building: Its Nature, Problems, and Forms* of 1937, he directly compared the continuous flow of volumes in Mies's Brick Country House to the spatial flow in Wright's interiors.[103] In an essay for the Museum of Modern Art's Wright exhibition catalog of 1940, Behrendt was careful not to mention any European connections but rather concentrated on Wright's "new concept of organic architecture" by studying "the plans and buildings themselves." He claimed that Wright's rooms "flow into each other, penetrating each other and interlacing with indissoluble cohesion. And their uninterrupted flow does not stop at the enclosing walls, but continues over terraces, loggias and balconies into the outer space of the surrounding landscape." Wright, who had insisted on reading the catalog essays before anything went to print, was greatly displeased. Any connection to his European peers, even indirectly through the use of critical terms, was not welcome. Wright redacted Behrendt's piece and completely eliminated the above quoted paragraph. When the curators balked at this, Wright threatened to cancel the entire show. Instead, the museum abandoned the catalog.[104]

Hitchcock stepped in and wrote a "sort of *ex post facto* catalogue" for the exhibition in 1942 called *In the Nature of Materials: The Buildings of Frank Lloyd Wright, 1887–1941.* It was, finally, the first American book on Wright—thirty-two years after the Wasmuth portfolio, sixteen years after the Dutch and German monographs. Hitchcock credited Wright as his coauthor and, not surprisingly, was much kinder in his judgment than he had been in his 1929 publication. He also avoided references to the "flow of spaces" that he had used in his 1932 essay on Wright for the "Modern Architecture" exhibition. Of course, the situation had changed dramatically in the interim. Fallingwater (1935–39) and the Johnson Wax Building had brought renewed recognition, and, so he wrote, "the unity of modern architecture and the pre-eminence of Wright are once again generally recognized."[105] Wright was "happily as busy as in the days of his greatest activity before 1910 . . . [and] poised for new triumphs at the opening of a great phase of his career."[106] Instead of directions of influence and national identities, Hitchcock now emphasized "parallelisms" between Wright and the European modernists and defended Wright's use of ornament. While some critics in the 1920s, he wrote, "literally could not see the architecture for the hollyhocks," Wright was now recognized as the "long-term leader of modern architecture" and played an important role as the "master to all the younger generation."

Mies and Wright met for the last time at the former's 1947 show at MoMA. Mies's prewar work dominated the room in wall-high photographs (fig. 8). After the opening, Wright wrote: "My dear Mies: Somebody had told me you were hurt by remarks of mine when I came to see your New York show. . . . you know you have frequently said you believe in 'doing next to nothing' all down the line. Well, when I saw the enormous blow-ups the phrase 'Much ado about "next to nothing"' came spontaneously from me. Then I said the Barcelona Pavilion was your best contribution to the original 'negation' and you seemed to be still back there where I was then. . . . it does seem to me that the whole thing called 'Modern Architecture' has bogged down with the architects right there on that line."[107] But, he added: "You are the best of them all as an artist and a man," and he invited him to come up to Taliesin and talk. Mies responded: "It was an exaggeration if you heard that my feelings were hurt. . . . If I had heard the crack 'Much ado about next to nothing' I would have laughed with you. About 'negation'—I feel that you use this word for qualities that I find positive and essential."[108] Wright's somewhat cryptic statement: "you seemed to be still back there where I was then" makes sense in the light of his 1925 letter to the European colleagues, where he recalled that his early work had used straight lines and empty surfaces of machine-made materials as a concession to the mechanistic method, but that he then discovered the need for humanizing ornament.

The different design approaches of Mies and Wright and related questions of European versus American cultural identity continued to occupy critics in the following years.[109] Vincent Scully created an unexpected controversy in 1954 with a spirited essay titled "Frank Lloyd Wright and the International Style" about the mutual influences between Wright and his European peers. While a plausible assertion today, the time was not yet ripe (and Wright was still alive) for Scully's claim to be accepted. The Barcelona Pavilion played a major role in Scully's argument. It was, he said, strongly influenced by Wright's 1902 Yahara Boat Club project for Madison, Wisconsin, via the 1910 Wasmuth publication (fig. 9). The pavilion then in turn inspired Wright's early Usonian houses.[110]

FIG. 8. Exhibition of the work of Mies van der Rohe, Museum of Modern Art, New York, 1947. Photograph Herbert Matler. (Museum of Modern Art, New York, and Artists Rights Society, 2018)

According to the (no doubt delighted) editor of *Art News,* Scully's essay "aroused a tempest and spawned a number of impassioned letters to the editor." Edgar Kaufmann Jr., Wright's former apprentice and son of the client of Fallingwater, for instance, suggested that Scully had mixed up "crustaceans" and "vertebrates," the latter being the more developed species. The Barcelona Pavilion, he argued, uses "its screens to enclose space," thus being a primitive crustacean, while Wright would expand, almost explode, space from a nucleus: "Wright's walls are always flowing out, Mies's always returning on themselves." In addition, he said, the flat roof and the base at Wright's boat club and Mies's Barcelona Pavilion were entirely different. Interior designer T. H. Robsjohn-Gibbings simply found the idea that Wright was "now being influenced by those he influenced . . . too preposterous to be taken seriously."[111] Similarly, Elizabeth Gordon, the outspoken editor of *House Beautiful,* who had recently identified Mies as a "threat to the next America," saw "neither truth nor poetry" in the notion of Wright "imitating his imitators . . . as though the block playing Mies were literally the father of the man who fathered him."[112] Scully rushed to respond to his critics, and

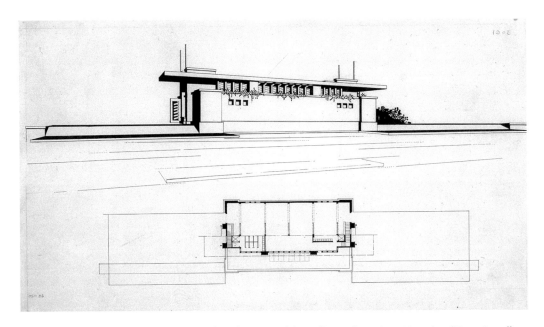

FIG. 9. Frank Lloyd Wright, Yahara Boat Club, Madison, Wisconsin, 1902, project (Henry-Russell Hitchcock, *Frank Lloyd Wright,* 1928, fig. 79). (© The Frank Lloyd Wright Foundation, AZ/Art Resource, NY)

a year later he made a strong case for the *American* origins of what he considered one of Wright's (and also much of Modern architecture's) most central qualities, namely the "flow of space" and "spatial interpenetration." They had been around in American architecture long before Mies, he pointed out, namely in the Shingle Style of the 1880s, with houses by Wilson Eyre, Bruce Price, and McKim, Mead & White leading up to Wright's work, such as the Willits and Martin houses.[113] This was exactly the kind of argument that the youthful Henry-Russell Hitchcock had laid out in an unpublished manuscript of 1927, which might not be entirely coincidental, as Hitchcock was a member of Scully's dissertation committee.[114] Wright, of course, had no interest in the metaphor of "spatial flow," which he probably considered an invention of European modernists just as affected as their exaggerated simplicity.

The process of cross-fertilization was complex and multifaceted. The critical reception of those mutual influences was enriched by and fraught with concerns about cultural identities on both sides. Returning to my initial quote by Hegemann who had, tongue-in-cheek, declared that Wright was "a product made in Germany," one might concede that at the very least some of the critical language that we routinely apply to Wright had emerged from the German and Dutch discourse on movement and architecture in the

1920s, which had seen its first convincing European example in the work of Mies van der Rohe.

NOTES

1. Werner Hegemann, "Baumeister: Frank Lloyd Wright," *Die Weltbühne* 25 (25 June 1929): 982. Hegemann's flippant remark suggests that he was unaware of the fatal fire at Taliesin in 1925 that destroyed the living quarters and the remaining copies of Wright's Wasmuth publication. See Henry-Russell Hitchcock, "Wright's Influence Abroad," in Peter Reed and William Kaizen, eds., *The Show to End All Shows: Frank Lloyd Wright and The Museum of Modern Art, 1940* (New York: Museum of Modern Art, 2004), 144–50.

2. Hitchcock's papers contain four somewhat similar versions of this early manuscript, which the twenty-three-year-old, freshly minted art historian began to work on after receiving his master's of art from Harvard. Two versions are called "American Architecture in Europe," an outline is titled "Modern Architecture: History and Criticism," another manuscript is called "Modern Architecture and After: History and Criticism." The above quote is from the fourth version of the manuscript "Modern Architecture and After: History and Criticism," dated 24 September–1 October. Henry-Russell Hitchcock Papers, 1919–1987, Archives of American Art, Smithsonian Institution, mss. "Modern Architecture."

3. The Dutch response to Wright has so far received more attention than his German reception. See, for example, Mariëtte van Stralen, "Kindred Spirits: Holland, Wright and Wijdeveld," in Anthony Alofsin, ed., *Frank Lloyd Wright: Europe and Beyond* (Berkeley: University of California Press, 1999), 45–75. See also Herman van Bergeijk, ed., *Amerikaanse Dromen: Frank Lloyd Wright en Nederland* (Rotterdam: Uitgeverij 010, 2008). For the German reception, see Anthony Alofsin, "Wright, Influence and the World at Large," in Alofsin, *Frank Lloyd Wright: Europe and Beyond,* 1–23; and Donald Langmead and Donald Leslie Johnson, *Architectural Excursions: Frank Lloyd Wright, Holland and Europe* (Westport, Conn.: Greenwood, 2000).

4. These two publications are known as *Ausgeführte Bauten und Entwürfe von Frank Lloyd Wright* (Berlin: Ernst Wasmuth, 1910) and *8. Sonderheft der Architektur des XX. Jahrhunderts: Frank Lloyd Wright Chicago.* (Berlin: Ernst Wasmuth, 1911). On Wright and Europe, see Anthony Alofsin, *Frank Lloyd Wright: The Lost Years, 1910–1922, A Study of Influence* (Chicago: University of Chicago Press, 1993). Two photographs of Wright's work made it into another Wasmuth publication in 1910 (albeit without any mention in the text and with misspelled attributions), the Winslow house of 1893–94 and the Williams house of 1895, both in River Forest, Illinois, in R. Rudolf Vogel, *Das Amerikanische Haus* (Berlin: Wasmuth, 1910), 221.

5. "Beilage für Vereine. Berichte über Versammlungen und Besichtigungen. Vereinigung Berliner Architekten," *Deutsche Bauzeitung* 44 (1 October 1910): 641.

6. Alofsin, *Frank Lloyd Wright: The Lost Years,* 34.

7. Walter Curt Behrendt, "Frank Lloyd Wright, Chicago," *Kunst und Künstler* 11 (1913): 487.

8. In particular, Gropius's design for the office building at the 1914 Cologne Werk-

bund Exhibition, which apparently takes some inspiration from the Park Inn Hotel in Mason City, Iowa (1909–10), and his Sommerfeld house in Berlin of 1920, which bears a certain resemblance to the Winslow house in River Forest.

9. Gropius lectured on "Monumentale Kunst und Industriebau" on 29 January 1911 at the Folkwang Museum in Hagen. His lecture notes have survived in the Bauhaus Archive, Berlin. His 1913 essay in the *Werkbund Jahrbuch* followed the same lines: Walter Gropius, "Die Entwicklung Moderner Industriebaukunst," in *Die Kunst in Industrie und Handel* (Jena: E. Diederichs, 1913), 17–22.

10. See Hendrik Petrus Berlage, "Neuere amerikanische Architektur: Reiseeindrücke," *Schweizerische Bauzeitung* 60:11 (1912): 148–50 and pls. 33–36; 60:12 (1912): 165–67 and pls. 37–40; 60:13 (1912): 178 and pls. 41–44. Berlage's essay was based on a slide lecture he had given at the Architects and Engineers Association in Zürich on 30 March 1912.

11. Berlage, "Neuere amerikanische Architektur," 150.

12. J. J. P. Oud, "Architectural Observations Concerning Wright and the Robie House," *De Stijl* 1:4 (1918): 39–41, reprinted in H. Allen Brooks, ed., *Writings on Wright: Selected Comment on Frank Lloyd Wright* (Cambridge: MIT Press, 1983), 135–37.

13. Jan Wils, "Frank Lloyd Wright," *Elsevier's Geïllustreerd Maandschrift* 61:4 (1921): 217–27, reprinted in Brooks, *Writings on Wright,* 139–48.

14. Ludwig Hilberseimer and Udo Rusker, "Amerikanische Architektur," *Kunst und Künstler* 18:12 (1920): 537–46.

15. Adolf Behne, "Amerikanische Architektur," *Vossische Zeitung,* 14 April 1923, morning edition, 2 (translation by the author).

16. Adolf Behne, "The Modern Functional Building" (translated from *Moderne Zweckbau,* 1926) (Santa Monica, Calif.: Getty Research Institute, 1996), 99.

17. Erich Mendelsohn to his wife, Luise, 31 October 1917, Erich Mendelsohn Archiv, Kunstbibliothek, Staatliche Museen zu Berlin, online at http://ema.smb.museum /de/briefe/?id=553.

18. Erich Mendelsohn to Luise Mendelsohn, 5 November 1924, Erich Mendelsohn Archiv, Kunstbibliothek, Staatliche Museen zu Berlin, online at http://ema.smb .museum/1927. (Mendelsohn published the text of this letter to his wife almost verbatim two years later: Erich Mendelsohn, "Besuch bei Wright," *Baukunst* 2 [February 1926]: 56.)

19. Frank Lloyd Wright, *An Autobiography*, revised and enlarged edition (New York: Duell, Sloan & Pearce, 1943), 260.

20. Architect and critic Hermann Sörgel mocked the flood of new architecture books as an escapism from the contemporary malaise and lack of work. Eighty percent of them were superfluous, he claimed. Hermann Sörgel, "Bücherschreiben und Verlegerverantwortung," *Baukunst* 2 (1926): 70.

21. Walter Gropius, *Internationale Architektur* (Munich: Albert Langen, 1925), 44–45, 68–69.

22. Werner Moser, "Frank Lloyd Wright und Amerikanische Architektur," *Werk* 12:5 (1925): 129–42. Moser's essay was followed by Richard Neutra's brief comments on "Architects and Architecture in Chicago" ("Architekten und Bauwesen in Chicago"), *Werk* 12:5 (1925): 143–44, which sketched out a lineage from Burnham & Root to Sullivan and Wright.

23. Roland Jäger, *Heinrich de Fries und sein Beitrag zur Architekturpublizistik der*

Zwanziger Jahre (Berlin: Gebrüder Mann, 2001), 101; Heinrich de Fries, "Junge Baukunst," *Städtebau* 16 (1920): 17–19, quote p. 17.

24. Jäger, *Heinrich de Fries,* 102.

25. Heinrich de Fries, *Moderne Villen und Landhäuser* (Berlin: Ernst Wasmuth, 1924), vii.

26. It is important to note that the 1925 volume (seventh series) of *Wendingen* appeared with much delay between May 1925 and September 1926, the seven Wright issues between October 1925 and April 1926 (all still labeled seventh series, 1925). Because of the delay and editorial disagreements about the exorbitant costs (not the least of the Wright project), there was no 1926 series, and series eight started only in June 1927. Wijdeveld had presented the project to the editorial board in the meeting on 13 February 1925. See Martijn F. Le Coultre, *Wendingen—A Journal for the Arts, 1918–1932* (New York: Princeton Architectural Press, 2001), 14, 164–68.

27. J. J. P. Oud, "The Influence of Frank Lloyd Wright on the Architecture of Europe," *Wendingen* 7 (June 1925, published February 1926): 85–89, reprinted in Hendricus Theodorus Wijdeveld, ed., *The Life Work of the American Architect Frank Lloyd Wright* (Santpoort, Netherlands: C. A. Mees, 1925), 85–89. To his credit, Wijdeveld gave room to Oud's critical essay in both his magazine *Wendingen* and in the subsequent book. The essay also appeared in J. J. P. Oud, *Holländische Architektur* (1926; reprint ed., Mainz and Berlin: Florian Kupferberg, 1976), 77–83.

28. In his then recent history of American architecture, Lewis Mumford had given rather short shrift to Wright. His "pleasure pavilions and hotels do not resemble either factories or garages or grain elevators" but rather reject the "whole world of engineering" and instead respond to "human purposes" and the American prairie. Lewis Mumford, *Sticks and Stones* (New York: Boni and Liveright, 1924), 181–82. It appeared in German in 1925 under the title "Vom Blockhaus zum Wolkenkratzer."

29. Levis [*sic*] Mumford, "The Social Background of Frank Lloyd Wright," *Wendingen* 7 (May 1925, published January 1926): 65–75, and (June 1925, published February 1926): 78–79, reprinted in Wijdeveld, *The Life Work,* 65–79.

30. Jaeger, *Heinrich de Fries,* 110.

31. Heinrich de Fries, "Zu den Arbeiten des Architekten Frank Lloyd Wright," in de Fries, *Frank Lloyd Wright* (Berlin: Ernst Pollak, 1926), 29–31. De Fries had published the essay previously in the journal *Baugilde,* which he edited: Heinrich de Fries, "Zu einigen Arbeiten des Architekten Frank Lloyd Wright," *Baugilde* 7:1 (1925): 15–16.

32. Heinrich de Fries, "Reisebilder aus Holland," *Baugilde* 6 (1924): 272. De Fries also made his claim about Wright's China connection in the introduction to his book *Moderne Villen,* vii.

33. The article was one of the first, perhaps *the* first, to discuss Wright's pinwheel planning technique, which de Fries referred to as a windmill plan.

34. De Fries to Wright, 11 August 1926, quoted from Jaeger, *Heinrich de Fries,* 108.

35. In fairness, Wright had actually told Wijdeveld in January 1925 about "two recent projects," given to de Fries, "for reproductions in color . . . which could not possibly be got into *Wendingen* and are not executed," material de Fries "had anxiously awaited long since." Wijdeveld to Wright, 25 April 1926, Frank Lloyd Wright Archives, quoted from Anthony Alofsin, "Frank Lloyd Wright and the Dutch Connection," in van Bergeijk, *Amerikaanse Dromen,* 30. See also a letter from Wright

to Wijdeveld, 7 January 1925, telling him about the reproductions that he had sent to de Fries: "I think, the Wendingen should be pushed so as not to be behind these things of DeFries if possible." See Bruce Brooks Pfeiffer, ed., *Letters to Architects: Frank Lloyd Wright* (Fresno: California State University Press, 1984), 57.

36. Jaeger, *Heinrich de Fries,* 114.

37. Frank Lloyd Wright, "To My European Co-Workers," *Wendingen* 7 (September 1925, published April 1926): 162.

38. Several scholars have made this assumption; see Alofsin, "Frank Lloyd Wright and the Dutch Connection," 33n11; and Jaeger, *Heinrich de Fries,* 110.

39. The essay is included in neither Donald Langmead, *Frank Lloyd Wright: A Bio-Bibliography* (Westport, Conn.: Praeger, 2003); nor Bruce Brooks Pfeiffer, ed., *Frank Lloyd Wright: Collected Writings, vol 1, 1894–1930* (New York: Rizzoli, 1992). Langmead, however, does mention the later publication of that same essay in German in the Swiss journal *Werk* 13 (1926): 375, 377–80.

40. See Neil Levine, "Abstraction and Representation in Modern Architecture: The International Style and Frank Lloyd Wright," *AA Files* 11 (Spring 1986): 3–21.

41. Frank Lloyd Wright, "An die europäischen Kollegen," in de Fries, *Frank Lloyd Wright,* 43–44.

42. Werner Hegemann and Elbert Peets, *The American Vitruvius: An Architects' Handbook of Urban Design* (New York: Architectural Book Publishing, 1922).

43. Werner Hegemann, "Holland, Wright, Breslau," *Wasmuths Monatshefte für Baukunst* 9:4 (1925): 165–67.

44. Werner Hegemann, *Entlarvte Geschichte* (Leipzig: Jakob Hegner, 1933).

45. See Jaeger, *Heinrich de Fries,* 62–63.

46. Adolf Rading, "Buchbesprechung: Amerikanische Architektur und Stadtbaukunst," *Baugilde* 7:1 (1925): 37. Hegemann's response and Rading's rejoinder: *Baugilde* 7:4 (1925): 206–207, 208–210, respectively. Not surprisingly, Rading heaped exuberant praise on de Fries's book when it appeared the next year ("one of the most essential publications of our time"). Adolf Rading, "Frank Lloyd Wright: Herausgegeben von Architekt H. de Fries," *Die Form* 2 (1927): 127–28. About Werner Hegemann and his opinion on Frank Lloyd Wright, see Christiane Crasemann Collins, *Werner Hegemann and the Search for Universal Urbanism* (New York: W. W. Norton, 2005), 157–67.

47. The book by Hegemann that the Nazis burned was the above mentioned *Entlarvte Geschichte.*

48. Werner Hegemann, "Weimarer Bauhaus und Ägyptische Baukunst," *Wasmuths Monatshefte für Baukunst,* 8: 3–4 (1924): 69–86.

49. Hegemann, "Weimarer Bauhaus," 81. Hegemann followed up with a lengthy editorial in his own magazine: "Holland, Wright, Breslau," see n. 43.

50. Werner Hegemann, *Amerikanische Architektur und Stadtbaukunst,* 2nd ed. (Berlin: Ernst Wasmuth, 1927), 148.

51. Heinrich de Fries, *Frank Lloyd Wright: Aus dem Lebenswerke eines Architekten* (Berlin: Ernst Pollak, 1926), 30.

52. Hegemann, *Amerikanische Architektur,* 172, 173. See a similar reference by Hegemann to Wright's "Chinese Pylons" in his response to an article on Belgian architecture: Emile Henvaux, "Modernistische Baukunst in Belgian ausserhalb Gross-Brüssels," *Wasmuths Monatshefte für Baukunst* 111:1 (1927), 12–23 (Hegemann's remarks on pp. 16 and 23). Hegemann here adopted verbatim the argument

that his collaborator, architect Leo Adler, had made during the previous year. See
Leo Adler, "Zuschriften an die Herausgeber: Frank Lloyd Wright's Neue Baukunst
und Mendelsohns Logik," *Wasmuths Monatshefte für Baukunst* 10:7 (1926): 308–9.
With the help of three illustrations of Chinese architecture from a recent book
(Ernst Boerschmann, *Chinesische Architektur* [Berlin: Wasmuth, 1925]), Adler
compared houses in Shenzi and Canton provinces with vertical piers in front and a
comparable motive at the Larkin Building and the Martin house in order to contra-
dict Mendelsohn, who had praised Wright for an architecture without precedent
and the final step after Sullivan in America's move toward modernity. See Erich
Mendelsohn, "Frank Lloyd Wright," *Wasmuths Monatshefte für Baukunst* 10:6
(1926): 244–45.

53. Henry-Russell Hitchcock, "American Architecture in Europe," manuscript, ca.
1927, p. 6, Henry-Russell Hitchcock Papers, Modern Architecture, Archives of
American Art, Smithsonian Institution (hereafter HRH). Outline and Introduction, several drafts, all 1927.

54. Hitchcock, "American Architecture," HRH, 32.

55. Henry-Russell Hitchcock, "Modern Architecture: I, The Traditionalists and
the New Tradition," *Architectural Record* 63 (April 1928): 340, 347; Hitchcock,
"Modern Architecture: II, The New Pioneers," *Architectural Record* 63 (May 1928):
452–60.

56. Henry-Russell Hitchcock, *Frank Lloyd Wright* (Paris: Editions Cahiers d'Art,
1928), n.p.

57. Henry-Russell Hitchcock, *Modern Architecture: Romanticism and Reintegration*
(New York: Payson & Clarke, 1929), 155.

58. Hitchcock, *Modern Architecture,* 104, 115, 116–17, 118.

59. Max Osborn, "Frank Lloyd Wright," *Vossische Zeitung,* 17 June 1931, evening ed., 3.
Wilhelm Lotz defended Wright against Osborn's critique in the Werkbund journal:
W. L. "Unter der Lupe: Frank Lloyd Wright und die Kritik," *Die Form* 6:9 (1931):
357–58.

60. Paul. F. Schmidt, "Grösse und Niedergang eines Bahnbrechers der modernen
Architektur," *Baukunst* 7 (August 1931): 278–79.

61. Frank Lloyd Wright, "To My Critics in the Land of the Danube and the Rhine,"
in Pfeiffer, *Frank Lloyd Wright: Collected Writings, Vol. 3, 1931–19* (New York:
Rizzoli, 1993), 18–20.

62. Frank Lloyd Wright to Philip Johnson, 19 January 1932, in Pfeiffer, *Letters to
Architects,* 89.

63. "Oral History of George Danforth," interviewed by Pauline Saliga, Chicago Architects Oral History Project, Art Institute of Chicago, 90, online at http://digital
-libraries.saic.edu/cdm/compoundobject/collection/caohp/id/2697/rec/3.

64. See, for example, Mies's Perls, Werner, Urbig, Eichstädt, Ryder, Kempner, Feld-
mann, and Mosler houses.

65. Werner Hegemann, "Schräges oder Flaches Dach," *Wasmuths Monatshefte für
Baukunst* 11:3 (1927): 120.

66. Mies to Berlage, 13 December 1923, Mies Papers, private correspondence 1923–40,
Manuscript Division, Library of Congress (hereafter Mies Papers). The original
letter is in the Berlage Papers, Het Nieuwe Instituut (formerly Netherlandish
Architecture Institute), Rotterdam (hereafter Berlage Papers).

67. Mies to Werner Jakstein, 13 September 1923, Mies Papers.

68. Adolf Meyer to Mies, 22 November 1923; Mies to Gropius, 29 September 1923; Gropius to Mies, 2 October 1923, Mies Papers.

69. Vincent L. Michael, "Expressing the Modern: Barry Byrne in Europe," *Journal of the Society of Architectural Historians* 69 (December 2010): 541.

70. Barry Byrne, "Frank Lloyd Wright," *Baukunst* 2 (1926): 54–55.

71. Ludwig Mies van der Rohe to J. J. P. Oud, 10 June 1924, Berlage Papers.

72. Heinrich Wölfflin, *Renaissance und Barock: Eine Untersuchung über Wesen und Entstehung des Barockstils in Italien* (Munich: Theodor Ackermann, 1888), 18, 40, 52.

73. August Schmarsow, *Das Wesen der architektonischen Schöpfung* (Leipzig: Hiersemann, 1894), English trans. in Harry Francis Mallgrave and Eleftherios Ikonomou, eds., *Empathy, Form, and Space: Problems in German Aesthetics, 1873–1893* (Santa Monica, Calif.: Getty Center for the History of Art and the Humanities, 1994), 291, 292.

74. Hendrik Petrus Berlage, "The Foundations and Development of Architecture," in *Hendrik Petrus Berlage: Thoughts on Style, 1886–1909* (Santa Monica, Calif.: Getty Center for the History of Art and the Humanities, 1996), 249.

75. Paul Frankl, *Die Entwicklungsphasen der neueren Baukunst* (Leipzig: Teubner, 1914); English ed., *Principles of Architectural History*, trans. J. F. O'Gorman (Cambridge, Mass.: MIT Press, 1968), 148.

76. Frankl, *Principles of Architectural History*, 46.

77. J. J. P. Oud, "Architectural Observations Concerning Wright and the Robie House," *De Stijl* 1:4 (1918): 39–41; reprinted in Brooks, *Writings on Wright*, 135–37.

78. Adolf Behne, "The Modern Functional Building" (translated from *Das Moderne Zweckbau*, 1926), (Santa Monica, Calif.: Getty Research Institute, 1996), 99.

79. Arthur Stanley Eddington, *Raum, Zeit und Schwere* (Brunswick: Vieweg + Teubner, 1923), 114–25.

80. The mathematician Hermann Minkowski had first published this idea in his 1908 lecture "Space and Time," which provided the basis for the General Theory of Relativity of his former pupil Albert Einstein in 1915. In an attempt to explain his complex model to the general public, Minkowski wrote: "Henceforth space by itself, and time by itself, are doomed to fade away into mere shadows, and only a kind of union of the two will preserve an independent reality. . . . No one has ever noticed a place unless at a certain time, neither a time without a distinct place." Hermann Minkowski, *Raum und Zeit*, 1908, in Hendrik Anton Lorentz, *Albert Einstein, Hermann Minkowski, Das Relativitätsprinzip 1913* (Leipzig: Teubner, 1915), 57.

81. Fritz Schumacher, "Die Zeitgebundenheit der Architektur," *Deutsches Bauwesen* 5:16 (1929): 238–43. See also Paul Zucker, "Der Begriff der Zeit in der Architektur," *Repertorium für Kunstwissenschaft* 44 (1924): 237–45, quoted from Andreas Denk, Uwe Schröder, and Rainer Schützeichel, eds., *Architektur. Raum. Theorie. Eine kommentierte Anthologie* (Tübingen: Ernst Wasmuth, 2016), 301–11.

82. Theo van Doesburg, "Towards Plastic Architecture" (1924), in Joost Baljeu, *Theo van Doesburg* (New York: Macmillan, 1974), 144. See also John G. Hatch, "Some Adaptations of Relativity in the 1920s and the Birth of Abstract Architecture," *Nexus Network Journal* 12 (2010): 131–47; Linda Dalrymple Henderson, *The Fourth Dimension and Non-Euclidean Geometry in Modern Art* (Cambridge, Mass.: MIT Press, 2013).

83. Els Hoek, *Theo van Doesburg oeuvre catalogus* (Utrecht: Centraal Museum, 2000), 370.

84. In his essay on the Third Dimension for the Wendingen volume, Wright wrote, "A sense of the third dimension in the use of the 'box' and the 'slab'—and a sense of the room within as the thing to be expressed in arranging them are what made Unity Temple." Frank Lloyd Wright, "In the Cause of Architecture: The Third Dimension," in Pfeiffer, *Frank Lloyd Wright: Collected Writings*, vol. 1, *1894–1930* (New York: Rizzoli, 1992), 212.

85. Frank Lloyd Wright, "In the Cause of Architecture: IX, The Terms," *Architectural Record* 64 (December 1928): 509.

86. Wright, "In the Cause of Architecture: IX," 510.

87. Hans Soeder, "Architektur auf der Berliner Kunstausstellung 1924," *Neubau* 6 (1924): 153–58; Hans Richter, "Der Neue Baumeister," *Qualität* 4 (January–February 1925): 3–9; Walter Curt Behrendt, *Der Sieg des neuen Baustils* (Stuttgart: Dr. Fr. Wedekind, 1927), 51.

88. Günther Kühne, "Der Skelettbau ist keine Teigware: Sergius Ruegenberg berichtet von Mies van der Rohes Berliner Zeit," *Bauwelt* 11 (28 February 1986): 346–51, quote p. 350.

89. Jeanne Bailhache, "Deutschland auf der Internationalen Ausstellung in Barcelona," *Frankfurter Nachrichten* 208 (2 June 1929): n.p.; Walther Genzmer, "Der Deutsche Reichspavillon auf der Internationalen Ausstellung in Barcelona," *Die Baugilde* 11 (October 1929): 1654–55; Justus Bier, "Mies van der Rohes Reichspavilion in Barcelona," *Die Form: Zeitschrift für gestaltende Arbeit* 16 (15 August 1929): 423–30. Vs., "Der Pavillon des Deutschen Reiches auf der Ausstellung in Barcelona: Architekt Ludwig Mies van der Rohe," *Stein Holz Eisen* 41 (26 September 1929): 609–13. See also Francisco Marroquin, "Hacia una nueva arquitectura: El Pabellón de Alemania en la Exposicion de Barcelona," *ABC* 26 (26 January 1930): 13–14; Nicolas M. Rubió i Tudurí, "Le Pavillon de l'Allemagne à l'Exposition de Barcelone par Mies van der Rohe," *Cahiers d'Art*, nos. 8/9 (1929): 408–11.

90. Bier, "Mies van der Rohes Reichspavillon in Barcelona," 423–30.

91. Gustav Adolf Platz, *Die Baukunst der Neuesten Zeit*, 2nd ed. (Berlin: Propyläen, 1930), 80–81.

92. Philip C. Johnson, "Mies van der Rohe," in *Modern Architecture: International Exhibition* (New York: Museum of Modern Art, exhibit cat. 1932), 115.

93. Henry-Russell Hitchcock, "Frank Lloyd Wright," in *Modern Architecture: International Exhibition*, 32.

94. Carbon copy of letter from Wright to Johnson, 26 February 1932, fiche #M029B03, Frank Lloyd Wright Foundation Archives, Avery Architectural & Fine Arts Library, Columbia University, and Museum of Modern Art, New York (hereafter FLWFA).

95. Letter from Wright to Johnson, 26 February 1932.

96. Barry Bergdoll, "The Nature of Mies' Space," in Terence Riley and Barry Bergdoll, eds., *Mies in Berlin* (New York: Museum of Modern Art, 2001), 67–105.

97. Colin Rowe, "Neo-Classicism and Modern Architecture II" (written 1956–57, first published in *Oppositions* 1 [1973]), reprinted in Rowe, *The Mathematics of the Ideal Villa and Other Essays* (Cambridge, Mass.: MIT Press, 1976), 143–44.

98. Peter Eisenman, "miMISes READING: does not mean A THING," in John Zukowsky, ed., *Mies Reconsidered: His Career, Legacy, and Disciples* (Chicago: Art Institute of Chicago, and New York: Rizzoli, 1986), 93.

99. Kenneth Frampton, "Modernism and Tradition in the Work of Mies van der Rohe," in Zukowsky, *Mies Reconsidered*, 35–53.

100. William H. Jordy, *American Buildings and Their Architects*, vol. 5, *The Impact of European Modernism in the Mid-Twentieth Century* (New York: Oxford University Press, 1972), 148–49.

101. Letter from Wright to Johnson, 26 February 1932.

102. Behrendt followed here the above-mentioned Paul Frankl. See Frankl, *Principles of Architectural History*, 46.

103. "As in Wright's most advanced examples of organic building, the boundaries of the rooms are loosened, their outer walls are fully opened, their volumes flow into one another, penetrate each other, and thereby achieve a connection more intimate than the mechanical one of geometric order, accomplished by the mere relation of axes." Walter Kurt Behrendt, *Modern Building: Its Nature, Problems, and Forms* (New York: Harcourt, Brace, 1937), 155.

104. Reed and Kaizen, *The Show to End All Shows*, 72, 74, 127–28.

105. Henry-Russell Hitchcock, *In the Nature of Materials: The Buildings of Frank Lloyd Wright, 1887–1941* (New York: Duell, Sloan & Pearce, 1942), 72.

106. Hitchcock, *In the Nature of Materials*, xxix, 102–03.

107. Wright to Mies, 25 October 1947, Mies van der Rohe Papers, Museum of Modern Art.

108. Mies to Wright, 25 November 1947, Mies van der Rohe Papers, Museum of Modern Art.

109. Bruno Zevi, *Poetica dell'architettura neoplastica* (Milan: Libreria Editrice Politecnica Tamburini, 1953), 133.

110. Vincent J. Scully Jr., "Wright vs. the International Style," *Art News* 53 (March 1954): 32–35, 64–66, reprinted in Neil Levine, ed., *Vincent Scully: Modern Architecture and Other Essays* (Princeton: Princeton University Press, 2003), 54; letters to Edgar Kaufmann jr., T. H. Robsjohn-Gibbings, and Elizabeth Gordon and Scully's response: "The Wright—International Style Controversy," *Art News* 53 (September 1954): 48–49. Scully doubtlessly picked up on the importance that Hitchcock had placed on the Yahara Boat Club design in his 1942 monograph; Hitchcock, *In the Nature of Materials*, 49.

111. "The Wright-International Style Controversy: T. H. Robsjohn-Gibbings," *Art News* 53 (September 1954): 48.

112. Elizabeth Gordon, "The Threat to the Next America," *House Beautiful* 95 (April 1953): 126–30, 240, 250–51; "Wright—International Style," 48–49.

113. Vincent J. Scully Jr., *The Shingle Style: Architectural Theory and Design from Richardson to the Origins of Wright* (New Haven: Yale University Press, 1955; expanded ed., 1971), 99, 121, 123, 127, 133.

114. I would like to thank Richard Longstreth for pointing out this fact to me. Hitchcock's 1927 manuscripts are cited in n. 2 above.

JEAN-LOUIS COHEN

Wright on the Scene in France, Russia, and Italy
Observation and Instrumentalization

In his article "Amerikanizm in European architecture," published in 1925, the Russian artist and architect El Lissitzky reiterated the scathing statement Le Corbusier made two years earlier against American architects. Lissitzky condemned the "artists-architects" who were "clothing the living skeleton of the skyscrapers with ostentatious embellishments." But, in contrast to his Parisian colleague, he did not see a radical alternative in the works of the engineers. Instead, he mentioned "Frank Lloyd Wright, America's only architect, who dared to discard all text-book precepts and to create a new type of dwelling, which has revealed him as the father of modern architecture."[1]

Lissitzky's knowledge had been acquired neither in America nor Russia, but in the Netherlands. He was undoubtedly familiar with the 1925–26 *Wendingen* publications of Wright's buildings—more than many of his contemporaries—as he had himself designed the cover of one of the issues devoted by Hendricus Theodorus Wijdeveld to Wright's architecture in 1921.[2] It is true that, by the mid-1920s, journals and books had widely informed professional audiences throughout Western Europe about Wright's buildings, designs, and ideas. He was already inserted in the first narratives establishing a genealogy of the new architecture, such as Gustav Adolf Platz's 1927 *Baukunst der neuersten Zeit*.[3] The echo his work received in Germany and Holland, the main contexts in which he was known, have been repeatedly discussed since the 1970s, yet new considerations are revising the earliest studies, as shown by Dietrich Neumann's contribution to this volume.[4] Other European countries, such as France, Russia, and Italy, where the "discovery" of Wright was to some extent delayed, have not received the same attention and deserve to be scrutinized.[5]

Despite the geographic distance, I suggest that, far from being considered as an exotic figure, Wright can be seen almost as an internal protagonist of the architectural discourse in these countries from the late 1920s to the 1970s, the shadow cast by his changing design strategies extending sometimes to unexpected circles, not all of them engaged in the most innovative projects. In reference to Hans-Robert Jauss's theories on the aesthetic of reception, it could be said the horizons of expectation in which the reception of Wright was inscribed were widely different.[6] He was inscribed in critical perspectives that were not necessarily his own. Yet the various roles he was unwillingly invited to play were sometimes strikingly similar. Before considering these multiple roles, a focus on his reception in France, Russia, and Italy allows for an understanding of the expectations to which Wright seemed to respond.

BELATED FRENCH ECHOES

While the discovery of Wright in France was later than in Germany and Holland, it was informed by previous developments in both countries. The first echoes of his work were indirect.[7] Wright was, for instance, absent from the two monumental volumes published by the landscape architect Jacques Gréber in 1920, in which the main goal was to celebrate the impact of French "genius" on American architecture.[8] One of the earliest agents was none other than the young Charles-Édouard Jeanneret, who had not yet opted for the pseudonym of Le Corbusier. In the first volume of his *Oeuvre complète,* published in 1930, he affirmed that he had become aware of Wright's work before 1914.[9] Early traces of Wright appear in Jeanneret's designs, particularly in the Jeanneret-Perret house built in 1912 for his parents in his hometown of La Chaux-de-Fonds, Switzerland, where he designed a fenestration pattern reminiscent of the Winslow house in River Forest, Illinois (1893–94), which he had discovered in 1910 while working in the office of Peter Behrens in Berlin (fig. 1). Also, the library of the École d'Art at La Chaux, where he was teaching, owned the *Sonderhefte der Architektur des XX. Jahrhunderts* published by Ernst Wasmuth in Berlin, including the 1911 monograph devoted to Wright. In a letter sent to his mentor Auguste Perret in August 1915, he confirmed having bought this book in Switzerland, as German publications could not enter wartime France.[10]

Asked in 1925 by Wijdeveld to contribute to the issue of *Wendingen* he was dedicating to Wright, Le Corbusier mentioned the strong impressions the Prairie houses and the Larkin Building (1902–6) had made on him, underlining Wright's relationship to the École des Beaux-Arts, only to further Le Corbusier's lingering hostility to that institution: "One perceived in Wright's plans the good school of the École des Beaux Arts, that is an inclination towards order, towards organization, towards a creation of pure ar-

JEAN-LOUIS COHEN

FIG. I. Charles-Edouard Jeanneret, Jeanneret-Perret house, La Chaux-de-Fonds, 1912. Photo Richard Pare, 2011. (© Richard Pare)

chitecture." It was perhaps less related to Wright's work built in Japan than to the Japanese influence he detected in the Prairie houses: "I was almost completely ignorant of Wright, yet I remember clearly the shock that struck me with these spirited and smiling villas . . . with their Japanese laughter."[11]

Auguste Perret never explicitly expressed his interest in Wright. They met in 1937 at a dinner organized by the director of the École des Beaux-Arts and again in 1939 during the only trip he made to the United States.[12] The distinguished Princeton University architecture professor Jean Labatut reported a response Perret gave to a student asking him his thoughts on Wright's use of concrete at Taliesin West: he said he considered it as "un peu bâtard" [rather impure].[13] Perret was one of the sponsors of Jean Badovici's journal *Architecture vivante,* where the first significant French images of Wright's works were published in 1924, for the most part borrowed from the 1911 Wasmuth volume.[14] In his later articles, Badovici considered that Wright was by then passé and that he could only be seen as a somewhat odd precursor unable to perceive emerging issues.[15] When he devoted an entire portfolio of the journal to Wright in 1930, recycling for the most part plates reproduced from *Wendingen,* and even from the Wasmuth portfolio, he insisted that Wright's relevance did not go beyond North America, while also asserting that he was "one of the greatest, if not the greatest among modern architects."[16]

Robert Mallet-Stevens and André Lurçat, then considered two of the main figures of Modern architecture in Paris, not only had a good knowledge of Wright's work but also engaged in critical comments. Mallet-Stevens expressed his point of view in an issue of *Wendingen,* affirming that Wright was "one of the first to dare to break with tradition reduced to routine in order to create," and considered his work as "grand, rich, and logical."[17] He discussed the Robie house (1908–10) in a lecture delivered in 1925. Describing the building in a worldwide panorama of new ideas, he acknowledged having been (mistakenly) struck by this "desire of long horizontal lines, lines that only reinforced concrete allows."[18] Mallet-Stevens kept observing the production of Wright and met him in Paris in 1939, when he took him on a citywide tour of recent Modern buildings.[19] Pierre Vago, the founder of the Rencontres internationales d'architectes, a moderate rival of CIAM (Congrès internationaux d'architecture modern), had invited Wright, who was then in London, to give a lecture before a Parisian audience. Only half of the auditorium's seats were occupied—in the eyes of Vago a confirmation of Wright's modest popularity in France.[20]

In 1927, André Lurçat, who was then engaged in a personal competition with Le Corbusier, had convinced Christian Zervos, publisher of the monthly *Cahiers d'Art,* to produce an issue devoted to Wright. In the journal, Lurçat published a set of photographs and celebrated a genius "who knows admirably how to combine the data of reason with the unexpected effects of imagination and the subtlest sensitivity."[21] Thanks to his contacts with J. J. P. Oud and through Peter van der Meulen Smith, an American working in his office, Lurçat got in touch with the young architectural historian Henry-Russell Hitchcock and asked him to author the introduction to a selection of photographs documenting Wright's California work. Hitchcock wrote, somewhat ponderously, that "Wright is not only an architect, that is to say an artist who draws and creates his buildings, who is perhaps greater than his contemporary European colleagues—who are not always devoid of that kind of restraint to which he occasionally abandons himself—but he is also a brilliant engineer and a brilliant technician."[22] In the preparation of the book, Lurçat negotiated the delivery of the photographs with Wright, who boasted in his letters about the "new principles in the use of reinforced concrete" at work in his West Coast houses and declared his delight at being at last acknowledged in Paris, affirming: "it *will* be great to see myself in France."[23] This volume would remain for decades the only one readily available to French readers.

In the early 1930s, the only reaction to the ideas Wright expressed in a 1931 essay in *Schweizerische Bauzeitung,* which was intended as a response to the emergence of European modernism, came a year later from Sigfried

JEAN-LOUIS COHEN

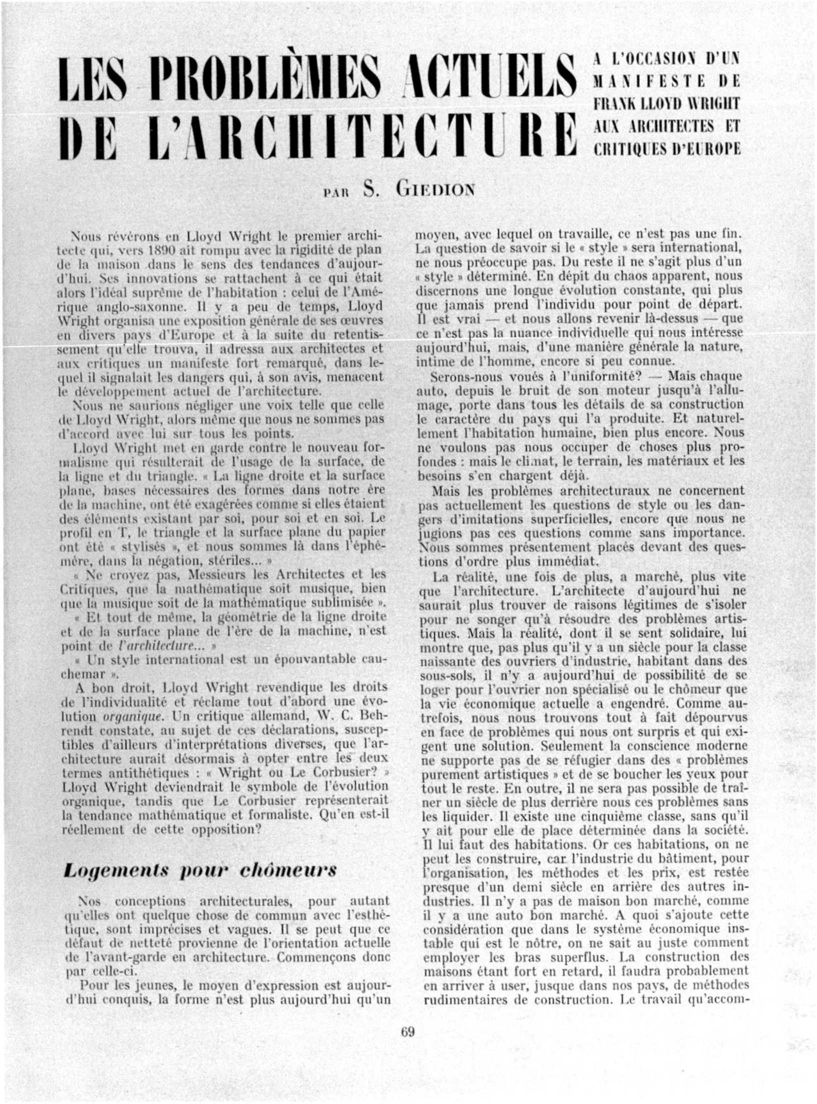

LES PROBLÈMES ACTUELS DE L'ARCHITECTURE

A L'OCCASION D'UN MANIFESTE DE FRANK LLOYD WRIGHT AUX ARCHITECTES ET CRITIQUES D'EUROPE

PAR S. GIEDION

Nous révérons en Lloyd Wright le premier architecte qui, vers 1890 ait rompu avec la rigidité de plan de la maison dans le sens des tendances d'aujourd'hui. Ses innovations se rattachent à ce qui était alors l'idéal suprême de l'habitation : celui de l'Amérique anglo-saxonne. Il y a peu de temps, Lloyd Wright organisa une exposition générale de ses œuvres en divers pays d'Europe et à la suite du retentissement qu'elle trouva, il adressa aux architectes et aux critiques un manifeste fort remarqué, dans lequel il signalait les dangers qui, à son avis, menacent le développement actuel de l'architecture.

Nous ne saurions négliger une voix telle que celle de Lloyd Wright, alors même que nous ne sommes pas d'accord avec lui sur tous les points.

Lloyd Wright met en garde contre le nouveau formalisme qui résulterait de l'usage de la surface, de la ligne et du triangle. « La ligne droite et la surface plane, bases nécessaires des formes dans notre ère de la machine, ont été exagérées comme si elles étaient des éléments existant par soi, pour soi et en soi. Le profil en T, le triangle et la surface plane du papier ont été « stylisés », et nous sommes là dans l'éphémère, dans la négation, stériles... »

« Ne croyez pas, Messieurs les Architectes et les Critiques, que la mathématique soit musique, bien que la musique soit de la mathématique sublimisée ».

« Et tout de même, la géométrie de la ligne droite et de la surface plane de l'ère de la machine, n'est point de *l'architecture...* »

« Un style international est un épouvantable cauchemar ».

A bon droit, Lloyd Wright revendique les droits de l'individualité et réclame tout d'abord une évolution *organique*. Un critique allemand, W. C. Behrendt constate, au sujet de ces déclarations, susceptibles d'ailleurs d'interprétations diverses, que l'architecture aurait désormais à opter entre les deux termes antithétiques : « Wright ou Le Corbusier? » Lloyd Wright deviendrait le symbole de l'évolution organique, tandis que Le Corbusier représenterait la tendance mathématique et formaliste. Qu'en est-il réellement de cette opposition?

Logements pour chômeurs

Nos conceptions architecturales, pour autant qu'elles ont quelque chose de commun avec l'esthétique, sont imprécises et vagues. Il se peut que ce défaut de netteté provienne de l'orientation actuelle de l'avant-garde en architecture. Commençons donc par celle-ci.

Pour les jeunes, le moyen d'expression est aujourd'hui conquis, la forme n'est plus aujourd'hui qu'un moyen, avec lequel on travaille, ce n'est pas une fin. La question de savoir si le « style » sera international, ne nous préoccupe pas. Du reste il ne s'agit plus d'un « style » déterminé. En dépit du chaos apparent, nous discernons une longue évolution constante, qui plus que jamais prend l'individu pour point de départ. Il est vrai — et nous allons revenir là-dessus — que ce n'est pas la nuance individuelle qui nous intéresse aujourd'hui, mais, d'une manière générale la nature, intime de l'homme, encore si peu connue.

Serons-nous voués à l'uniformité? — Mais chaque auto, depuis le bruit de son moteur jusqu'à l'allumage, porte dans tous les détails de sa construction le caractère du pays qui l'a produite. Et naturellement l'habitation humaine, bien plus encore. Nous ne voulons pas nous occuper de choses plus profondes : mais le climat, le terrain, les matériaux et les besoins s'en chargent déjà.

Mais les problèmes architecturaux ne concernent pas actuellement les questions de style ou les dangers d'imitations superficielles, encore que nous ne jugions pas ces questions comme sans importance. Nous sommes présentement placés devant des questions d'ordre plus immédiat.

La réalité, une fois de plus, a marché, plus vite que l'architecture. L'architecte d'aujourd'hui ne saurait plus trouver de raisons légitimes de s'isoler pour ne songer qu'à résoudre des problèmes artistiques. Mais la réalité, dont il se sent solidaire, lui montre que, pas plus qu'il y a un siècle pour la classe naissante des ouvriers d'industrie, habitant dans des sous-sols, il n'y a aujourd'hui de possibilité de se loger pour l'ouvrier non spécialisé ou le chômeur que la vie économique actuelle a engendré. Comme autrefois, nous nous trouvons tout à fait dépourvus en face de problèmes qui nous ont surpris et qui exigent une solution. Seulement la conscience moderne ne supporte pas de se réfugier dans des « problèmes purement artistiques » et de se boucher les yeux pour tout le reste. En outre, il ne sera pas possible de traîner un siècle de plus derrière nous ces problèmes sans les liquider. Il existe une cinquième classe, sans qu'il y ait pour elle de place déterminée dans la société. Il lui faut des habitations. Or ces habitations, on ne peut les construire, car l'industrie du bâtiment, pour l'organisation, les méthodes et les prix, est restée presque d'un demi siècle en arrière des autres industries. Il n'y a pas de maison bon marché, comme il y a une auto bon marché. A quoi s'ajoute cette considération que dans le système économique instable qui est le nôtre, on ne sait au juste comment employer les bras superflus. La construction des maisons étant fort en retard, il faudra probablement en arriver à user, jusque dans nos pays, de méthodes rudimentaires de construction. Le travail qu'accom-

69

FIG. 2. "Les problèmes actuels de l'architecture," article by Siegfried Giedion, *Cahiers d'Art,* January-February 1932, 69–70. (Bibliothèque national de France)

Giedion, who took note of Wright's "organic evolution" in *Cahiers d'Art* but criticized his indifference to modern art (fig. 2).[24] Giedion linked the contributions of the American to what he knew best: "Wright's ideas are extended in the work of Le Corbusier, but one can scarcely tell this from the outside. No architect of his time has like Wright from the outset situated the problem of dwelling at the very center of his work. He showed for the first time how to break with the traditional rigidity of the plan, to link the various levels of a house, to restore liberty to the elements of the cubic mass, to destroy the notion of the façade, and to orchestrate the passage from house to landscape. It is not by chance that Le Corbusier's efforts bear upon the same matters." Giedion had some reservations about the potential developments of Wright's work: "Not having been able to see in reality the curious structures of Wright in recent years, we will not risk taking any distinct position. Certainly, there is, in the way he respectfully takes into account the slightest fold in the terrain—with which his building sometimes meld—a sort of renunciation of the notion of architecture, a tendency to the cosmic that in the future will no doubt be called upon to play an important role. But it is equally possible that there be, in these houses that purposely avoid any pronounced structure, a flight into solitude and individuality with which we would be unable to align ourselves."[25]

The French interest for Wright went beyond the realm of architecture and architectural criticism, as art historians began to insert his work into their surveys of contemporary practice. In his history of art in Canada and the United States, Louis Gillet affirmed that the Larkin Building (1902–6) allowed for the "explosion" of the "American feeling" of the "leader of modern architecture," equivalent to Perret and Le Corbusier: "in this austere and admirably legible composition, the laconic masses stylize the organs and reveal the usage as clearly as the labels of a filing cabinet."[26]

Perhaps the most original reflections to be found on the world scene is the analysis made by French novelist Jean Prévost, an active protagonist of left-wing culture in interwar Paris, who would die resisting the Nazis. Among the small phalanx of writers interested in architecture, he had published a monograph on Gustave Eiffel in 1929 and, ten years later, an account of an eight-month trip throughout the United States he had made the previous year.[27] He did not credit Wright for the title he chose for the latter book—*Usonie*— but characterized him as one of the emblematic figures of "American Civilization." Prévost also dedicated a full chapter to Wright's biography in this travelogue: "His first years as an architect were happy and hard ones. Like Balzac, Wright fueled his ardor for work with debts. He attained originality; his houses, admired by some, mocked by others, occasionally frightened his patrons, who requested of him concessions to traditional taste. He explained to them, and he sometimes succeeded in realizing for them, his model for the Prairie house, his first original creation—a sort of new standard model, capable of being adapted depending on the site, and on the size of the family. No more traditional house in the form of a cube: there was no lack of ground;

on the flat prairie, the slightest rise indeed makes effects enough. All the interior layouts are calculated on a human scale—five feet, eight inches, according to Wright. To within a half-inch, that is his own height. They said that if he had been two inches taller, his homes would have been different. 'Maybe,' he replied, good naturedly."[28]

Prévost drew an interesting parallel between Walt Disney, to whom he devoted another chapter, and Wright. In the work of this "man of tyrannical genius," shaped by the great outdoors and fond of movement, he identified a new "form of spirit," which contrasts to the "vertical line" thanks to the richness of its "geometric form." He did not discuss the smaller Usonian houses, but mentions perceptively the buildings he saw during his trip: "Tiny masterpieces—Fallingwater, the Kaufmann House in Bear Run, Pennsylvania [1935–39], which expresses the affinity between the house, the forest, and the waterfall that the house has laid hold of; Wingspread [1938–39], or the Johnson cottage, the new Prairie House, and Honeycomb, the Hanna House in Stanford, California [begun 1937], which speak of the intimate union of house and landscape, are of human scale, are capable of instructing all minds. They teach a pride more intimate than the naïve vanity of the skyscrapers: the sense of the present, the sense of leisure. Cruel enemies of all routine, they are little temples from man to purified man, to the new man."[29]

After the Second World War, as the groups active on the French architectural scene focused their attention on the most minute aspects of the American scene, a remarkable change took place in the discourse on Wright. The most radical modernists, who had rallied around Wright, had shifted their attention—and their enthusiasm—to Richard Neutra, to whom the first postwar monographic issue of *L'Architecture d'aujourd'hui* was devoted, featuring inflamed praise by the functionalist architect Marcel Lods and others.[30] Wright was then, unwillingly, recruited by the conservative wing in its effort to rescue architecture as art from the technology-oriented work of Neutra and his generation. Rome Prize laureate André Remondet, who had spent time in the United States and was teaching with Perret at the École des Beaux-Arts, offered one of the first postwar panoramas of American architecture. He celebrated in *L'Architecture française,* a journal created in 1940 with a definitely anti-modernist agenda, the virtues of Wright's administrative building for the S. C. Johnson Company (1936–39).[31]

When his exhibition "Sixty Years of Living Architecture" opened at the École des Beaux-Arts in 1952, Wright had the opportunity of meeting with a wide range of colleagues, including Perret (fig. 3). His recent work was discussed in *L'Architecture française,* which underlined the contrast between his "organic" forms and those of the "fetishists" of technology such as Marcel

FIG. 3. Frank Lloyd Wright (left) and a group of French officials at opening of the "Sixty Years of Living Architecture" exhibition, Paris, April 1952. (The Frank Lloyd Wright Foundation Archives [The Museum of Modern Art | Avery Architectural & Fine Arts Library, Columbia University, New York])

Lods (fig. 4).[32] Upon his return from France, Wright supported the conservatives and condemned Le Corbusier's barely completed Unité d'habitation (1946–52), in which he saw a "Massacre on the Marseilles Waterfront."[33] From that moment onward, Wright's work would be included in the surveys of twentieth-century architecture, from those published by the journals to historical narratives, but in a rather acritical and celebratory mode. It would take a certain time to see a new generation of designers and scholars dedicate its attention to Wright. Among the former, the most dedicated followers were Hervé Baley and Dominique Zimbacca, who created a sort of loose French Usonia with their villas spread throughout the Paris region, while Edmond Lay was shaping his own interpretation in southwest France.[34]

In parallel to the comprehensive lectures given by Gilbert Cordier, documenting Wright's buildings photographed in situ, the most perceptive analysis of his work—in particular the earliest part—was proposed by Jean Castex, a young faculty member at the School of Architecture in Versailles,

ARCHITECTURE
FRANÇAISE

123-124
(8oo frs)

FRANK LLOYD WRIGHT

FIG. 4. *L'Architecture
française,* issue devoted to
Wright, March 1952, cover.
(Canadian Centre for Archi-
tecture/© Durand-Souffland)

who had been the recipient of the AIA's Delano and Aldrich Fellowship in
1968–69 and had traveled to see most of Wright's major buildings.[35] He would
admit many years later that he had made these trips "with much discretion,
as it was unfashionable at that time to go see famous architects."[36] Within
a research team by the name of "Syntaxe," Castex undertook in the 1970s
with his Ecole classmate Philippe Panerai a structural analysis of Wright's
plans.[37] He extended his interpretation by shaping imaginative graphic
representations of the Prairie houses, deconstructing their mode of composition (fig. 5). He underlined the analogy with the patterns of germination
and growth of plants, which he traced back to the reflections of Louis Sullivan and the French theorist of ornament Victor-Marie Ruprich-Robert.[38]
With Castex, a new phase in the reception of Wright had begun, in which
scholarly, comparative investigations replaced the celebrative writings of
earlier authors.

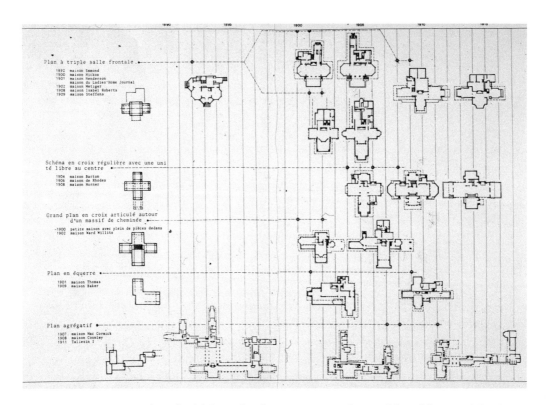

FIG. 5. Chart of Prairie house plans in Jean Castex, *Le printemps de la Prairie House,* 1987, 152–53. (Canadian Centre for Architecture/© Jean Castex)

WRIGHT'S RUSSIAN ECHO

The Russian response to Wright was rather different from the French one, as it involved both individuals and institutions. Even if Soviet culture was in its entirety permeated by an unquestionable idealization of America, the interest in the New World, its technology, art, and architecture fluctuated according to the political situation and the prevailing ideological discourse. Themes and architects who were popular at a given moment would be the object of a sort of *damnatio memoriae* a few years later, only to resurface in the next phase. The reception of Wright did not escape these cycles, in particular from the 1920s to the 1970s.

In late Czarist Russia, American architecture had received less attention than British, French, or German production, yet several observers reported on new developments in the United States, directly or otherwise. The publication of Wasmuth's *Ausgeführte Bauten* was not reported by the main professional journal *Zodchii,* but in 1911 it mentioned the publication of F. Rudolf Vogel's *Das amerikanische Haus,* in which several early houses by Wright were illustrated.[39]

Lissitzky's knowledge of Wright, acquired in Holland and also probably during the course of his studies in Darmstadt before 1914, has been mentioned. Among the other innovative architects of his generation, early Wrightian themes appear in 1915 in the project of Moisei Ginzburg and Naum Kopelyovich for the Lokshin villa in Crimea (fig. 6). If the basic parti remains compact and symmetrical, in contrast with the modular principle and horizontal expansion of the Prairie houses, the arched entrance, the plinth, and the vases framing the steps seem to be borrowed from the 1902 Heurtley house in Oak Park or the Dana house in Springfield, Illinois (1902–4).[40]

Once he had become the main theoretician of constructivism, Ginzburg consistently mentioned Wright in his articles for *Sovremennaia Arkhitektura.* When he defined in 1927 the "functional method" of architectural design, he gave the same status of an inspiring model to modern airplanes and the work of an architect he pictured as representing the American "farmer-pioneers."[41] When he devoted a full article to Wright, Ginzburg affirmed that the Robie house presented a "completely new plan—simple, open, bathed by air and light, that develops freely in space." Endorsing the then fashionable discourse of *Amerikanizm,* he presented the building as a challenge comparable to the machine, mentioning in passing Wright's early essays, that the Russians, cast as having "a still more pioneering spirit than the Americans," needed to face urgently.[42] Once constructivism had been excised from the discourse of Soviet architecture, Ginzburg published a summary of his research on housing, in which he inserted illustrations of the Robie, Coonley, and Freeman houses. As an indication of the ambiguous status of the American examples in 1930s Soviet Russia, he dispensed with any comment.[43] The provenance of the third house's images is undoubtedly the translation of Neutra's *Wie baut Amerika?,* published in Moscow in 1929, where the first views of Wright's California work were directed to a Russian audience.[44]

The relationship between the USSR and the USA became more intense at the precise moment in which the Stalinist line prevailed in culture, leading to the taming of the avant-garde. Albert Kahn was invited to shape the nascent discipline of industrial architecture by opening a branch of his office in Moscow. And Wright continued to be part of the landscape of capitalist culture. His recent work was featured in the art historian David Arkin's 1933 book *Arhitektura sovremennogo zapada,* together with that of Le Corbusier, Gropius, and Neutra.[45] Arkin engaged a correspondence with Wright, asking him, for instance, in 1935 to send a contribution to the first issue of *Arkhitekturnaia Gazeta,* a bi-monthly newspaper published by the newly cre-

XXIX. М. Я. Гинзбург и Н. А. Копелиович

Макет дома Локшиных в Евпатории 1917 год

FIG. 6. Moisei Ginzburg and Naum Kopelyovich, Villa Lokshin, 1915, project. *Stil'i epokha,* 1924, pl. 14.

ated Union of Soviet Architects.[46] In 1934, the union's journal, *Arkhitektura SSSR,* inserted an article by Wright in its series "How Do I Work," alongside Russian and European designers such as Lurçat, Mallet-Stevens, Hannes Meyer, and Oud. Wright rejected firmly the notion of "composition" about which he was questioned: "In organic architecture composition, as such, is dead. We no longer compose. We conceive the building as an entity. Proceeding from generals to particulars by way of some appropriate scheme of

JEAN-LOUIS COHEN

construction we try to find the equation of expression best suited, that is to say most natural, to all the factors involved." [47] In this illuminating text, only available in the published Russian version, he also refused to view historical precedent as the main source of architectural invention: "The only way classical or modern architectural monuments can be helpful to us is to study that quality in them which made them serviceable or beautiful in their day and be informed by that quality in them. As ready-made forms, they can only be harmful to us today. What made them great in their day is the same as what would make great buildings in our own day. But the buildings we should make would be very different, necessarily." [48]

Throughout the 1930s, Wright was asked to send messages in support of Soviet politics and to make statements about the dire state of capitalism in the West. He played the role of the foreign expert previously enjoyed by Le Corbusier, who fell from favor after the 1932 competition for the Palace of the Soviets. After a first attempt at extracting a text from him in 1932, the daily newspaper of the Communist party, *Pravda,* questioned Wright on the life of intellectuals in America and the effects of the Depression. He described the former as "hapless beneficiaries of a success-system they have never clearly understood, but a system that has worked miracles for them while they slept." Wright went on to declare that "the present economy has practically eliminated our profession, such as it was," without, however, fully endorsing the Soviet system: "I view the USSR as a heroic endeavor to establish more genuine human values in a social state than any existing before. Its heroism and devotion move me deeply and with great hope. But I fear that machine worship to defeat capitalism may become inverted capitalism in Russia itself and so prostitute the man to the machine." [49]

The reorganization of the profession reached a new stage with the preparation of the first congress of Soviet architects, scheduled for 1937. A significant number of Western architects were invited at the initiative of the Union and VOKS, the Society for the Cultural Relationships in charge of international exchange. The pivotal figure in the lengthy process of establishing the list of guests was Arkin, who edited in 1936 the Russian translation of Lewis Mumford's *Sticks and Stones,* a short history of American architecture published twelve years before, in which the legacy of Sullivan in Wright's work was discussed. In his foreword, Arkin identified the different directions of the "contradictory" architecture of the United States, including the most recent one: "the attempt at a local folkloric archaism in the so-called 'Prairie Style' to which the last of the innovators—Frank Lloyd Wright—has widely contributed." [50]

Notwithstanding this critique, Arkin was instrumental in the invitation made to Wright the following year to attend the congress of Soviet architects in 1937. Initially a rather broad search for foreign guests developed, as documented by the meetings of VOKS and the Union of Soviet Architects. Wright was in the very first list—supported by short notes about his life and work—for a rather long period of time together with Neutra. In fact, four categories of professionals were meant to be invited: the representatives of the institutions such as the AIA, the leaders of major corporate firms, the best-known innovators, and, on the side of the political friends of the USSR, architects "related to the Popular Front." Names such as those of William B. Lamb, noted as "the architect of the Empire [State] Building," and of Frederick Kiesler and Knud Lönberg-Holm, in the category of the radical designers, were mentioned.[51] In the end, only Wright and Simon Breines, a young New York architect who had taken part in the competition for the Palace of Soviets, showed up (fig. 7).

Accompanied by his wife, Olgivanna (Olga Ivanovna per their hosts), who spoke fluent Russian, Wright was given a special status among the foreign guests of the congress. He was taken to visit the last buildings of the constructivists, such as the Vesnin brothers' palace of culture of the ZIL factory, and was received at the Union of Soviet Architects' country club in Sukhanovo (fig. 8). Wright brought drawings to Moscow and had the opportunity

FIG. 7. Boris Iofan, Olga Sasso-Ruffo, and Wright in Moscow, 1937. (The Frank Lloyd Wright Foundation Archives [The Museum of Modern Art | Avery Architectural & Fine Arts Library, Columbia University, New York])

FIG. 8. Viktor Vesnin and Wright visiting ZIL workers' club, Moscow, 1937, RGALI, Moscow. (© Courtesy of the Russian State Archive for Literature & Art, Moscow, Russia)

to show his recent work to a select audience, offering to host three dozen Russian apprentices at Taliesin. But the climax of the trip was his address to the congress.

Speaking to the participants of a monumental event meant to confirm the shift toward socialist realism, in which the representatives of the former avant-garde were humiliated by having to apologize for their previous work, Wright acknowledged rather enthusiastically the developments of the Soviet economy but also dismissed both the radicals and the conservatives: "The USSR must now construct buildings on a scientific basis, guided by common sense and making the most efficient use of high quality building materials. The left wing of the so-called 'new' architecture also advocated the principles of creating an organic architecture but, to all intents and purposes, did not proceed beyond plain wall panels, flat roofs, and ornamental corner windows; and the right wing of said 'new' architecture turned the buildings into ornaments. Both tendencies are generated by decaying old cultures. The correct path to the creation of organic architecture consists of the scientific organization of building activity and animating it with a genuine spirit of humanity."[52]

Despite the friendly relationship he had established with Boris Iofan, Wright did not spare his design for the Palace of the Soviets, hitting two birds with one stone when he related it to the eclectic American skyscrapers that he hated: "this palace—only proposed I hope—is good if we take it for a modern version of St. George slaying the Dragon: that is to say the leonine Lenin stamping the life out of a capitalistic skyscraper."[53] Needless to say, this passage of his address was censored by both the official newspapers and the architectural press.[54] After his return from Moscow, Wright was asked by *Soviet Russia Today,* a propaganda magazine based in New York, to publish his text, which was now entitled "Architecture and Life in the USSR" and contained only an allusion in passing to that architecture's "grandomania."[55]

Wright continued to respond positively to requests from the Soviet press, sending an article to the government newspaper *Izvestia* through his most frequent contact in the United States, Vladimir Verinsky—the director of Amkino, who frequently lent him Soviet films.[56] In this piece, Wright sought to teach the Russians a lesson in organicism and democracy, providing rather condescending advice: "Study Russian nature for your forms, my Russians. Throw the musty text-books away. Close these morgues you were taught to call museums. Learn the basic principles of the new reality you profess as these principles apply to buildings, sculpture, painting, planting and clothing."[57] Taking the posture of a loyal friend of Stalin's Russia, he endorsed the new Soviet constitution, as reported by the communist organ, the *Daily Worker,* in August 1937.[58] He also tried to invite Karo Alabian, the architect in charge of building the Soviet pavilion at the New York World's Fair of 1939, to visit Taliesin, still longing for a contingent of Russian apprentices.[59]

On the Soviet side, a negative perception of Wright's Broadacre City (1929–35) would be pervasive. In his account of American architecture, Iofan had labeled it, ironically, a "utopian project for an agricultural village" meant to "rescue humankind from capitalism."[60] In the months preceding Russia's and America's entry into the war, *Arkhitektura SSSR* went further, when it criticized the lectures given by Wright on organic architecture in London in 1939. The journal reported with delight that the "very nebulous thoughts of this idealist architect"—namely Broadacre City—had been "bitterly attacked by the progressive component of the British architectural youth—a reaction that underlined the unreality of his plans in the conditions of capitalism."[61]

After the Nazi invasion of the Soviet Union, foreign celebrities were asked to express support for Russia. Despite the polemics of the 1930s, Iofan sent a message to Wright, asking for an expression of sympathy.[62] Wright responded positively to a request of the filmmaker Joseph Losey, made on behalf of the Russian War Relief Committee, and sent a message to a meeting held on 27 October 1941 at New York's Madison Square Garden without, however, deigning to appear in person. Dedicated to Iofan, his text was a rather generic plea for democracy.[63]

Despite the unflattering Russian response to Broadacre City, Wright's disurbanism remained a term of reference for the planners preparing the reconstruction of the Soviet Union. Moreover, when the Architects' Committee of the National Council of American-Soviet Friendship sent an exhibition on American architecture to Moscow in 1945, one of the forty panels of an exhibition featured a set of Usonian houses. *Architectural Forum* editor Douglas Haskell selected the buildings; the prominent New York architect Harvey Wiley Corbett oversaw production of the show, which Frederick Kiesler designed.[64]

Ten years later, after the xenophobic parenthesis of the postwar period, in which American architecture was conspicuously ignored and its "agents," such as Arkin, publicly condemned, the popularity of Wright among Russian architects was measured in 1955 thanks to a bizarre incident. Following Nikita Khrushchev's vibrant critique of Stalinist buildings, a first group of architects and engineers was sent to the United States to study construction methods.[65] The daily press and the professional journals reported on what *Architectural Forum* called the "Grim End" to the tour.[66] While he was in Washington, D.C., the rumor spread that Alexander Vlasov, president of the Academy of Architecture, had been demoted from his responsibilities because of an unauthorized, extracurricular visit to Taliesin. The news hit the press in Kentucky and in the Midwest. Wright declared to the *Milwaukee Sentinel:* "He believed he could learn something from me. He was too good to be a Russian."[67]

It would take five more years for the first translation of one of Wright's books to appear in Russian. *The Future of Architecture* was published with an introduction by the translator, Arkady Gol'dshtein, and Alexander Gegello, a prolific, but by no means innovative, architect from Leningrad. They emphasized that "Wright is interesting for us first of all as an innovator who understood, still at the end of the previous century, that the proper development of architecture had to shun the imitation of old forms and methods in order to invent solutions that responded to real conditions and expectations." Paying the indispensable lip service to the critique of his "formalism," they considered that if the "limitations of Wright tarnish his achievements, they do not cancel them. He was a superior master, in the same rank as the greatest architects in history."[68] The renewed acceptance of Wright's work

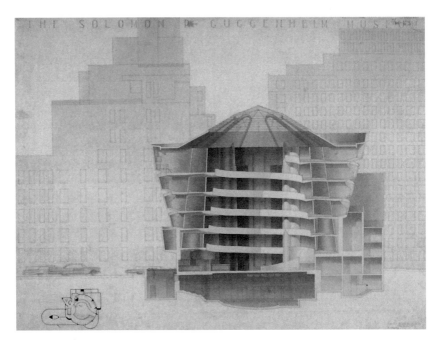

was further revealed by the student work at the Moscow Architecture Institute, where the Guggenheim Museum (1943–59) became a theme for the first-year drawing course, together with the Parthenon and Palladio's villas (fig. 9). In 1963, the same building was fully featured in the first Soviet book entirely devoted to American architecture.[69] Finally, in 1973, more than fifty years after the Wasmuth publications, the first complete monograph on Wright's work, compiled by Gol'dshtein, was released.[70]

WRIGHT'S ITALIAN AURA

The Italian discovery of Wright was much delayed in relation to what had taken place in Germany, the Netherlands, France, or Russia but was in the end far more impactful. Wright was almost completely absent from the publications in the first two decades of the twentieth century; the first significant mention to his work was made in passing by the Roman architect Marcello Piacentini in 1921.[71] As noted by Federica Lehmann and Augusto

Rossari, Otto Wagner was still considered by Italian critics as the main precursor of the new architecture.[72] A deliberate opportunist at the service of Fascism's nationalist discourse, Piacentini excluded Wright from his panoramic *Architettura d'oggi* of 1930. However, a turning point in the reception of Wright was reached when the 1933 Milan Triennale devoted a booth-size exhibition to his work, together with ones devoted to eleven other architects, among them Willem Marinus Dudok, Walter Gropius, Le Corbusier, Adolf Loos, Ludwig Mies van der Rohe, Konstantin Melnikov, and Perret.

From that moment, the leading modernist critics focused their attention on Wright. Unquestionably the most perceptive of them, the anti-fascist Edoardo Persico, who was one of the directors of the monthly journal *Casabella,* considered his buildings in an original light in his 1935 lecture, "Profezia dell'architettura," based on the Triennale exhibit. Attempting rather unprecedented genealogy, he cleverly related Wright's "open-air architecture" to Impressionist painting and to Sherwood Anderson's stories. He observed: "I know why the work of Wright induces such thoughts. Wright says it himself when his writings on architecture call for the freedom of the human spirit. I know how much Ruskin and Morris there are in this American who designs houses floating on rivers and is preaching the standard."[73]

In 1938 the Milanese architect Giuseppe de Finetti, another enemy of the Fascist regime, praised Wright's "unique inventive spirit" and "unbreakable courage."[74] However, the critic Rafaelle Giolli celebrated at the same moment the Kaufmann house in Mill Run, Pennsylvania: "here architecture fights against nature, and it is on another level in order to defeat it. Wright's appeal to nature is not that of the American elegies, but that of the unyielding pioneers who felt that their work could have a life of its own only after it had faced and eventually vanquished nature."[75] Another mention of Wright in the Italian press of the Fascist period is an article the art historian Carlo Giulio Argan devoted to his *Autobiography* in *Casabella,* where he insisted on Wright's engagement and his morality, a clear allusion to the political situation of a country then aligned with the Third Reich.[76]

The most fertile period began after the liberation and the return to Rome of the young Bruno Zevi, who put Wright at the center of his first book, *Towards an Organic Architecture,* published in 1945, arguing that "Organic architecture is the antithesis of the monumental architecture enslaved to the states' mythologies" (fig. 10).[77] Zevi affirmed in retrospect that all the credit for his book should have gone to Giedion: "I have just translated *Space, Time and Architecture,* with a single modification. I have inserted the chapter on F. L. Wright after the one devoted to Le Corbusier," implying that the American had cured architecture from the simplistic formulas of the

FIG. 10. Bruno Zevi, *Verso un architettura organica,* 1947, cover. (Canadian Center for Architecture; HB-04414–5D3, Chicago History Museum, Hedrich-Blessing Collection; © Giulio Einaudi Torino, 1945; © Chicago Historical Society, published on or before 2015, all rights reserved)

Parisian prophet.[78] This led him to the creation of the APAO—the Association for Organic Architecture—which intervened in the political arena when some of its members became candidates in local elections. He also founded the review *Metron,* in which an important "Introduction to Wright" by Argan was published in 1947.[79]

Zevi wrote about Wright in popular magazines, while maintaining an extensive correspondence with the architect, in which the latter sometimes shared the blandest personal reactions to his contemporaries. Confirming the rivalry that was at the center of the postwar French view of America, Wright cast Neutra as a sort of inverted cuckoo, an "immoral bird trying to lay my eggs in his own nest."[80] In 1947, Zevi published the first Italian monograph on Wright in the small collection devoted by the publishing house Il Balcone to the "architects of the modern movement." In this modest volume, he praised the "exceptional merit" Wright had of putting the "problem of space" at the very foundation of his work. Zevi also expressed his belief that Wright "will escape" from the framework he was himself delineating, because of his "extraordinary ability in his passion for making things, his continuing ability at invention."[81]

Zevi was also involved in the organization of the Italian venue of the mammoth exhibition of Wright's oeuvre, organized in 1951 by the art historian Carlo Ludovico Ragghianti and its initial curator, architect Oskar Stonorov, at Florence's Palazzo Strozzi (fig. 11).[82] In the preparation of this first stop of the exhibition in Europe, before Paris, Wright wrote to Zevi: "So glad you are heading the exhibition. It is the grandest show in Architecture ever, they say! No exaggeration."[83] Zevi kept a friendly relationship with Stonorov, to whom he devoted a posthumous issue of his magazine *Architettura,* while remaining a loyal, active agent of Wright in Italy, engineering his reception of an honorary doctoral degree in Venice and continuing to publish his work widely. The cult of Wright found numerous recruits in Italy, which was unquestionably for him the most hospitable national scene throughout his last years, even if the palazzo he designed in 1952 on Venice's Canal Grande in memory of the young architect Angelo Masieri remained unbuilt (see Alice Thomine-Berrada's essay, this volume). In contrast to the other two scenes discussed here, the Italian reception went beyond the discussion of Wright's status and ideas to shape significant designs.

FIG. II. Wright and Zevi, Venice, 1951. (© Fondazione Bruno Zevi)

Wright's European presence during the last three decades of his life can be interpreted through parallel analyses of the main national scenes. I could also have proposed a comparative discussion of the reception of Broadacre City, the Usonian houses, Fallingwater, or the Guggenheim Museum in order to detect the main themes of the readings they inspired to critics and designers. Yet, given the extraordinary identification between the man and the work, perhaps the most stimulating approach is to identify the diverse roles Wright played on the three changing scenes just scanned.

Wright's first role was the one of a precursor, a sort of fatherly figure. He seems to have enjoyed it, not missing an opportunity to highlight the debt that the following generations owed to him. Many critics, historians, and protagonists have paid homage, albeit not without certain ambiguities, to the founding father featured in all the genealogies of Modern architecture, even if the causal chain in which he was inserted differed greatly according to the writers. Le Corbusier affirmed to have detected in his work the effect of the "best" of the Beaux-Arts, perhaps taking at face value H. P. Berlage's mistaken statement that Wright had attended the Ecole.[84] He was most probably unaware of the Parisian background of Louis Sullivan but had read, like Wright, Eugène Emmanuel Viollet-le-Duc's *Dictionnaire raisonné*. Ginzburg saw in the Robie house one of the sources of the constructivists' concept of domestic architecture. And for Persico, Wright was simply "the Cézanne of the new architecture"—announcing, of course, several Picassos to come. [85]

The second role played by Wright was a political one. Unwillingly recruited to serve contradictory causes, he was considered a revolutionary in the USSR during the 1930s to the point of being often interviewed by the official press, before being viewed for two decades as a naive supporter of capitalism. At the same time, he was cast in the United States as a supporter of the Soviets. In his 1939 book *Usonie,* Prévost cast him as standing in opposition to the American establishment, underlining the convergence of his ideas with the social policies of the New Deal.[86]

In Rome, Zevi promoted organic architecture as an expression of democracy, antithetical to the programs of Fascism. In a "Declaration of Principles" published in the second issue of *Metron,* Zevi wrote in 1945: "Organic architecture is altogether a social, technical, and artistic activity aimed at creating the environment of a new democratic civilization. . . . It is opposed to the major and the minor axes of contemporary neoclassicism, of the neoclassicism of arches and columns, and to the falsity hidden behind the pseudomodern forms of today's monumental architecture."[87] It must also be said that the 1951 exhibition, held in a city such as Florence, ruled by the Italian

Communist Party, was inscribed within the vigorous propaganda campaign organized by the United States in Europe during the early stages of the Cold War that was used by Zevi in support of his endeavors.[88]

The third role played by Wright was an architectural one. His spatial concepts and his geometries and aesthetics were used by European architects either in an implicit or an explicit way. The latent derivations were structural and allusive, as in the Cavrois house built by Mallet-Stevens in 1935 near Lille, in which the latter relied on the process of "expansion" toward the landscape he had observed in the Prairie house, without, however, relating it to a real spatial fluidity indoors (fig. 12). His relationship to the master was not overlooked at the time. In his *New World Architecture* of 1930, Sheldon W. Cheney wrote that Mallet-Stevens "is frankly indebted to the American Wright," acknowledging also what he had in common with the "posteresque Modernists of Vienna and Munich."[89]

The manifest derivations tended to recycle more explicitly the syntactic and the lexical elements of Wright's buildings. One of the most outspoken users of Wrightian forms within French architectural culture was Jean-François Zevaco, active in Morocco during and after colonization. His courthouse in Mohammédia (1958–62) crystallizes the North-African echo of Wright's work in Arizona. In Bordeaux, the 1974 postal bank of Edmond Lay, with its large

FIG. 12. Robert Mallet-Stevens, Villa Cavrois, Croix, 1929–33, garden elevation. (Author's photo)

FIG. 13. Edmond Lay, Meriadeck Savings Bank, Bordeaux, 1976–80, postcard. (David Liaudet Collection)

cylindrical drum, takes its cue from the Guggenheim Museum (fig. 13) As a recipient of the Delano and Aldrich Fellowship, he had met Wright in 1958. But perhaps the most accomplished derivation of both the Prairie and the Usonian houses can be found in the many villas built from the mid-1960s to the 1980s by Hervé Baley and Dominique Zimbacca, who had a firsthand knowledge of their models and provided elegant interpretations of their plans and main features, in particular, the fireplaces.[90]

In the absence of any ambitious single-family house construction, Soviet architects had very few opportunities to use themes derived from Wright, even after the post-Stalinist thaw. The Moscow Architecture Institute provided the greatest freedom, even if biting critiques shot down designs inspired by Wright. When a student of Ilia Lezhava based his design on the Guggenheim Museum, he got a bad grade because of his "sensationalism."[91]

Italy provided the largest spectrum of literal relationships between Wright and his followers.[92] Carlo Scarpa gave many examples of his ability at playing with Wright's shapes, from his project for an apartment building at Feltre (1949) and his pavilion for Venezuela at the Venice Biennale (1954–56) to the church at Corte di Cadore (1956–61) (fig. 14). Ignazio Gardella's Italian Pavilion at the Brussels Exposition of 1958 and Carlo Mollino's mountain buildings were more on the latent side, while Marcello d'Olivo drifted

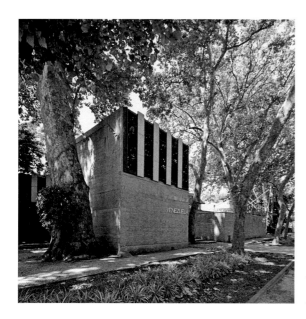

FIG. 14. Carlo Scarpa, Venezuela Pavilion, Venice Biennale, 1954–56. (Photograph by Andrea Jemolo)

toward the manifest with his Spezzotti house in Lignano Pineta (1958) (fig. 15). Often missing the subversive imagination of their role model, these buildings nonetheless form together a loose, pervasive component of late twentieth-century architecture. Scarpa, who designed a posthumous exhibition of Wright at the Milan Triennale in 1960, was well-aware of the limits of his interpretations, when he declared in an often-quoted 1978 interview: "Wright's work struck me like a lightning bolt. I'd never experienced anything like it. It carried me away, as though I was riding a wave, it can be seen in some of my projects for houses. Wright's work really left me in awe. I don't like those houses much anymore, because I don't believe you should imitate so shamelessly."[93]

More than simple mimesis, the Italian derivations of Wright could perhaps be ascribed to mannerism, a design strategy based on the borrowing and distortion of linguistic elements and on the search for exacerbated personal expression, which was, by the way, discounted by Giuseppe Samonà, one of Wright's hosts in Venice. In reaction to these derivations, Samonà wrote in 1949: "I don't believe that this great architecture . . . lends itself very well to mannerisms, facile languages, second-hand poetics."[94] In contrast, Zevi had lucidly foreseen, if not encouraged, this attitude four years earlier when he wrote: "we have to control ourselves, and to guide in a certain way, also generate the organic mannerism, knowing however that it will only be generated by works with manner."[95] He gave himself a glimpse at his method

The following text appears within the figure:

3. Villa Spezzotti a Lignano Pineta
architetto Marcello D'Olivo

In alto: scorcio del fronte sud della Villa Spezzotti.

A destra: veduta del lato sud, sul quale si affaccia il corpo delle camere da letto e un lato del soggiorno.

La villa sorge ad est della Villa Mainardis, illustrata all'inizio di questa rassegna, con orientamento nord-sud, addossata alla duna verso il mare. La pianta si sviluppa secondo archi di cerchio aventi i centri su assi a 45°. Le strutture verticali sono costituite da muri in calcestruzzo a vista, le strutture orizzontali sono in parte in cemento armato monolitico, in parte in laterizio armato.

Al pianterreno sono sistemati i servizi e l'abitazione del custode. Al piano padronale si accede dalla strada situata a nord, attraverso una rampa in terra con sentiero in lastre di calcestruzzo lavato. La rampa dà accesso all'atrio comunicante con il soggiorno-pranzo e con la balconata antistante le camere da letto. Il primo piano è a livello della duna posta a sud ed è disimpegnato con il pianterreno da una scala di servizio.

Alla terrazza di copertura praticabile si accede dalla balconata del soggiorno per mezzo di una rampa. La terrazza nella parte sud è a sbalzo e ha funzione di frangisole per le camere ed il soggiorno.

Il pranzo-soggiorno occupa la parte est ed è delimitato da due muri convessi aprentisi a sud verso il mare ed a nord sulla strada di accesso. I serramenti sono realizzati mediante una doppia cortina di oscuri ed invetriate. Gli oscuri in perline irregolari di larice, rovere e mogano, si aprono a libro e scorrono contro i muri d'ala; le invetriate sono su perni a sfere. Nella zona dei soggiorni i pavimenti sono in graniglia grigia e bianca e si sviluppano a fasce concentriche; nella zona notte sono realizzati in pulchetti di rovere.

Come il Villaggio del Fanciullo e la Villa Mainardis, questa villa è stata costruita dai fratelli Ursella, i quali hanno assecondato l'architetto con fiducia cieca, impiegando tutta la loro energia. I muratori friulani sono famosi in tutto il mondo.

L'a IV 302

FIG. 15. Marcello d'Olivo, Spezzotti house, Lignano Pineta, 1955–57, view and floor plans, in *L;Architettura, cronache, storia.* (Canadian Centre for Architecture; © Fondazione Bruno Zevi)

when defining in 1973 the "seven invariants" of Modern architecture, which were all present in Fallingwater and many buildings of Wright's, as he concluded in a paper delivered at the Museum of Modern Art in 1994 (fig. 16).[96] As enumerated by Zevi in his own terms, these invariants were listing of functional requirements; asymmetry and dissonance; anti-perspective

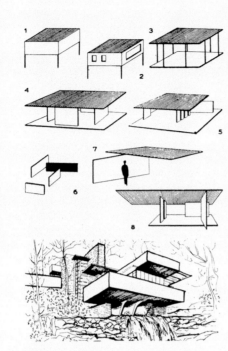

13. Eight sketches to illustrate a lecture by Frank Lloyd Wright on the involvement of every architectural element in the structural scheme. *Below:* the Kaufmann House, Falling Water, at Bear Run, Pennsylvania (1936–39), which incorporates all seven invariables of the modern language of architecture.

FIG. 16. Bruno Zevi, diagram of "seven invariants," in *Il linguaggio moderno dell'archittura,* 1973. (© Guido Einaudi editore, Torino, 1973; Canadian Centre for Architecture; © Fondazione Bruno Zevi)

three-dimensionality; four-dimensional composition; cantilever, shell, and membrane structures; space-in-time; and integration of building, city, and landscape.[97] A comprehensive, worldwide exploration of the "organic mannerism" of Wright both in its latent and in its manifest versions, remains to be undertaken through a more detailed, comparative investigation of the many contexts in which it was received.

NOTES

1. Le Corbusier, *Vers une architecture* (Paris: G. Crès, 1923), 29; El Lissitzky, "Amerikanizm v evropeiskoi arkhitekture," *Krasnaia Niva* 2 (29 November 1925): 1188.
2. *Wendingen* 4:11 (November 1921).
3. Gustav Adolf Platz, *Baukunst der neuersten Zeit* (Berlin: Propyläen, 1927), 65–69.
4. Heidi Kief-Niederwöhrmeier, *Frank Lloyd Wright und Europa Architekturele-*

mente, Naturverhältnis, Publ., Einflusse (Stuttgart: Karl Kramer, 1983); *Neder-landse architectuur 1880–1930: Americana* (Otterlo, Netherlands: Rijksmuseum Kroller-Muller, 1975).

5. I made a first attempt in this direction with my essay "Useful Hostage: Constructing Wright in Soviet Russia and France," in Anthony Alofsin, ed., *Frank Lloyd Wright, Europe and Beyond* (Berkeley: University of California Press, 1999), 100–120.

6. Hans-Robert Jauss, *Toward an Aesthetic of Reception* (Minneapolis: University of Minnesota Press, 1982).

7. See Jean-Louis Cohen, "Wright et la France, une découverte tardive," preface to *Ausgeführte Bauten und Entwürfe von Frank Lloyd Wright* (Paris: Herscher, 1986), 5–15.

8. Jacques Gréber, *L'architecture aux États-Unis, preuve de la force d'expansion du genie français* (Paris: Payot, 1920). During the early twentieth century Gréber designed several formal gardens for country houses by the Philadelphia architect Horace Trumbauer. He also completed plans in 1917 for the grand Benjamin Franklin Parkway, connecting Philadelphia's City Hall to Fairmount Park. See David Brownlee, *Building the City Beautiful: The Benjamin Franklin Parkway and the Philadelphia Museum of Art* (Philadelphia: Philadelphia Museum of Art, 1989).

9. Le Corbusier, preface to Willi Boesiger and Oskar Stonorov, eds., *Le Corbusier et Pierre Jeanneret: Ihr Gesamtwerk von 1910–1929* (Zurich: Girsberger, 1930), 10.

10. Charles-Edouard Jeanneret to Auguste Perret, 30 June 1915, in Le Corbusier, *Lettres à ses maîtres,* vol. 1, *Lettres à Auguste Perret,* ed. Marie-Jeanne Dumont (Paris: Éditions du Linteau, 2002), 142.

11. Le Corbusier to Hendricus Theodorus Wijdeveld, 5 August 1925, Wijdeveld Archive, Het Nieuwe Instituut, Rotterdam, quoted in Paul V. Turner. "Frank Lloyd Wright and the Young Le Corbusier," *Journal of the Society of Architectural Historians* 42 (December 1983): 359.

12. Karla Britton and Kenneth Frampton, "Frank Lloyd Wright," in *Encyclopédie Perret,* ed. Joseph Abram, Jean-Louis Cohen, and Guy Lambert (Paris: Éditions du Patrimoine, 2002), 295; Auguste Perret to Marie Dormoy, 27 October 1949, in *Auguste Perret—Marie Dormoy: Correspondance 1922–1953,* ed. Ana Bela de Araujo (Paris: Editions du Linteau, 2009), 509.

13. Auguste Perret, quoted by Jean Labatut in "Lecture for the Opening of the Exhibition of Auguste Perret, Sponsored by French Embassy," 18 May 1950, in Britton and Frampton, "Frank Lloyd Wright," 295.

14. Jean Badovici, "L'Art de Frank Lloyd Wright," *Architecture vivante* 2 (Winter 1924): 26–27 and pls. 34–35.

15. Jean Badovici, "Frank Lloyd Wright," *Cahiers d'art* 1 (January 1926): 30–32.

16. Jean Badovici, "Frank Lloyd Wright," *Architecture vivante* 8 (Spring–Summer 1930): 50.

17. Robert Mallet-Stevens, "Frank Lloyd Wright et l'architecture nouvelle," in Hendricus Theodorus Wijdeveld, ed., *The Life Work of the American Architect Frank Lloyd Wright* (Santpoort, Netherlands: C.A. Mees, 1925), 92.

18. Robert Mallet-Stevens, "Les raisons de l'architecture moderne dans tous les pays," lecture given at the Colisée in Paris in 1925, *Conferencia* 1 (December 1928): 592–93.

19. Pierre Vago (Rencontres internationales d'architectes), to Frank Lloyd Wright,

31 May 1939, Frank Lloyd Wright Foundation Archives, Avery Architecture & Fine Arts Library, Columbia University, and Museum of Modern Art, New York (hereafter FLWFA).

20. Pierre Vago, *Une Vie intense* (Brussels: Archives d'architecture moderne, 2000), 143–44.

21. [André Lurçat], "Frank Lloyd Wright," *Cahiers d'art* 2 (November 1927): 322.

22. Henry-Russell Hitchcock Jr., *Frank Lloyd Wright* (Paris: Éditions Cahiers d'Art, 1928), n.p.; my translation.

23. André Lurçat to Frank Lloyd Wright, 27 October 1927, FLWFA; Frank Lloyd Wright to André Lurçat, undated [1927], Lurçat Archive, Cité de l'architecture et du patrimoine, Paris.

24. Frank Lloyd Wright, "An meine Kritiker!" *Schweizerische Bauzeitung* 98:11 (1931): 136–37; initially sent to the *Frankfurter Allgemeine Zeitung* as "To My Critics in the Land of the Danube and the Rhine," in Bruce Brooks Pfeiffer, ed., *Frank Lloyd Wright: Collected Writings* (New York: Rizzoli, 1993), 3:18–20.

25. Sigfried Giedion, "Les problèmes actuels de l'architecture; à l'occasion d'un manifeste de Frank Lloyd Wright aux architectes et critiques d'Europe," *Cahiers d'art* 7 (January–February 1932): 70–72.

26. Louis Gillet, "L'Art au Canada et aux États-Unis," in André Michel, ed., *Histoire de l'Art depuis les premiers temps chrétiens jusqu'à nos jours,* vol. 8. (Paris: Armand Colin, 1929), 1168.

27. Jean Prévost, *Eiffel* (Paris: Rieder), 1921; Jean Prévost, *Usonie, esquisse de la civilisation américaine* (Paris: Gallimard, 1939). He was executed by the Nazis in 1944.

28. Prévost, *Usonie,* 154.

29. Prévost, *Usonie,* 157.

30. Marcel Lods, "Visite à Neutra," and Alexandre Persitz, "Un architecte d'aujourd'hui," *L'Architecture d'aujourd'hui* 13 (May–June 1946): 4–5, 9.

31. André Remondet, "Évolution de l'architecture américaine," *L'Architecture française* 7 (January 1946): 29–33.

32. Louis-Georges Noviant, "L'architecture organique regarde l'architecture moderne," in "Frank Lloyd Wright," special issue, *L'Architecture française* 14 (October 1952); 71–72.

33. Frank Lloyd Wright, "Massacre on the Marseilles Waterfront," in Pfeiffer, *Frank Lloyd Wright: Collected Writings* (New York: Rizzoli, 1995), 5:59. The piece makes clear Wright was referring to the Unité d'habitation even though the building lies some distance from the waterfront.

34. Anne-Laure Sol, ed, *Hervé Baley & Dominique Zimbacca, architectes: Pour une autre modernité* (Lyon: Lieux-Dits, 2018).

35. Caroline Maniaque, "Les architectes français et la contre-culture américaine (1960–1975)" (Ph.D. diss., Université de Paris, 2006), 185.

36. Jean Castex, in conversation with Caroline Maniaque, "Les architects français," 254.

37. Jean Castex and Philippe Panerai, "Frank Lloyd Wright, de la Prairie House à la Maison Usonienne," *L'Architecture française* 35 (May–June 1974): 21–23; Jean Castex, "Morphologie et syntaxe dans les œuvres de la première période de F. L. Wright," in Institut de l'environnement, *Sémiotique de l'espace* (Paris: Denoël-Gonthier, 1979), 43–69.

38. Jean Castex, *Le printemps de la Prairie House* (Liege: Mardaga, 1987).

39. F. Rudolf Vogel, *Das amerikanische Haus,* vol. 1, *Der Entwicklung der Baukunst und des amerikanischen Hauses* (Berlin: Wasmuth, 1910).

40. Model views are published in Moisei Ginzburg, *Stil i Epokha, problemy sovremennoi arkhitektury* (Moscow: Gos. Izdatelstvo, 1924), pl. 14.

41. Moisei Ginzburg, "Tselovaia ustanovka v sovremennoi arkhitekture," *Sovremennaia Arkhitektura* 2:1 (1927): 7.

42. [Moisei Ginzburg], "Frank Lloyd Wright," *Sovremennaia Arkhitektura* 2:2 (1927): 51. On the ideal representation of the United States in Russia, see Jean-Louis Cohen, *Building a New World: Amerikanizm in Russian Architecture* (New Haven: Yale University Press, 2020).

43. Moisei Ginzburg, *Zhilishche* (Moscow: Gosstroiizdat, 1933), 38–39.

44. Richard Neutra, *Kak stroit Amerika?* (Moscow: MAKIZ, 1929), 137–38, 140.

45. David Arkin, *Arhitektura sovremennogo zapada* (Moscow: OGIZ-IZOGIZ, 1932), 86–92.

46. David Arkin, telegram to Frank Lloyd Wright, 1 January 1935, FLWFA.

47. Frank Lloyd Wright, "Kak ia rabotaiu," *Arkhitektura SSSR* 2 (February 1934): 71; English text: "Categorical Reply to Questions by 'Architecture of the USSR'," in Pfeiffer, *Frank Lloyd Wright Collected Writings,* 3:145.

48. Pfeiffer, *Frank Lloyd Wright Collected Writings,* 3:145.

49. Frank Lloyd Wright. "First Answers to Questions by *Pravda,*" in Pfeiffer, *Frank Lloyd Wright Collected Writings,* 3:141–42.

50. David Arkin, "Amerikanskaia arkhitektura I kniga Mumforda," foreword to Lewis Mumford, *Ot brevenchatogo doma do neboskreba, ocherk istorii amerikanskoi arkhitektury* (Moscow: Izd. Vses. Akademii Arkhitektury, 1936), 11. The book was translated from the German edition: *Vom Blockhaus zum Wolkenkratzer* (Berlin: Bruno Cassirer, 1926).

51. Archives of the Union of Architects, Russian State Archive for Literature and Art, Moscow, Op. 2, 22, p. 30.

52. "Frank Lloyd Wright," *Arkhitektura SSSR* 5 (August 1937): 49–50; English translation in Donald Leslie Johnson, *Frank Lloyd Wright versus America: The 1930s* (Cambridge, Mass.: MIT Press, 1994), 229.

53. Frank Lloyd Wright. "Address to the Architect's World Congress—Soviet Russia 1937," in *An Autobiography* (New York: Duell, Sloan & Pearce, 1943), 573.

54. Edited excerpts of Wright's address are published in *Izvestia,* June 26, 1937, and *Arkhitektura SSSR;* see n. 47 above.

55. Frank Lloyd Wright, "Architecture and Life in the USSR," *Soviet Russia Today* 6 (October 1937): 14–19; also published in *Architectural Record* 82 (October 1937), 58–63; and in *An Autobiography,* 549–56.

56. Vladimir Verlinsky to Frank Lloyd Wright, 21 October 1937, FLWFA.

57. Frank Lloyd Wright, "For 'Izvestia'," 1937, in Pfeiffer, *Frank Lloyd Wright Collected Writings,* 3:214–15.

58. Paul Romaine, "Wright Praises New Soviet Constitution," *Daily Worker,* 12 August 1937.

59. Frank Lloyd Wright, cable to the Soviet Consulate in New York, 15 June 1939, FLWFA.

60. Boris Iofan, "Materialy o sovremennoi arkhitekture SShA i Italii," *Akademia Arkhitektury* 2:4 (1936), 47.

61. "Organicheskaia arkhitektura Franka Lloida Raita," *Arkhitektura SSSR* 9 (February 1941): 70.

62. Boris Iofan, cable to Frank Lloyd Wright, 6 July 1941, FLWFA.

63. Joseph Losey to Frank Lloyd Wright, 14 October 1941; Frank Lloyd Wright to Boris Iofan, 23 October 1941, FLWFA.

64. Douglas Haskell Papers, box C119, Avery Architecture & Fine Arts Library, Columbia University.

65. A report was published in the wake of the trip: *Opyt stroitel'stva za rubezhom. V Soedinennykh Shtatakh Ameriki* (Moscow: Gos. Izd. Literatury po Stroitel'stvu i Arkhitekture, 1956).

66. "Purge Report Puts Grim End to Soviet Experts' US Tour," *Architectural Forum* 103 (December 1955):16.

67. "Wright Fears Russian Architect Sacked for Admiring Him," *Milwaukee Sentinel,* 15 November 1955, 6.

68. Frank Lloyd Wright, *Budushchee Arkhitektury,* trans. Arkady F. Gol'dshtein (Moscow: Gos. Izd. Literatury po Stroitel'stvu, Arkhitekture i Stroitel'nym Materialam, 1960).

69. Alexandra M. Khristiani, *Noveishaia Arkhitektura SSha (1945–1960)* (Moscow: Gos. Izd. Literatury po Stroitel'stvu, Arkhitekture i Stroitel'nym Materialam, 1963), 246–47.

70. Arkady Gol'dshtein, *Frank Lloyd Wright* (Moscow: Stroiizdat, 1973).

71. Marcello Piacentini, "Il momento architettonico all'estero," *Architettura e arti decorative* 1 (May–June 1921): 32–76.

72. Federica Lehmann and Augusto Rossari, *Wright e l'Italia, 1910–1960* (Milan: Edizioni Unicopli, 1999), 61–65.

73. Edoardo Persico, "Profezia dell'architettura," *Casabella* 9 (June-July 1936): 4.

74. Giuseppe de Finetti, "L'America di Frank Lloyd Wright," (*Rassegna d'architettura,* February 1938) in Lehmann and Rossari, *Wright e l'Italia,* 70–71.

75. Rafaele Giolli, "L'ultimo Wright," (*Casabella,* March 1938), in Lehmann and Rossari, *Wright e l'Italia,,* 72.

76. Giulio Carlo Argan, "L'autobiografia di Wright," *Casabella* 14 (June 1941): 2–3.

77. Bruno Zevi, *Verso un'architettura organica; Saggio sullo sviluppo del pensiero architettonico negli ultimi cinquant'anni* (Turin: Einaudi, 1945); English trans.: *Towards an Organic Architecture* (London: Faber & Faber, 1950). See also Bruno Zevi, "Wright and Italy, A Recollection," in Alofsin, *Frank Lloyd Wright, Europe and Beyond,* 68–75.

78. Bruno Zevi, "Della cultura architettonica," *Metron* 5, nos. 31–32 (1949): 22.

79. Giulio Carlo Argan, "Introduzione a Wright," *Metron* 3:18 (1947): 9–24. See Francesco Dal Co's statement in *SaveWright* 8 (Fall 2017): 12–13.

80. Frank Lloyd Wright to Bruno Zevi, 18 March 1953, Fondazione Zevi, Rome.

81. Bruno Zevi, *Frank Lloyd Wright* (Milan: Il Balcone, 1947), 12, 9.

82. Francesca Tondello, "L'architettura di Wright in mostra a Firenze: Le complesse vicende di un'esposizione: I progetti culturali di Ragghianti, Zevi e Stonorov, 1948–1951" (M.A. thesis, Università degli studi di Trieste, 2014); Kathryn Smith, *Wright on Exhibit: Frank Lloyd Wright's Architectural Exhibitions* (Princeton: Princeton University Press, 2017), 169–209.

83. Frank Lloyd Wright to Bruno Zevi, 1 February 1953, Fondazione Zevi, Rome.

84. Le Corbusier to Hendricus Theodorus Wijdeveld, 5 August 1925, Wijdeveld Archive, Nieuwe Institut Rotterdam.

85. Persico, "Profezia dell'architettura," 4.

86. Prévost, *Usonie,* 157.

87. Bruno Zevi, "Dichiarazione di principi," *Metron* 1, no. 2 (September 1945).

88. On Zevi's contribution to Italian architecture, see Pippo Ciorra and Jean-Louis Cohen, eds., *Zevi's Architects: History and Counter-History of Italian Architecture, 1944–2000* (Rome: MAXXI, Macerata, Quodlibet, 2018).

89. Sheldon W. Cheney, *The New World Architecture* (New York: Longmans, Green, 1930), 221.

90. Sol, *Hervé Baley & Dominique Zimbacca,* 84, 91, 95, 101, 107.

91. Ilia Lezhava, 2015 interview in Masha Panteleyeva, "Re-Forming the Socialist City: Form and Image in the Work of the Soviet Experimental Group NER, 1960–1970" (Ph.D. diss., Princeton University, 2018), 16.

92. See the excellent survey: Maristella Casciato, "Wright and Italy: The Promise of Organic Architecture," in Alofsin, *Frank Lloyd Wright, Europe and Beyond,* 76–99.

93. Carlo Scarpa, interview, quoted in Lehmann and Rossari, *Wright e l'Italia,* 94.

94. Giuseppe Samonà, 1949, quoted in Lehmann and Rossari, *Wright e l'Italia,* 94.

95. Bruno Zevi, "L'architettura organica di fronte ai suoi critici," *Metron* 4:23–24 (1948): 43.

96. Zevi, "Wright and Italy," 75; Bruno Zevi, *The Modern Language of Architecture* (1973; reprint ed., New York: Da Capo Press, 1994).

97. Zevi, *The Modern Language of Architecture.*

CAMMIE MCATEE

Wright

The Postwar Form Giver

On 23 April 1959, the exhibition "Form Givers at Mid-Century" opened in Washington, D.C., at the Corcoran Gallery of Art. Organized by *Time* magazine in celebration of the fiftieth anniversary of the American Federation of Arts. It showcased the work of thirteen "form givers"—Alvar Aalto, Marcel Breuer, R. Buckminster Fuller, Walter Gropius, Wallace K. Harrison, Philip Johnson, Le Corbusier, Ludwig Mies van der Rohe, Richard Neutra, Eero Saarinen, Edward Durell Stone, Frank Lloyd Wright, and the firm of Skidmore, Owings & Merrill. Curated by *Time* staff writer Cranston Jones, the exhibition offered a panorama of the work of those figures considered by their peers and followers to have made the most significant contributions to postwar architecture.

György Kepes, who was brought in as the installation designer, harnessed the diversity of architectural expression through a display system of open frames and illuminated columns that supported large-scale photographic reproductions. Brightly lighting some rooms and plunging others into darkness, Kepes skillfully balanced the material and the immaterial, the glossy images of buildings given architectural weight through elements that included a bronze mullion, cast concrete block and grill elements, a stained glass template, a geodesic tensegrity sphere and tension-compressed beam, and tabletops made of stone, various woods, concrete, bronze, marble, and stainless steel (figs. 1, 2). Further life was brought to the exhibition through a short motion picture made by *Time*. Titled *The New Age of Architecture,* the forty-minute film featured many of the architects speaking about their work and ideals. The wealth of material on display—the models alone included Wright's Solomon R. Guggenheim Museum (1943–59), Mies's Seagram Building (1954–58) and S. R. Crown Hall (1950–56), Johnson's Glass House (1945–49), Fuller's Union Tank Car Company in Baton Rouge, Louisiana (1958), and Stone's U.S. Embassy in New Delhi (1954–59)—spoke of the extraordinary success of American architects.[1] The exhibition drew crowds of visitors as it toured fifteen U.S. cities as well as a Canadian one over the next two years.[2]

FIGS. I AND 2. "Form Givers at Mid-Century" exhibition, general view of installation at the Art Institute of Chicago, 12 April to 15 May 1960, György Kepes, installation designer. (The Art Institute of Chicago/Art Resource, NY)

CAMMIE MCATEE

Despite the fact it was an immensely popular exhibition that went far in educating the public about contemporary architecture, "Form Givers at Mid-Century" has received scant attention in histories of postwar architecture.[3] The unabashedly triumphalist tone adopted by Jones in the accompanying catalog may partially explain why it has been sidelined. As a veteran *Time* writer, Jones held Henry Luce's "American Century" line, taking as his guiding statement for the exhibition project two phrases from Luce's 1957 speech to the American Institute of Architects on the occasion of its one hundredth anniversary. Luce had prophesied that the country, having achieved a vital democracy, would "succeed in creating the first modern, technological, humane, prosperous, and reverent civilization. This creative response to challenge will be most vividly expressed in and by architecture."[4] Jones then narrated a history of Modern architecture that had all but moved to the United States. The press release proclaimed: "Behind this exhibition is the realization that architecture . . . has reached a stage of high fulfillment within the United States."[5] It was also regularly mentioned that all but two of the form givers were working in the country, five of them émigrés. It is here where the Cold War rhetoric can be felt. Who was left out smacks of mid-century geopolitics—the exclusion of the undeniably powerful form giver (and communist) Oscar Niemeyer was especially egregious.

The reception of the exhibition was generally positive. The *New York Times* reviewer, Stuart Preston, accepted the premise that Modern architecture had moved to the United States and saw the exhibition as "no more than a sharp and brilliant focus on the kind of buildings springing up everywhere. In a sense the whole country is an architectural exhibition."[6] If architecture commentators had qualms—the British-born Canadian historian Peter Collins opined that "form giver" was "simply Madison Avenue's euphemism for a 'good architect'"—their reservations were generally put aside in deference to the favorable light the exhibition shone upon architecture.[7]

While more than a little American chauvinism was on display in the exhibition and catalog, there is more to the project's content than that. "Form Givers at Mid-Century" came at the end of an extremely successful period for the architecture profession in the United States. Even taking into account Luce's great personal interest in and support of architecture (his *Architectural Forum* was arguably the most significant U.S. journal of its kind in the 1950s and 1960s, but also a consistent money loser), that a major news publisher would both organize and financially support an exhibition on contemporary architecture speaks to a meteoric rise of the field in postwar American culture.[8]

Where the deeper significance of the exhibition lies is in its privileging of form. To put it in its simplest terms, the 1950s saw the conceptual dyad "form follows function" broken and replaced by "form follows *form.*" Coined by the architect Matthew Nowicki, a rising figure in American architecture culture who died tragically in 1950, this expression came to characterize a new vision of the design process in the years that followed.[9] Architects and critics of very different ideological stripes embraced Nowicki's brilliant summation of the situation. It seemed to capture the realities of postwar design as well as to represent a step forward in the maturation of Modern architecture. Function, however, had not been left out; by the early 1950s most architects would likely have argued that what had once been seen as a driving force of design had simply been assimilated into problem solving. Recognized as the generator as well as the product of the design process, form had gained its full autonomy by the end of the decade. Thus whatever the superficiality of the content or underlying biases of the 1959 exhibition, the explicit foregrounding of form as the creative goal of postwar architectural production demands deeper consideration, as do the individual architects and designers selected for distinction.

As a photograph of Eero Saarinen and Walter Gropius admiring the Guggenheim model suggests, Frank Lloyd Wright was a central actor in the gradual foregrounding of form in the 1950s (fig. 3). Indeed, the figure of Wright stood out, positioned by Jones as the greatest "form giver of mid-century." It was one of the last honors paid to the architect, who did not live to see the exhibition open. How Wright was perceived in the 1950s is closely tied to the broad shift in architecture culture that saw form triumph over function, and the

FIG. 3. Walter Gropius and Eero Saarinen viewing model of the Solomon R. Guggenheim Museum at "Form Givers" exhibition at Corcoran Gallery of Art, Washington, D.C., 23 April 1959. *Evening Star* [Washington], 24 April 1959. (Reprinted with permission of the DC Public Library, Star Collection © Washington Post)

architect, now a form giver, reclaim the position of the artist. In a climate in which form as a bearer of feeling and emotion was increasingly valued and the idea of personal expression cautiously readmitted into architecture, the eyes and ears taking in Wright's buildings and statements perceived him in a new light.

FORMING THE FORM GIVERS

How the exhibition materialized reveals much about shifts in architectural concerns. The catchy title was borrowed from Eero Saarinen. Cranston Jones readily admitted to "snitching" the title phrase from Saarinen, who had introduced it into popular architectural discourse in an *Architectural Forum* essay published in July 1953.[10] Presenting his views of what he defined as "six broad currents of modern architecture," Saarinen singled out, in this order, the architects Wright, William Wurster, Pietro Belluschi, Aalto, Le Corbusier, Gropius, Mies, and the "engineer-scientists" Pier Luigi Nervi and Fuller as the "form givers" who were pushing architecture forward.[11] If letters to the editor can be taken as evidence of a general response, American architects warmly embraced the designation. While one respondent noted the appropriateness of the term—"it is through form that architecture may realize the fulfillment of itself as a creative human activity"—another replied with cartoons that gently satirized Saarinen's at times awkward prose (fig. 4).[12] That Saarinen received the Architectural League of New York's prestigious Howard Myers Award for architectural writing three years after the article's publication speaks to its ongoing impact.

But what did "form," "form giver," and even "form giving" mean in the 1950s? The term as noun and verb proved both useful and stimulating to the practice of architecture. On a pragmatic level, form giver offered an elegant way out of the increasingly thorny problem of differentiating between architects, engineers, and other design professionals, all of whom were transforming the built environment. Form giving perfectly captured what was understood as the central challenge of architecture: designing buildings that would touch their users in ways that transcended the demands of functionalism to answer what Sigfried Giedion had termed during the war years the human need for "emotional expression."[13]

Jones, a consummate Luce-trained journalist, recognized a compelling tagline when he saw one, and first used the designation in a *Time* profile on Saarinen published in July 1956. To contextualize Saarinen's contributions in a period of great diversity and accomplishment in architecture, Jones provided a list of fourteen architects that he designated "The 20th Century

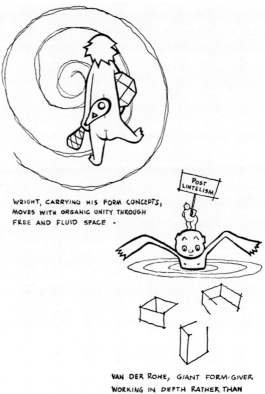

WRIGHT, CARRYING HIS FORM CONCEPTS, MOVES WITH ORGANIC UNITY THROUGH FREE AND FLUID SPACE.

VAN DER ROHE, GIANT FORM-GIVER WORKING IN DEPTH RATHER THAN BREADTH, BRINGS PROUD ORDER OUT OF FORM WORLD, ENRICHING THE VOCABULARY WITH EMPTY REGULAR SPACES.

FIG. 4. Cartoon satirizing Saarinen's term "form giver," showing Wright and Mies, 1953, John MacFayden, cartoonist. *Architectural Forum,* September 1953. (Author's collection)

Form Givers." Jones's selection differed from Saarinen's through its inclusion of many up-and-coming architects as well as older, more established "masters."[14] He also made a point of the fact that only one "20th century master" (Le Corbusier) did not live and work in the United States. The main contribution of the article is in how it helped introduce the idea of the form giver to mainstream American culture. Sales records for the issue with Saarinen on the cover were reportedly on a par with the high ones for the May issue featuring Marilyn Monroe.

Thus encouraged, Jones decided to explore the topic further. Working with architecture colleagues at Time-Life, he prepared a questionnaire about the current state of architecture that was sent to leading architects, architecture schools, and the publisher's national and foreign news bureaus in June 1956. Three months later, *Architectural Forum* published the poll results. The responses to the question "Whom would you consider the leading 'form-givers'?" yielded yet more names.[15] If still inconclusive, the poll made two things clearer: most architects believed that Wright, Le Corbusier, and Mies van der Rohe were the most significant form givers; and diversity in architectural expression was now seen as, if not a wholly positive trend, one that held promise for a great future for Modern architecture. The place of Gropius in these approval ratings is also worth noting. Though he was cited in this "pulse-taking," Gropius's reputation as a creative artist was beginning a downward slide, a descent that would reveal much about what was considered important for postwar architecture.

Jones's research unexpectedly proved useful for another project. In the spring of 1958, the American Federation of Arts (AFA) approached *Time* editors about organizing an exhibition on architecture in honor of the AFA's fiftieth anniversary the following year. Operating as a museum without walls, the AFA worked to raise awareness of art, photography, design, and architecture through exhibitions organized with other institutions and the federal government that were circulated nationally and internationally. The AFA also brought exhibitions from other parts of the world to the United States. Jones's 1956 article seems to have directly inspired the AFA's request. Demonstrating the power of an impactful label, the AFA's director, Harris K. Prior, suggested that the exhibition take the "form givers" as its theme.[16] Jones, who was appointed curator, was acutely aware that moving from a short descriptive article to a well-developed curatorial argument would be very demanding. To arrive at a tight, rigorous, and defensible list of form givers, he invited Belluschi to work with him as professional adviser, a role the dean of the MIT School of Architecture regularly played throughout the period. Jones settled into the task, likening it to being "as much fun as picking the next Pope."[17] Belluschi took the project seriously and demanded a high standard for selection. Jones assured his superiors at *Time* and the AFA: "That when you use the expression 'Form Givers,' you mean just that. Architecture begins with genius. It becomes the vernacular of an age through a process of adaption, modification, commercialization." If the reference to commercialization might raise a cynical eyebrow today, Jones and Belluschi meant it in the sense of that which was taken up by many and thus diffused.

The final list for the exhibition comprised thirteen form givers, including one architectural firm, which solved the diplomatic problem posed by the singling out of one partner.[18] If representing architectural democracy—that is, principles of social equality—was the stated goal of the exhibition, the catalog's table of contents and organization tells another story, for the form givers were presented in an order that suggests, through the number of pages and degree of voice granted to each designer/firm, three more-or-less distinct hierarchies: Wright, Mies, and Le Corbusier occupy the highest level; Gropius, Neutra, Aalto, and Breuer stand in the next tier; in almost alphabetical order Harrison, Johnson, SOM, Saarinen, and Stone occupy the third level, with the sole outsider to the architectural profession, Fuller, placed at the end. It is hard not to draw symbolic (if not biblical) significance out of the number of form givers and Wright's position at their head, especially in light of the way Jones's narrative of the development of Modern architecture was presented in the catalog.

As the country's most well-known and only home-grown architect in the first tier, it was absolutely crucial that Wright participate in "Form Givers at Mid-Century." Jones was overjoyed when he accepted the invitation. But, as Kathryn Smith has discussed in her rigorous study of Wright's exhibitions, the architect's initial approbation seems to have been based on a misunderstanding, and only after extensive negotiation did he finally agree to be included, and then only in a limited way.[19] With the Guggenheim Museum nearing completion but still arousing controversy, Wright was really only interested in the exhibition's second venue, the Metropolitan Museum in New York, where it was scheduled to open on 8 June, his ninety-second birthday. When he was granted his own room, Wright agreed to allow his work, which was drawn from another exhibition, to "join . . . the travelling show" in New York (fig. 5).[20] His sudden death on 9 April, less than two weeks before the opening at the Corcoran, had the unexpected consequence of securing his participation for the entire tour.[21] Jones quickly moved to intensify Wright's presence at the Metropolitan, adding many more drawings, including those for the never completed project for Wright's own mausoleum. The New York presentation became, in effect, a memorial for the architect many believed the greatest form giver of them all.

These demands and gestures, however, only partially explain why Wright, who had maintained a pugnacious "me against the world" attitude, accepted, if in a carefully circumscribed way, to enter into what he termed "a competitive exhibition."[22] It is all the more curious since the exhibition also celebrated his arch nemesis. So important was Wright's cooperation that Jones, encouraged by Prior, briefly considered leaving Le Corbusier out. At least two architects, SOM's Gordon Bunshaft and Edward Durrell Stone, dissuaded him, arguing that "Lever House [was] as much Corbu as Mies," and the "stilts on which the Museum of Modern Art rests, with its open ground floor, is Corbusier."[23]

We may surmise that the depth to which Wright was written into the overall exhibition narrative helped lower the walls he had built to maintain his cherished status as an architectural outsider and mitigate his outrage upon discovering he was to share the limelight with others. He was repre-

FIG. 5. "Form Givers" exhibition, gallery devoted to Wright, Metropolitan Museum of Art, New York, 8 June to 7 September 1959. (American Federation of Arts Records, Archives of American Art, Smithsonian Institution)

sented by the earliest work in the show—a drawing for the Cooper house (1887) that Wright claimed to have shown Louis Sullivan when applying to work in his office—and the most recently built project in the exhibition, the Guggenheim Museum.[24] In this sense, he appeared to embody the whole history of Modern architecture, his status as its progenitor confirmed in the narrative in the exhibition catalog. It was a corrective to the historical record that Wright would have approved of, especially as it implied that the contributions of Le Corbusier, Mies, and Gropius were stimulated by his inventions. He was also undoubtedly moved by the reverence Jones expressed toward Sullivan, who was placed at the beginning of Modern architecture, with John Szarkowski's photograph of the Wainwright Building (1890–91) serving as a graphic illustration of what Wright described as the "death blow" Sullivan had given to the Ecole des Beaux-Arts.[25]

However, there is also reason to believe that the label "form giver" likewise appealed to Wright. His writings, after all, were about the creation of form, which had a special significance for him through his close relationship to Sullivan. He embraced it as his own, adapting its connotations to suit his purposes and enshrining it within his personal lexicon. In the 1950s his words found a broader audience.

FORM AND FUNCTION ARE ONE

Wright was a self-anointed form giver. In a Sunday morning Taliesin talk in 1950 he stated: "An architect is a builder, a constructor, a form-giver, and he's got to be a master of idea-giving."[26] As the date of this talk alone shows, Eero Saarinen was not the originator of the potent catch-phrase. Indeed, he never asserted authorship, for the concept came to him from his father, Eliel, who had laid out his belief in an eternal "search for form," as his 1948 book was titled. Nor could the elder Saarinen make any claims, for the concept of the form giver, if not the phrase itself, is deeply rooted in eighteenth-century German and nineteenth-century French theories about form.[27]

Both Eliel Saarinen and Wright saw form as a living force, infused with "sense and spirit," as Goethe described *lebende Gestalt* (living form). Wright read Goethe when he was young and translated the poem "A Hymn to Nature," attributed to him, with Mamah Borthwick around 1910. His thinking about form was furthered by the writings of Eugène-Emmanuel Viollet-le-Duc, who used the word *forme* to denote idea, style, order, structure, and shape, but also imbued it with emotional sensibilities. Viollet's pronouncements on form have generally been read from the perspective of his structural rationalism, but he also equated spirit and feeling with form, a message that resonated with Wright, who built these associations into his own discourse. That a reprint of Henry Van Brunt's 1875 translation of the *Discourses on Architecture*— Viollet referred to "feeling for form" in three places—was issued in 1959 might suggest that others believed there was a new audience for such ideas. Wright's exposure to American Transcendentalism through the writings of Ralph Waldo Emerson surely only intensified these associations.

Wright and American architects more broadly in the 1950s came together around form through the tragic hero Louis Sullivan, whose work and writing underwent a major revival in the years leading up to and following the 1956 centenary of his birth. Celebrated that year in a major retrospective exhibition curated by Edgar Kaufmann jr., his buildings reentered contemporary architecture. The importance of Sullivan for the postwar period is also closely tied to the aphorism most associated with him. While many architects were beginning to see "form follows function" as a straitjacket to creativity, what Sullivan said about both sides of the equation in *Kindergarten Chats* (1901–2) appeared to offer an antidote to a conceptual dyad that was no longer productive. The significance he attributed to function also went beyond practical considerations to include symbolic meaning. Out of print for many years, an authoritative new edition of the book was released in 1947 by the art book publisher George Wittenborn as part of the "Documents of Modern Art" series edited by the painter Robert Motherwell. Given a fresh design by Paul Rand, the text of what was now titled *Kindergarten Chats and Other Writings* was free to speak to a new audience. While every architect knew that Sullivan was the author of "form follows function," it was there where knowledge of his writings generally began and ended.[28] The editor of *Progressive Architecture,* Thomas Creighton, was one of many commentators who pushed for a deeper reading of Sullivan's meaning, warning that "everyone who carelessly misuses the 'form follows function' cliché should be forced to read the two essays on Function and Form."[29] The fifty-nine essays in the volume offered much fodder for thinking about the purpose of architecture and of the architect in society. Sullivan's message that the dual faculties of intuition and imagination were critical to the creative work of architecture and his call that it should be reaffirmed as an "Art of Expression" fell on receptive ears.

Wright directly entered the fray with his 1949 memoir of Sullivan. The publication of *Genius and Mobocracy* motivated the newly appointed architectural editor, Douglas Haskell, to break *Architectural Forum*'s unofficial rule of only featuring recent work on its cover. The frieze of the remodeled interior of Adler & Sullivan's McVicker's Theater in Chicago (1883–85, 1890)—one of the many drawings that Sullivan gave Wright in 1924—appeared on the August 1949 cover. Wright's memoir was intended to set the record straight, return Sullivan's original meaning to the well-worn phrase, and attack those Wright perceived as enemies to what he and Sullivan saw as "truth." He confronted the perception of his *Liebermeister* as a "'form follows function' scientist," by a re-presentation of him as a "great lyric poet."[30] Though he did allow that the basic equation was correct—in nature form *did* follow function—Wright took the phrase back from the "dogma" of the "imported self-styled functionalists" and restored its sense of spiritual significance: "Use both the word organic and the word Nature in deeper sense—essence instead of fact: say *form and function are one.*"[31] Four years later, Wright included the phrase in a lexicon of words and phrases that he felt were needed at that moment in time. He put his imprimatur on the revitalized equation and, placing it in third position after "nature" and "organic," elaborated on its "real" meaning in his 1953 book *The Future of Architecture.* An excerpt, published in the May 1953 issue of *Architectural Forum,* pulled the threads closer together: "Form *is* predicated by function but, so far as poetic imagination can go with it without destruction, transcends. 'Form follows function' has become spiritually insignificant: a stock phrase. Only when we say or write *'form and function are one'* is the slogan significant. It is now the password for too much sterility. Internationally."[32] That Haskell retrospectively positioned the essay as the first in a series of important "think pieces" by contemporary architects on "The Future of Modern Architecture" leaves little doubt that Wright's corrective reached its intended audience.[33] And just as his role as Sullivan's defender benefited his postwar image, so did Wright's company among younger practitioners, more so since it included Eero Saarinen, who had launched "form giver" into popular architectural parlance. Form was becoming a basis for exchange.

RECONCILING WITH WRIGHT

If any doubt that Wright was a formidable force in architecture had been put aside by the masterworks that came off his drafting board in the 1930s, 1940s, and the 1950s, his never-ending battle against the International Style and what he saw as the overall mediocrity of the profession continued to be divisive. Given this, it is all the more surprising that the last decade of Wright's life saw reconciliation between the architectural profession and the architect who had spent much of his career needling his presumed confrères for their limitations. It was the younger set of architects, among them Belluschi, Johnson, Louis Kahn, Saarinen, Stone, and Paul Rudolph, who led the way, recognizing the significance of his ideas as well as buildings and projects for what they were all engaging, to wit, in what was called the search for form.

Unexpected alliances were made between Wright's old supporters and new ones. Together they formed a coalition that successfully lobbied the American Institute of Architects to award Wright its Gold Medal in 1949.[34] In *Architectural Forum,* Haskell reported on the intense backroom plotting that took place in a Salt Lake City hotel at the 1948 AIA convention. Kahn and Belluschi were among the signatories, the latter making an especially persuasive appeal in favor of the resolution. What "had looked difficult and nervy and questionable at the start," Haskell wrote, was "not bad in the end," and the measure easily passed.[35] Despite the fact that Wright harangued the audience at the award ceremony in Houston the next spring, the RCA record of his acceptance speech quickly sold out just as virtually every publication associated with Wright had in the past.[36] Sigfried Giedion, whose assessment of Wright was undergoing significant revision, later likened the belated honor to those accorded by the French Academy to Ingres, "after having embittered his whole career as a painter."[37] While there was some truth to this backhanded comparison, Wright had found a way to thrive on negative reception, discovering, as Ada Louise Huxtable aptly put it, "dissent suited him so well."[38] After a life of fighting against real, imagined, and invented threats, it was harder for him than anyone else to give up his oppositional position toward the architectural profession.

Eero Saarinen was among the younger architects opening up to Wright. If this did not represent an about-face as it did for some others, the disparaging remarks Wright had made about his father, Eliel, over the years had strained the younger Saarinen's regard.[39] His romantic relationship with Aline Louchheim, whom he met in January 1953 and married at the end of the year, brought his unresolved feelings about Wright out into the open. A longtime supporter of Wright, Louchheim, who was associate art editor at the *New York Times,* played an especially important part in his career in the 1950s: her spirited defense of the Guggenheim Museum project helped him win the battle that was waged in print.[40] But while letters chronicle her determination to bring her new lover around to her architectural hero, it was a weekend visit to Fallingwater in 1953 that deeply moved Saarinen. Photographs taken from below the house capture his excitement over Wright's daring cantilevered trays and their relationship to the rock ledge above which they hover (fig. 6). Visits to other sites followed, with Saarinen photographing—

FIG. 6. Fallingwater's cantilevered trays seen from the rock ledge below. Eero Saarinen, photographer. (Eero Saarinen Collection [MS 593], Manuscripts and Archives, Yale University Library)

FIG. 7. Frank Lloyd Wright and Eero Saarinen at Taliesin, Spring Green, Wisconsin, likely May 1954. Aline B. Saarinen, photographer. (Eero Saarinen Collection [MS 593], Manuscripts and Archives, Yale University Library)

and being photographed at—Taliesin in Spring Green, Wisconsin (begun 1911); the Unitarian Meeting House in Madison, Wisconsin (1946–52); and Taliesin West in Scottsdale, Arizona (begun 1938) (fig. 7).[41]

While these images demonstrate a fascination for Wright's work, what Saarinen identified as the architect's greatness is revealing of what was considered important in the 1950s. In a letter to Louchheim, he stated that Wright's real contribution was in giving expression to the "spiritual" side of architecture, seeing this as a "bridge to the future."[42] His summation placed Wright's work very much in the present; simultaneously liberating him from Philip Johnson's famous displacement to the nineteenth century and from a vague future importance for architectural directions, what "some-day will be" as Wright's friend Henry Wright Jr. had put it in a 1948 *Architectural Forum* editorial.[43] A force of the present, Wright, Saarinen believed, could now "show the way forward." But at the same time, he also held strong reservations, dramatically warning Louchheim, "don't go near his form; it's vicious." When it came to articulating these feelings in his *Architectural Forum* essay, the writing of which he was assisted by Louchheim as well as Haskell, Saarinen ranked Wright and "organic unity" as the first of "The Six Broad Currents of Modern Architecture."[44] He accepted Wright's "very personal form" but questioned whether "a lasting school" could grow from it "because this form in the hands of others seems, already, anachronistic."[45]

In 1953, an anonymous writer in a British journal made an intriguing pro-posal, suggesting that the late Matthew Nowicki "was in many ways, though not the obvious ones, a true heir to Frank Lloyd Wright."[46] The author tied the two architects together through a shared position on a fundamental problem that "has to do with the place of conscious aesthetic expression in contemporary architecture." Naming monumentality as this uniting concern, the writer posited that Nowicki had been able to reach back through the "Internationalist generations" to take up the "traditional modes and forms" developed by Wright. This proposition bears further consideration, especially since Nowicki had so perfectly summarized how form had taken over both sides of the form follows function equation and, in doing so, had recognized the autonomy that Wright had long claimed for form.

An accomplished architect, planner, and graphic designer in Warsaw, Nowicki came to the United States in 1945 to work on the master plan for the Polish capital's reconstruction. He and his wife, the architect and graphic designer Stanislava Sandecka Nowicki, applied for asylum after the communist takeover in 1948 and settled in Raleigh, North Carolina.[47] In the matter of just a few years, Matthew Nowicki rose from obscurity to be considered one of the brightest architects of his generation. After his death in an airplane crash in Egypt while on his way back from India, where Nowicki was working with Albert Mayer on the planning of the new city of Chandigarh, Saarinen speculated: "If time had allowed his genius to spread its wings in full, this poet-philosopher of form would have influenced the course of architecture as profoundly as he inspired his friends."[48] Almost a decade later, Nowicki was still being mentioned as a designer who could have become a major form giver.

The connections between Nowicki and Wright were more concrete than the British writer could have known. Nowicki had first come into contact with Wright in the early 1920s, when his father was sent to Chicago as the consul general of Poland. Already interested in architecture, Nowicki studied at the Art Institute of Chicago and then enrolled in the architecture program at the Warsaw Technical University when the family returned in 1925. The influence of Le Corbusier and Auguste Perret, combined with rigorous engineering training and an awareness of Eastern European Constructivism, can be felt in Nowicki's work in the United States as well as in Poland. His thorough grounding in both the science and art of architecture put Nowicki in the perfect position to critically assess the state of Modern architecture, especially the relationship between function and form.

While the connections between Nowicki and Le Corbusier have been examined, little has been made of those with Wright. When Nowicki returned to Chicago after the war, he visited Taliesin and met Wright. Lewis Mumford, Nowicki's biographer, stated that the experience "overwhelmed" him.[49] Whether Nowicki's interest in the architect had developed during his early years in Chicago is unknown, but his admiration for Wright's recent work is readily apparent in a wartime project for a church in Prandocin, Poland. As Tyler Sprague has analyzed, the tapered mushroom columns indicate that Nowicki was very much aware of the S. C. Johnson & Son Administration Building (popularly known as the Johnson Wax Building, 1936–39) (fig. 8).[50] Nowicki's American work, most of which was still on the drawing boards when he died, shows that he continued to consider Wright's forms very closely for their monumental power, much as the *Architectural Review*'s commentator had suggested. A central ramp within his project for a Museum of Art, History, and Science for the state of North Carolina (1949–50) evokes the spiral Wright had first used in the Gordon Strong Automobile Objective project (1924–25) and that organized two recent projects, the Guggenheim Museum and the David and Gladys Wright house in Phoenix (1950–52) (fig. 9).

Nowicki's writings also reflect a careful, unbiased reading of Wright's writings. His first important published essay, "Composition in Modern Architecture" of March 1949, began to open up the problem of the form-function equation. He took Wright's corrective "form and function are one" as his starting point, noting that Wright's clarification of the interdependent

FIG. 8. Matthew Nowicki and S. S. Putowski, sketch for a church in Prandocin, Poland, competition entry, ca. 1944, from Tadesuz Baruki, *Matthew Nowicki: Poland, USA, India,* 1980.

CAMMIE MCATEE

FIG. 9. Matthew Nowicki, sketch for the main floor rotunda, with helix ramp, for a Museum of Art, History, and Science, Raleigh, 1949–50, project. (Special Collections Research Center, North Carolina State University Libraries)

relationship of the two quotients would allow "problems of form in modern architecture" to be studied just as those of function were.[51] This went far in leveling the playing field between function and form and setting the stage for what Nowicki would famously state as the reality of the situation. In considering the future of Modern architecture without the blinders of functionalism, he cited the very mushroom columns that had characterized his own church design as a step toward freedom. In addition to citing the Johnson Wax Building's columns as a "precursor" to "a future wave that will bring unpredicted solutions in form," he included photographs of Fallingwater and Taliesin West in his illustrations.[52] Since neither of the figures is keyed to the text, it is difficult to draw a precise meaning from each, but the fact that the view of Taliesin West, taken from the "prow," came last might tie it to Nowicki's conclusion. Titled "Search for Truth," a phrase that comes from both Sullivan and Wright, the final section opened with a statement that went far in fueling changes in how architecture was perceived in the 1950s: "Architecture may be considered a science, a profession, a craft, a hobby, a way of life and many other things, but it is also an art." In the eyes of Nowicki and subsequently many other architects, Wright offered much stimulus for contemporary and future directions.

Increased concern for the psychological and emotional as well as "spiritual" content of architecture also made Wright's work attractive to one of the most influential critics of the period, Sigfried Giedion, whose wartime call for a more "emotional architecture" intensified in the postwar years. This led the historian back to Wright, an architect he had previously placed in a carefully circumscribed box, nowhere more so than in *Space, Time and Architecture* (1941), where Wright appears as a lonely pioneer in a distant land. Just a few months after his arrival at Harvard University in October 1938 to deliver the Norton Lectures that would form the basis for the book, Giedion traveled to Oak Park, Chicago, and Racine, Wisconsin, where he saw the Johnson Wax Building, which was then nearing completion, and in the summer of 1939 he returned to the region to visit Wright at home in Spring Green.[53] Giedion's first impressions registered amazement at the hall of the Johnson Wax Building: "it is the most fantastic thing that has been conceived in the architectural imagination for a long time."[54] Despite his evident admiration, Wright remained an enigma to him, for in later editions of the book, even as Giedion accepted that the United States had become the locus for the further development of Modern architecture, he continued to isolate Wright, forever casting him as a significant influence (especially on Mies) rather than a significant actor whose work continued to evolve. This being said, the unwieldy size and controlling structure of *Space, Time and Architecture* may have hampered any attempt to make a substantial change.

In the early 1950s, by which time an interest in the archaic and primordial had seized him, Giedion had new things to praise about Wright's work. Excited by the powerful curves exemplified in the plan of the project for the McCord house in North Arlington, New Jersey (1948), in 1954 he now commended Wright for "plunging so deeply into problems that concerned the human spirit" and praised him specifically as "an artist" who was showing what he now believed Modern architecture needed most, *"imagination."*[55] What can be taken away from such revisions is that what had once been found deeply suspect in Wright's work and personality—too personal, too subjective, too emotional, too egotistical—were now the valuable attributes of the form giver, the artist-architect.

As many scholars have discussed, the Museum of Modern Art made significant contributions to how Wright's work was understood and valued in the postwar years.[56] Philip Johnson, director of the Architecture and Design Department from its inception in 1932 until 1934 and again from 1946 until 1954, played a major role in shaping and reshaping perceptions of Wright.[57] Having completed a degree in architecture at Harvard's Graduate School of Design in 1943, Johnson wore two hats during his second tenure as A+D director. Part of Johnson's turn toward Wright, with whom he had had a legendarily tempestuous relationship, may be explained by his experience as an architect rather than as a curator. In 1947, midway through the design of what would become the Glass House, Johnson was drawn to what he called Wright's "California numbers" where the houses "dripped over the ravine."[58] Facing the challenge of a site abutting a significant drop, he was likely referring to the Ennis and Freeman houses (both 1924–25) in Los Angeles and, especially, the Millard house in Pasadena (1923–24).

Johnson's writings about Wright soon reflected an architectural understanding of his work. In 1949, he published the first of several articles drawing attention to the complexity of the spatial experience of Wright's architecture. The first one, which appeared in the *Architectural Review,* extolled the experiential richness of Wright's spaces and shapes. The spatial complexity of Wright's two homes and the Johnson Wax Building drew his admiration; Johnson wrote of "the cumulative impact of moving through his organized spaces, the effect of passing though low space into high, from narrow to wide, from dark to light."[59] He also stated what would become a commonplace in reviews of Wright's work: "His buildings can rarely be appreciated correctly except at first hand." This somewhat searching article was a prelude to a much deeper analysis that was inspired by a day spent alone at Taliesin West in late 1949. Although at the time Johnson reported to Wright that it was "impossible to describe [the complex]; one can only feel it," in a lecture at the University of Houston some four years later he attempted to put into words what it felt like to "walk and walk and walk" from the parking lot to the "composition" of buildings through passages with steps that require you to advance "crossways, not straight down, you skip across them on the slant," to pass "around a fantastic rock," and then, just when "boredom sets in, . . . suddenly on your right are two great piers" and a view across a hundred miles, and you arrive at Wright's private space, and inside, "one table, two chairs, and there you talk with the genius of the place."[60] The experience of "what the art of architecture really can be when it's played on a full orchestra" stayed with Johnson, his language intensifying when he returned to the subject a few years later to account for changes at the complex. Arriving in the "cove" (Wright's private dining space), "you realize that you've been handled, and twisted very much as a symphony will, until you get to the crisis."[61] If, as Neil Levine and others have identified, Johnson's concept of the "processional" comes from Le Corbusier's *architectural promenade,* the "emotional impact" of architecture that Johnson found critical, increasingly so as the 1950s progressed, was deeply rooted in his firsthand experience of Wright's work.[62]

Following the rapprochement on Johnson's side, the 1953 "Built in USA: Post-war Architecture" exhibition he cocurated with Henry-Russell Hitchcock and Arthur Drexler positioned Wright as one of three major forces of contemporary architecture. Johnson and Hitchcock had prepared the ground for this project in a co-signed 1952 essay, "The Buildings We See," that was published in *New World Writing,* a popular anthology of literature and criticism. The essay focused on Mies, Wright, and Le Corbusier, along with Saarinen and Bunshaft. The "artist-architect" paradigm was put forward in the ways the authors described how each architect approached his specific problem "intuitively, like a painter or sculptor, rather than rationally, like technical experts on materials," and each situation inspired a different expression, "rather than *a priori* conviction."[63] The emphasis on the art of architecture was in perfect continuity with the 1932 "Modern Architecture" exhibition and concurrently published book, *The International Style,* which had directly challenged the premise that form was the result of function.

Importantly for Wright, whose influence was typically assigned to the past, in their analysis of recent buildings by the next generation, Hitchcock and Johnson pointed to subtle signs of his impact on contemporary work, notably at Eero Saarinen's General Motors Technical Center (1948–56), where they saw a debt that went beyond the oft-cited Mies to include "something of Wright's warmth in this free handling of color."[64] There were limits, however. For Hitchcock and Johnson, Wright remained the Michelangelo of Modern architecture, an intimate virtuoso who reacted against the dominant architectural trends of his time.[65] While there was a negative edge to this characterization, which was frequently repeated, the great master paradigm fed that of the form giver.

Arthur Drexler, who would follow Johnson as the next major force in the museum's A+D department, also made valuable contributions to repositioning Wright in contemporary architecture. Exactly a year before "Built in USA" opened, Drexler curated a small show on the Johnson Wax Building and its Research Tower (1943, 1947–50). It was one of his first exhibition projects after joining the department in 1951.[66] Drexler's interest in Wright was by no means simply a product of the museum's culture, for he had already proven himself to be sensitive to Wright. As the architectural editor of *Interiors + Industrial Design,* he had written about Wright's desert architecture using language that revealed him to be very much in tune with the contemporary form-speak: at one point he refers to the "significant content of Wright's form."[67]

"Frank Lloyd Wright: Buildings for Johnson Wax" was truly a testimony to what Johnson had argued in 1949, namely that Wright's work demanded firsthand knowledge. Again, it was an imperative that went far in helping confer upon architecture the status of being a work of art. The need to "experience" his architecture became almost standard fare in Wright's postwar interpretation. Significantly, Drexler's Wright show followed another small but equally potent exhibition on Le Corbusier. Held during the summer months of 1951, "Le Corbusier: Architecture, Painting, Design" was conceived to highlight the polyvalence of Le Corbusier and, to that end, presented just seven objects in a stark white, light-filled gallery.[68] In striking contrast, the Johnson Wax exhibition was held in a dramatically darkened gallery presenting thirty-seven "three-dimensional" day and night views of the buildings in individual stereoscopic slide viewers (fig. 10). Drexler, a remarkably perceptive photographer as well as an imaginative installation designer, took the 3D photographs, which were complemented by a print of an aerial night view of the Racine complex by Ezra Stoller.[69] Although the architectural tour was a technique Drexler had previously used to great effect in print media, he believed that the illusion of stereo photography offered a more realistic experience of the buildings. This method, he noted, "enables people to grasp the intention of the architect quite easily."[70] Peering through individual viewers, visitors were thus "conduct[ed . . .] through and around the buildings." The choice of a medium capable of communicating not only depth but also a heightened sense of scale, light, and materials was made with the explicit goal of representing the "real" experience of this masterpiece of Modern art.

The Johnson Wax exhibition was in many respects a prologue to "Built in USA." One of Ezra Stoller's powerful photographs of the Research Tower was selected to open the 1953 exhibition, rising up behind the introductory panel (fig. 11). The homage, however, was lost on the building's architect. As Kathryn Smith has chronicled, Wright, outraged by what he saw as an International Style bias within the exhibition, refused to attend the opening. The book published to accompany the show only exacerbated the already tense situation. Wright very publicly objected to the argument advanced by Hitchcock in the foreword. Although he was deeply unhappy with the way he

FIG. I0. "Frank Lloyd Wright: Buildings for Johnson Wax" exhibition, Museum of Modern Art, 15 January to 16 March 1952, Arthur Drexler, curator, stereoscopic photographer, and installation designer; Soichi Sunami, photographer. (Digital Image © The Museum of Modern Art/Licensed by SCALA/Art Resource, NY)

was positioned as just one of three leaders who would guide Modern architecture into the future, there were many subtle and not-so-subtle clues within the rest of the book that he was the most important among them. If Alvin Lustig's type-based cover avoided any favoritism, the image chosen for the frontispiece—again, the Research Tower—was the only color photograph in the book. The ten pages devoted to Wright's work—four more than any other architect—included a two-page spread of the tower, again, the only one in the book. Its implicit message—that Wright's work could not be contained—was transmitted internationally through translations.[71] When Drexler reprised the exhibition for the architecture section of the Museum of Modern Art and U.S. Department of State's "Fifty Years of American Art" at the Musée d'Art Moderne in Paris, he gave more space to Wright than to any other architect and presented the massive photomural of the tower.[72] If historians have interpreted such gestures as attempts to smooth the ruffled feathers of an irascible prima donna, there can, on the contrary, be no doubt that they expressed the sincerest admiration of all three curators.

FIG. 11. "Built in USA: Postwar Architecture" exhibition, Museum of Modern Art, 20 January to 15 March 1953. Arthur Drexler, Henry-Russell Hitchcock, and Philip Johnson, cocurators; Drexler, installation designer; David E. Scherman, photographer. (Digital Image © The Museum of Modern Art/Licensed by SCALA/Art Resource, NY)

Although the praise of the "un-American" International Style was the official tipping point in Wright's last feud with the Museum of Modern Art, he was probably most aggrieved by the way Hitchcock drew him into current architecture, presented as one among many great architects, rather than as a singular outsider, a position he cherished.[73] The battle elicited a strong defense from the museum's director, René d'Harnoncourt, who underlined the fact that the institution had previously presented Wright's work in no less than fourteen exhibitions, six of them solo shows.[74] Kathryn Smith has revised this figure, counting some twenty-six exhibitions organized by the museum that included work by Wright.[75] Even without this addition, the Museum of Modern Art had not only given him more exposure than any other architect, but more than it had given to any other artist. The message was that Wright was on par with, perhaps even more important than, Picasso, an affirmation that also fit well into the museum's ongoing project to keep architecture within the world of art. And in doing so, it reasserted the artist-architect designation.

THE RISE OF THE TRIUMVERATE

As the "Built in USA" exhibition demonstrates, Wright was not alone in benefiting from sea changes in what were considered the most important attributes of the architect. Opinions on Le Corbusier underwent a radical reversal as well. The Unité d'Habitation at Marseilles (1945–52) first and then the chapel at Ronchamp (1950–55) put the issue of functionalism firmly in the past. Le Corbusier's work in other fields of visual art—painting and sculpture—which had been previously interpreted as signs of a capricious and undisciplined mind, was now seen as an asset. Mies van der Rohe, too, began to rise in the eyes of American architects. Aided not only by Johnson, but also by allies at *Architectural Forum,* who were furthering the cause of form, Mies ascended through the ranks.

What is also telling in this shift from architecture as a response to function to being solely one of form is the postwar decline experienced by Gropius. Although he had been consistently cited as a major architectural force since his immigration to the United States in 1937, Gropius's contributions to design were gradually downgraded, replaced by his role as an educator. While Johnson's contempt for Gropius as a designer is well known, Irene Sunwoo has revealed that in 1947 Johnson went so far as to try to oust him from the subtitle of Nikolaus Pevsner's authoritative account, *Pioneers of Modern Design: From William Morris to Walter Gropius,* first published in 1936, arguing to the author that "Mr. Gropius has never designed any building. . . . In other words, to say From Morris to Gropius is too much of a compliment to our estimable and excellent pedagogue."[76] Even Giedion, Gropius's long-standing apologist, seemed hard pressed to keep up his praise of the architect's abilities as a designer; whereas the section on Gropius in the first two editions of *Space, Time and Architecture* had closed with an assessment of his creativity (if a rather lukewarm one that credited him with a "strong and solid rather than quick imagination"), the third edition of 1954 ended on his contributions as a teacher.[77] This message was amplified in Giedion's monograph *Walter Gropius: Work and Teamwork* (1954). Not surprisingly, when Jones turned to Gropius in the *Form Givers* catalog, he called him a "planner and method giver as well as architect."[78]

Out of the fall of Gropius a diverse triumvirate emerged. What can be taken away from its composition is that what counted most for American architects in this new phase of freedom were the architect's abilities as a form giver. The consolidation of Wright, Le Corbusier, and Mies as the foremost contemporary practitioners was a direct result of renewed appreciation of the architect as an artist. Significantly, this was a model that could embrace diversity. Thomas Creighton would write in *Progressive Architecture*'s 1955 issue devoted to the "Search for Form": "How boldly contrasting are the statements that some of the great of our time—Wright, Le Corbusier, and Mies van der Rohe, for example—have made as a result of their conscious experimentation with form expression."[79] The three soon became seen as the fundamental form givers. Jones's "Form Givers at Mid-Century" essay reinforced this exalted position. If each architect was treated slightly differently, they were prioritized by their position (Wright, Mies, Le Corbusier). Wright, however, was allotted six pages as compared to the four given to most of the other form givers. (Aalto, the least-known architect in the group, only had two pages.) The three were also given a "voice" through quotations; the ten other form givers had to let the captioned photographs of their buildings and projects speak for them. Wright again was distinguished from Le Corbusier and Mies: photographs of his work alone were accompanied by quotations from his writings that tied his ideas and ideals to realized buildings and projects that were still in the process of becoming.

Even when the term "form giver" began to wane in popularity in the 1960s as form took on the concerns of a new generation, the triumvirate held. For example, in his 1969 book on contemporary American architecture Robert A. M. Stern distinguished between the three as the "heroic generation of *form givers*," the "second generation of *formalists,* refiners and redefiners," which included Johnson, Saarinen, and Rudolph, and an up-and-coming third generation.[80] It was also during the 1950s that the descriptors "Wrightian," "Miesian," and "Corbusian" entered the vocabulary of Modern architecture. (In "Built in USA," Hitchcock attempted to coin "Gropiusite" but had second thoughts given that the aesthetics he was trying to describe belonged to Breuer.) Frequently used as shorthand for formal aesthetics or techniques, all three adjectives are very much still with us today.

While Wright's buildings struck a chord within an increasingly form-sensitized architectural public in the last decade of his life, his career-long discourse about the individuality and freedom of the artist made an especially important contribution to the construction of the postwar form giver. His railings against the conformity of the International Style had long corrupted this message for many, but appreciation of Wright after the war turned very closely on how Modern architecture was perceived, with personal expression and individuality privileged over systems and collectivity. A Taliesin lecture in the early 1950s might be taken as the zenith of form as individual expression. As the story goes, the unexpected gift of a large collection of seashells inspired Wright to present a lecture to the Fellowship in March 1953. He was not the only form giver to find architectural lessons in the detritus of sea life;

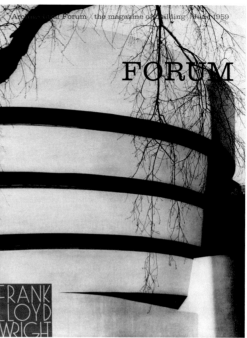

FIGS. 12 AND 13. Model and completed exterior of Solomon R. Guggenheim Museum (1943–59), as shown on covers of *Architecture Forum,* January 1946 and June 1959 (left and right). George Cserna, photographer (right). (Courtesy of Richard Longstreth [left]; author's collection, George Cserna photographs and papers, 1937–1978, Avery Architectural & Fine Arts Library © Columbia University in the City of New York [right])

Le Corbusier amassed a significant collection of shells that he called, drawing from Paul Valéry, "objets à réaction poétique."[81] But whereas the French architect was fascinated by the way the shells were transformed over time by nature, a process he superimposed on design, Wright found a different metaphor in their shapes. Working his way through the tray filled with "hundreds of beautiful, infinitely various little houses," Wright extolled the seemingly endless variety arising from a single idea and material, praising the brilliance of the hinge of the clam shell and the fantastic solution to the problem of housing offered by the design "genius" behind a more elaborate shell.[82] The range of expression, Wright claimed, came not from different ideas, but in having sufficient faith in individuality, a lesson he applied to architecture. The "inspired form" on display revealed everything that he believed was lacking in current architecture: genius, invention, variation, a clear relationship between form and the context in which it was made, an expression of the forces that created its form, and beauty.

CAMMIE MCATEE

This message could also be read in one project in particular. There is probably no more potent Wright building than the Guggenheim Museum in challenging either the concept of form follows function or asserting the architect's identity as an artist free to pursue a personal vision. Designed beginning in 1943 and completed after Wright's death in 1959, the project came to fruition during the years in which the metaphor of the architect as form giver rose to prominence. Significantly, *Architectural Forum* chose to open the postwar years with a view of its model and another of it completed to stand as Wright's memorial (figs. 12, 13). Read in its most basic formal terms—a circle set against the city's orthogonal grid—what is arguably the most iconic of Wright's buildings is nothing less than a manifesto of the artist's autonomy and individuality, a perfect representation of "genius against the mobocracy." But it represented much more to a younger generation of architects. They would see it as a testimonial to the unfettered creativity of the form giver.

NOTES

Like many students of Modern architecture, I was daunted by the formidable figure of Frank Lloyd Wright and the impressive scholarship on the architect and his buildings and projects. I thought I could "escape" Wright by working on a younger generation of Modern architects. How wrong I was! I am grateful to Neil Levine for encouraging and challenging my consideration of Wright's role in the postwar "search for form." I also thank him for the privilege of presenting my research to an audience as knowledgeable and engaged as the members of the Frank Lloyd Wright Building Conservancy are and in the auditorium of the institution that so stimulated and challenged Wright. I am also grateful to Richard Longstreth, Réjean Legault, and Jean-Louis Cohen for comments on earlier drafts, and Jess Ruefli and Judy Lew for timely help with an elusive image. The research on which this essay is based is drawn from my 2017 dissertation, "The 'Search for Form' in Postwar American Architecture," which was supported by grants from the Graduate School of Arts and Sciences, Harvard University, and a Wyeth Predoctoral Fellowship, Center for Advanced Study in the Visual Arts, National Gallery of Art.

1. More models were presented at the Corcoran Gallery of Art, Washington, D.C. (23 April–4 May 1959) and at the Metropolitan Museum of Art in New York (8 June–7 September) and some changes were made for the exhibition tour. See "59–15" exhibition files in boxes 36 and 37, Series 5: Exhibition Files, American Federation of Arts Records, Archives of American Art, Smithsonian Institution (hereafter, AFA Records).

2. After Washington and New York, the exhibition was presented in 1959 at the Boston Museum of Fine Arts (28 September–22 October); the Carnegie Institute (Carnegie Museum of Art), Pittsburgh (8 November–8 December); in 1960 at the

Minneapolis Institute of Arts (19 January–14 February); Virginia Museum of Fines Arts, Richmond (26 February–20 March): Art Institute of Chicago (12 April–15 May); Des Moines Art Center (26 May–12 June): Museum of Fine Arts, Houston (1–29 July); Municipal Art Gallery, Los Angeles (17 August–11 September); Seattle Art Museum (12 October–6 November); Portland Museum of Art, Maine (18 November–18 December); and in 1961 at the San Francisco Museum of Art (3–29 January); Montreal Museum of Fine Arts (15 February–6 March); Cranbrook Academy of Art (21 March–10 April); Commercial Museum, Philadelphia (21 April–14 May); box 36, AFA Records.

3. The few studies that have examined it have been monographs in which the exhibition is considered from the point of view of how it showcased the work of a single form giver. These studies include Mary Anne Hunting, *Edward Durell Stone: Modernism's Populist Architect* (New York: W.W. Norton, 2013), 92; Eeva-Liisa Pelkonen, "The Search for (Communicative) Form," in Eeva-Liisa Pelkonen and Donald Albrecht, eds., *Eero Saarinen: Shaping the Future* (New Haven: Yale University Press, 2006), 93; and Kathryn Smith, *Wright on Exhibit: Frank Lloyd Wright's Architectural Exhibitions* (Princeton: Princeton University Press, 2017), 213–21. Smith offers the most comprehensive history of the exhibition, but she does not broach the broader significance of the exhibition theme. Pelkonen briefly raises it in the context of form; her interpretation, however, is very different from the present one.

4. Quoted by Cranston Jones, confidential memo to James Linen, publisher of *Time,* and Harris K. Prior, director of the American Federation of Arts, 28 June 1958, box 37, AFA Records. The speech was reproduced in its entirety in the June 1967 issue of *Architectural Forum* (pp. 38–39) after Luce's death in February of that year.

5. Press release, Metropolitan Museum of Art, 9 June 1959, file 10, box 85, Douglas Putnam Haskell Papers, Avery Architectural & Fine Arts Library, Columbia University (hereafter Haskell Papers).

6. Stuart Preston, "Modern Architecture's New Look," *New York Times,* 21 June 1959, 12. Preston, who covered exhibitions and galleries for the *Times,* occasionally wrote about architecture after 1954, when Aline Saarinen recused herself from covering architecture, following her marriage to Eero Saarinen, and until 1963, when Ada Louise Huxtable joined the newspaper as its first full-time architecture critic.

7. Peter Collins, "The Form-Givers," *Perspecta* 7 (1961): 92.

8. Though *Time* owned *Architectural Forum,* it was the name of the news magazine that appeared on press materials related to the exhibition and its catalog. Through its cover stories and many articles on architecture and the technological developments that fueled its development, *Time* played an important role in raising the profile of architecture and many of its practitioners across the country.

9. The phrase appeared in a posthumously published article that broadly circulated under three different titles: Matthew Nowicki, "On Exactitude and Flexibility," *Student Publication of the School of Design* (North Carolina State College) 1:1 (1951): 11–18. It was republished as "Origins and Trends in Modern Architecture," in *Magazine of Art* 44 (November 1951): 273–79; and as "Function and Form," in Lewis Mumford, ed., *Roots of Contemporary American Architecture* (New York: Reinhold, 1952), 411–18.

10. Cranston Jones, letter to Aline Saarinen, 16 January 1959, box 37, AFA Records.

11. Eero Saarinen, "The Six Broad Currents of Modern Architecture," *Architectural Forum* 99 (July 1953): 110–15.

12. Charles B. Looker, "Letter to the editor," *Architectural Forum* 99 (November 1953): 64, 68. The cartoons were by John MacFadyen, who was following the story from Rome, where he was on a fellowship at the American Academy in Rome. Mac-Fadyen, "Letter to the editor," *Architectural Forum* 99 (September 1953): 64, 68.

13. Sigfried Giedion, "The Need for a New Monumentality," in Paul Zucker, ed., *New Architecture and City Planning* (New York: Philosophical Library, 1944), 549.

14. Jones included most of the architects to whom Saarinen had drawn attention, adding Marcel Breuer, Richard Neutra, Wallace Harrison, Gordon Bunshaft, Philip Johnson, Minoru Yamasaki, I. M. Pei, Paul Rudolph, and Eduardo Catalano, and dropping Wurster, Belluschi, Aalto, Nervi, and Fuller.

15. The "new" names were Edward Durell Stone, Louis Kahn, Ralph Rapson, Harry Weese, Charles Eames, and Vernon deMars. Cranston Jones, "Views Compared by Leading Architects," *Architectural Forum* 105 (September 1956): 146–49, 168, 172, 176.

16. As reported in a memo from *Time* journalist Frank Shea to AFA secretary Virginia Field, 28 October 1958, "Exhibition plan," box 37, AFA Records.

17. Cranston Jones, confidential memo to Linen and Prior, 28 June 1958. In an early exhibition description, Jones states that he also consulted Edgar Kaufmann jr., Peter Blake, Stone, Johnson, Saarinen, Breuer, Bunshaft, and the staffs of *Architectural Forum* and *House and Home*. "The Form Givers at Mid-Century," n.d., box 37, AFA Records. There are various lists of possible inclusions throughout the exhibition files.

18. Although Bunshaft was not named as he had been in Jones's *Time* article, the fact that all of the SOM buildings presented in the exhibition and three of the four reproduced in the catalog were all known as Bunshaft designs indicates he was considered the firm's form giver. On Bunshaft's chafing at the anonymity imposed by SOM, see Nicholas Adams, *Gordon Bunshaft and SOM: Building Corporate Modernism* (New Haven: Yale University Press, 2019), esp. 82–84.

19. Smith, *Wright on Exhibition,* 214–16.

20. Frank Lloyd Wright to Cranston Jones, 19 February 1959, Frank Lloyd Wright Correspondence, microfilm T089C05. Again, see Smith on Wright's possible motivations.

21. Wright's participation beyond the Met is documented in reviews of other presentations.

22. Frank Lloyd Wright to Cranston Jones, 9 February 1959, Frank Lloyd Wright Correspondence, microfilm T089B02.

23. Cranston Jones to Harris Prior, 2 July 1958, box 37, AFA Records.

24. I thank Neil Levine for pointing out that Wright's claims do not always match the historical record. The drawing for the Cooper house, La Grange, Illinois (1887, 1890–95), is reproduced in Smith, *Wright on Exhibition,* 215, fig. 6.2.

25. My use of "death blow" comes from Jones's essay: "Sullivan himself, with his dictum Form follows function, struck a death blow to the Beaux Arts tendency to view architecture as applied archaeology." Cranston Jones, "The Form Givers," *Form Givers at Mid-Century* catalog (Washington, D.C.: Corcoran Gallery of Art, 1959), 9. Wright first used the phrase in his 1901 address "The Art and Craft of the

Machine": "That the medicine has dealt Art in the grand old sense a death-blow, none will deny."

26. Wright in a Sunday morning talk, 18 June 1950. It is unclear whether this definition of the architect went beyond Taliesin until much later, as the text of the talk was not published until 1987, when Bruce Brooks Pfeiffer included it in *Frank Lloyd Wright: His Living Voice* (Fresno: Press at California State University, Fresno, 1987), 78 (not included in the accompanying cassette). In 1950 it had been included on a sound recording by the American Recording Company. But given that as few as fifty albums were pressed, this record is an unlikely source for a substantial diffusion of these ideas. I am grateful to Margo Stipe and the late Bruce Brooks Pfeiffer for identifying these sources of the quote.

27. Form has varied meanings in different Western architecture cultures. What a French architect meant by *forme* is distinct from what an architect trained in a German or English school of architecture meant by it. Emerging from Latin (*forma*) in the eleventh century and associated with that which is molded, *forme* was very early on closely related to art and by extension beauty. By contrast, the German meaning is complicated by the coexistence of two words—*Form* and *Gestalt*—that go back to Plato before being given much more nuance in the writings of Kant, Schiller, and Goethe. More semantic layers would be added in both German and French architecture in the nineteenth century and first two decades of the twentieth century. The architect in the English-speaking world, too, understands it first as shape, figure, or image—this first meaning coming from Old French into English—but this definition is complicated by an Aristotelian understanding of it in opposition to matter, thus becoming the essential creative quality. It also has a relationship to type, both as kind or genre and standard or typical forms, and a connection to style in terms of its arrangement and composition. For a German-leaning analysis, see the entry on form in Adrian Forty, *Words and Buildings: A Vocabulary of Modern Architecture* (London: Thames and Hudson, 2000), 149–72. How ideas about form gave rise to "form giving," "form giver," and related phrases is examined in Cammie McAtee, "The 'Search for Form' in Postwar American Architecture" (Ph.D. diss., Harvard University, 2017).

28. The roots of the phrase lie in the 1896 essay, "The Tall Building Artistically Considered," where Sullivan concluded that "form ever follows function, and this is the law." The phrase was reduced in an article by Sullivan's former partner Dankmar Adler, who streamlined it to "form follows function" in the first line of "The Influence of Steel Construction and Plate Glass upon Style," in *Proceedings of the Thirtieth Annual Convention of the American Institute of Architects,* 1896, 58. This article was subsequently reproduced and retitled as "Function and Environment" by Lewis Mumford in his anthology, *Roots of Contemporary American Architecture* (New York: Grove Press, 1959), 243–50.

29. Thomas Creighton, review of *Kindergarten Chats* by Louis H. Sullivan, *Progressive Architecture* 29 (January 1948): 106.

30. Frank Lloyd Wright, *Genius and the Mobocracy* (New York: Duell, Sloan & Pearce, 1949), 8.

31. Wright, *Genius and the Mobocracy,* 83.

32. Frank Lloyd Wright, "The Language of an Organic Architecture," *Architectural Forum* 98 (May 1953): 106. According to a note in the article, the essay, a lexicon of Wright's terms, was written in February 1953.

33. In May 1953, in the wake of Elizabeth Gordon's attacks on the International Style in the April issue of *House Beautiful,* the journal announced that it would publish a series of articles written by sympathetic observers. It began with Eero Saarinen's "review of today's trends," published as "The Six Broad Currents of Modern Architecture" (July 1953); followed by Robert Woods Kennedy's "After the International Style—Then What?" (September 1953). In his introduction to Kennedy's essay, Haskell referred to Wright's "The Language of an Organic Architecture" as the first in the series. Between 1949 and 1964, Douglas Haskell proved a powerful ally to the cause of form through his editorial direction of the most influential American architectural trade journal, *Architectural Forum*. On his promotion of the form givers, see McAtee, "The 'Search for Form.'" Concerning Haskell's previously unknown work as a designer, see Richard Longstreth, "Douglas Haskell's Adirondack Legacy," in Longstreth, *Looking beyond the Icons: Midcentury Architecture, Landscape, and Urbanism* (Charlottesville: University of Virginia Press, 2015): 133–49, 245–47.

34. "The AIA's decision is a follow-up of its convention resolution last spring . . . the next Gold Medal should go to Wright. The resolution was prompted by a group of AIA's younger, liberal members who took seriously the Institute's failure to recognize greatness in their profession." "News," *Architectural Forum* 90 (January 1949): 14.

35. Douglas Haskell to Helen Haskell, 25 June 1948, file 12, box 88, Haskell Papers. The real debate came after the decision was made to award Wright the Gold Medal. The various positions were aired in the major architecture journals in late 1948 and early 1949.

36. "Acceptance Speech of Frank Lloyd Wright," *Journal of the American Institute of Architects* 11 (May 1949): 199–207. Despite calling Wright's speech "an insult to the AIA" in May 1949, Henry H. Saylor, the journal's editor, later reported that "demand for the recording of Wright's Gold Medal acceptance speech far exceeded quantities and a new pressing has been made by RCA." *Journal of the American Institute of Architects* 16 (September 1951): 142.

37. Sigfried Giedion, *Space, Time and Architecture,* enlarged 3rd ed. (Cambridge, Mass.: Harvard University Press, 1954), 496.

38. Ada Louise Huxtable, *Frank Lloyd Wright* (New York: Viking Penguin, 2004), xvi.

39. This being said, there were friendly exchanges between Wright and Eliel and Eero Saarinen over the years. For example, Wright sent Eero and Lily Saarinen three Japanese prints on the occasion of their marriage in 1939. Wright also sent a telegram of condolence to Eero Saarinen when Eliel died in 1950.

40. On Aline Louchheim's role in the Guggenheim controversy, see Neil Levine, *The Architecture of Frank Lloyd Wright* (Princeton: Princeton University Press, 1996), 337, 343, 347. Franklin Toker has also credited her for being indirectly responsible for the Museum of Modern Art's 1938 exhibition on Fallingwater by introducing the Kaufmanns to the museum's architecture curator, John McAndrew, who was her thesis adviser at New York University. Through her, McAndrew was invited to visit the house, an event that sparked the idea of the exhibition and launched Edgar Kaufmann jr.'s relationship with the museum. Franklin Toker, *Fallingwater Rising: Frank Lloyd Wright, E. J. Kaufmann, and America's Most Extraordinary House* (New York: Knopf, 2003), 261–62.

41. Eero Saarinen's office calendars record the dates of two possible visits to Spring

Green: a dinner with Wright on 27 May 1954, and the inauguration of the Sullivan exhibition at the Art Institute of Chicago, at which Aline Saarinen as well as Wright had been invited to speak, on 24 October 1956. Folder 195, box 696, Eero Saarinen Collection, Manuscripts and Archives, Yale University Library.

42. Eero Saarinen to Aline Louchheim, n.d. [2 June 1953], folder 29, box 2, Aline and Eero Saarinen Papers, Archives of American Art.

43. Henry Wright Jr., unsigned editorial, *Architectural Forum* 88 (January 1948): 54. In the same vein, see also Henry-Russell Hitchcock's characterization of Wright's importance for contemporary architecture in the "What Is Happening to Modern Architecture?" symposium, *Museum of Modern Art Bulletin* 15 (Spring 1948): 10.

44. The text was based on a lecture Saarinen gave to the Cleveland Engineering Society, which, with Louchheim's writing help, was published as "Architecture of the Future," *Cleveland Engineering* 46 (May 1953): 6–8, 10–11. Saarinen then worked closely with Louchheim and Haskell to rework the essay for publication in *Architectural Forum*. The term "form giver" became much more prominent in the second version.

45. Eero Saarinen, "The Six Broad Currents of Modern Architecture," *Architectural Forum* 99 (July 1953): 112.

46. "Marginalia," *Architectural Review* 113 (May 1953): 337. The remark was prompted by Wright's essay, "Against the Steamroller," with commentary by J. M. Richards, which appeared in the same issue (pp. 283–85).

47. Some of the esteem with which Nowicki's American colleagues held him undoubtedly came from his wartime service. Active in the Polish resistance, Nowicki served in the Home Army, the 1944 Warsaw Uprising, and the underground teaching organization that was founded when the occupying Nazis closed most Polish educational institutions. After the Uprising failed, Nowicki was appointed chief planner for the reconstruction and, along with the planners Helena and Szymon Syrkus, was sent to the United States to promote the project. The Nowickis first settled in Chicago in late 1945, briefly lived in San Francisco, and in 1947 moved to New York after Matthew Nowicki was appointed to the UN Board of Design. Following the family's decision to stay in the United States, in the summer of 1948 he accepted a teaching position as acting head of the architecture department of the newly organized School of Design at North Carolina State College.

48. Eero Saarinen quoted in "From the Legacy of Matthew Nowicki," *Architectural Forum* 93 (October 1950): 207. For a recent discussion of Nowicki and Mayer's early planning work for Chandigarh, which preceded Le Corbusier and Pierre Jeanneret and Jane Drew and Maxwell Fry's work, see Tom Avermaete and Maristella Casciato, *Casablanca Chandigarh: A Report on Modernization* (Montreal: Canadian Centre for Architecture, 2014), 195–196.

49. Lewis Mumford recorded that the visit to Taliesin and meeting with Wright took place in 1947. Mumford, "The Life, Teaching and the Architecture of Matthew Nowicki: Part I," *Architectural Record* 115 (June 1954): 145.

50. Tyler Sprague connected Nowicki's 'mushroom' columns, the Johnson Wax Building, and the Geisshübel warehouse in Zurich (1910) by engineer Robert Maillart. See Sprague, "Expressive Structure: The Life and Work of Matthew Nowicki" (Ph.D. diss., University of Washington, 2013), 119–23.

51. Matthew Nowicki, "Composition in Modern Architecture," *Magazine of Art* 42 (March 1949): 108. The essay was republished by Mumford in *Roots of Contempo-*

rary American Architecture, 404–10. Interestingly, Mumford chose a photograph of the interior of the Guggenheim as the first image for the essay.

52. Nowicki, "Composition in Modern Architecture," 109. Nowicki included an illustration of another of his Johnson Wax–inspired projects—a chapel in Laski, Poland, described as a "study of a reinforced concrete ceiling for a country church" (111)—but the view does not show its mushroom columns.

53. On Giedion's first visit to Buffalo, Chicago, and St. Louis see Reto Geiser, *Giedion and America: Repositioning the History of Modern Architecture* (Zurich: gta Verlag ETH, 2018), especially 162–67. In *Space, Time and Architecture,* Giedion states that he visited Taliesin in July 1939 (413). He also reproduced his own photograph of the house: a somewhat unusual westward view of the tower belvedere (fig. 253). The timeline of his visit to Taliesin is supported by an exchange of letters in June 1939 between Giedion, Wright and Eugene Masselink, cited in Neil Levine, *The Urbanism of Frank Lloyd Wright* (Princeton: Princeton University Press, 2015), 222, 411n1.

54. Giedion, *Space, Time and Architecture,* 1st ed. (1941), 344. Giedion published his impressions of the Johnson Wax Building soon after visiting it. He classified it as a positive example of how luxury "makes sense when *it broadens emotional experience by means of new discovery. . . .* [Wright] shows us here, after half a century of building, how luxury can still be creative in architecrture." Sigfried Giedion, "The Dangers and Advantages of Luxury," *Focus* [London], no. 3 (1939): 34–39 (italics in original).

55. Sigfried Giedion, "The State of Contemporary Architecture: 1, The Regional Approach," *Architectural Record* 115 (January 1954): 137 (italics in original). The essay was included without illustrations in the collection of essays *Architecture You and Me: A Diary of a Development* (Cambridge, Mass.: Harvard University Press, 1958). However, the Italian translation did include the same plan. "Un nuovo regionalismo," in *Brevario di Architecttura* (Milan: Garzanti, 1961), 120, fig. 35.

56. Concerning Wright and the Museum of Modern Art, see Smith, *Wright on Exhibit,* 108–67; Hugh Howard, *Architecture's Odd Couple: Frank Lloyd Wright and Philip Johnson* (London: Bloomsbury, 2016); Nina Stritzler-Levine, "Curating History, Exhibiting Ideas: Henry-Russell Hitchcock and Architectural Exhibition Practice at the MoMA," in Frank Salmon ed., *Summerson and Hitchcock: Centenary Essays on Architectural Historiography,* Studies in British Art 16 (2006): 35–67; Peter Reed and William Kaizen, eds., *The Show to End All Shows: Frank Lloyd Wright and The Museum of Modern Art, 1940,* Studies in Modern Art 8 (New York: Museum of Modern Art, 2004); and various discussions in Levine, *The Architecture of Frank Lloyd Wright.* The 1938 Fallingwater exhibition is also discussed in Toker, *Fallingwater Rising,* 261–68, 273; and in Donald Hoffmann, *Frank Lloyd Wright's Fallingwater: The House and Its History* (New York: Dover, 1978), 91–92.

57. As Franz Schulze first chronicled, Johnson's abrupt departure from the museum in late 1934 was to pursue political goals inspired by the Nazi Party in Germany. As well as publishing articles espousing heinous ideas, Johnson offered his "showmanship" capabilities to those advancing fascism and anti-Semitism in the United States. In 1940, mostly because he had not been accepted by such figures as the right-wingers and anti-Semites William Lemke and Father Coughlin, and the populist Huey Long, Johnson returned to Harvard to study architecture. Increasingly aware of the negative perception of his political sympathies (it remains a

question if he truly regretted them), he began to make efforts to rehabilitate his image. After a stint in the army and a short period of laying low in his hometown of Cleveland, in 1946 Johnson returned to New York and the Museum of Modern Art, where friends such as Alfred Barr had been advocating on his behalf. He was accepted back into the fold of New York society with little censure. In addition to Franz Schulze, *Philip Johnson: Life and Work* (Chicago: University of Chicago Press, 1994), 104–68, see Mark Lamster's more historically grounded account of this period in *The Man in the Glass House: Philip Johnson, Architect of the Modern Century* (New York: Little, Brown, 2018), 275–385.

58. In a 1947 letter to Henry-Russell Hitchcock about progress on his design for his New Canaan house, Johnson reported that it "is turning out half Persius, half Wright. The Wright influence came from a two-week stay the master made a month ago [March 1947]. We got along swell. So the house drops over the ravine like the California numbers." Johnson to Hitchcock, n.d. [1947], "1947 Correspondence, I-K," box 3, Henry-Russell Hitchcock Papers, Archives of American Art. This description corresponds with drawings Stover Jenkins and David Mohney have identified as being made during the summer of 1947. Jenkins and Mohney, *The Houses of Philip Johnson* (New York: Abbeville Press, 2001), 82.

59. Philip Johnson, "The Frontiersman," *Architectural Review* 106 (August 1949): 105.

60. In a letter to Wright, Johnson related that he had taken "the opportunity to spend a good deal of the day at Taliesin West. Your brother-in-law was more than kind to me and let me wander around the place." Johnson to Wright, 1 December 1949, Frank Lloyd Wright Correspondence, microfilm J120A08. Kathryn Smith quotes Johnson's letter as well (158). On this visit, see also Tim Rohan's essay in the present volume. Philip Johnson, untitled lecture at the University of Houston, 1953; "Johnson / Houston / 1953," sound recording, folder 3, box 58, series IX, Philip Johnson Papers, Getty Research Institute. The lecture was likely the one given to the Student Chapter of the AIA on 17 November 1953. I am grateful to Sally McKay for making this recording accessible to me in 2007.

61. Excerpt from an interview with Johnson in John Peter, "Conversations Regarding the Future of Architecture," *Print* 11 (1957–58): 38–39.

62. Levine, *The Architecture of Frank Lloyd Wright,* 292.

63. Henry-Russell Hitchcock and Philip C. Johnson, "The Buildings We See," *New World Writing* (New York: New American Library of World Literature, 1952), 119.

64. Hitchcock and Johnson, "The Buildings We See," 124.

65. As Neil Levine has noted, the comparison with Michelangelo seems to have begun in 1948, when Hitchcock called Wright "the Michelangelo of the twentieth century." Though meant as praise, the comparison also allowed for some qualification, as he added "Michelangelo was not good for his contemporaries and, least of all for his students. But Michelangelo, in a period of considerable confusion, was a master who looked forward, not to what was going to happen in ten years, but what was going to happen in fifty years." Henry-Russell Hitchcock, statement in "What Is Happening to Modern Architecture?" *Museum of Modern Art Bulletin* 15 (Spring 1948): 10. See Levine, *The Architecture of Frank Lloyd Wright,* 423.

66. "Frank Lloyd Wright: Buildings for Johnson Wax" (exhibition #498), Drexler's second exhibition at the museum, ran from 15 January to 16 March 1952. "3-Dimensional Color Photographs of Buildings by Frank Lloyd Wright on Exhibition," press release, 9 January 1952, Press Release Archives, MoMA, https://www

.moma.org/momaorg/shared/pdfs/docs/press_archives/1580/releases/MOMA
_1952_0002_2.pdf.

67. Stated in Drexler's analysis of the interior of Wright's Pauson house (1938–41),
Phoenix, Arizona. Drexler, "The Contemporary Domestic Interior: Frank Lloyd
Wright," *Interiors + Industrial Design* 109 (July 1950): 68. On the importance of
the discussion of "significant form," see McAtee, "The 'Search for Form.'"

68. "Work by Le Corbusier to Be Shown at Museum," press release, 28 June 1951, Press
Release Archives, MoMA, https://assets.moma.org/documents/moma_press
-release_325785.pdf.

69. Although the exhibition press release only credits him as directing the photography, in a letter about the medium, Drexler unequivocally stated, "The photographs
were taken by myself with the technical assistance of the David White Sales
Company, manufacturer of the Stereo-Realist camera." Drexler to George S. James,
6 March 1952; MoMA Archives. These photographs are in the museum's slide
collection. Jonathan Lipman published five of Drexler's photographs in his book,
Frank Lloyd Wright and the Johnson Wax Buildings (New York: Rizzoli, 1986), pls.
2, 4, 6–8, but he does not discuss Drexler's role as either curator or photographer.
In 2000, seven of Drexler's stereo-realist photographs were included in a set of
three View-Master reels of the Johnson Wax Building. "Johnson Wax: The Wright
Buildings," Knoxville, Tennessee: View Productions, 2000. I am grateful to Michael Kaplan of View Productions for sharing with me his knowledge of Drexler's
stereo-realist photographs, his research on the 1952 exhibition, and his views on
stereo photography and Modern architecture more generally.

70. Drexler to James, 6 March 1952, MoMA Archives.

71. Italian, 1954; Croatian, 1956; Spanish (Argentina), 1957.

72. The exhibition was part of the "Salute to France" festival organized by the United
States Information Service. Directed by René d'Harnoncourt, the exhibition took
over gallery space in the Musée d'Art Moderne that was larger than the entire Museum of Modern Art in New York at that time. Press release, no. 11, 11 February
1955, Press Release Archives, MoMA, https://www.moma.org/momaorg/shared
/pdfs/docs/press_archives/1909/releases/MOMA_1955_0024_12.pdf. The emphasis on Wright in the Paris exhibition is apparent in a plan of the architecture
section; see Gay McDonald, "Selling the American Dream: MoMA, Industrial
Design and Post-War France," *Journal of Design History* 17 (2004): 397–412; see
p. 405, fig. 4. The use of stereoscopic viewers attracted attention; see comments in
"Marginalia," *Architectural Review* 117 (June 1955): 361–62.

73. On Wright's outsider status, see the concluding chapter of Levine, *The Architecture
of Frank Lloyd Wright.*

74. René d'Harnoncourt's statement was published in two journals in September 1953:
the opinion section of *Architectural Record* 114 (September 1953): 12; and *Interiors
+ Industrial Design* 113 (September 1953): 163–65.

75. Smith includes the twelve exhibitions of Wright's work prepared by the Department of Circulating Exhibitions; Smith, *Wright on Exhibition*, 109.

76. Philip Johnson to Nikolaus Pevsner, 3 October 1947; quoted in Irene Sunwoo,
"Whose Design? MoMA and Pevsner's Pioneers," *Getty Research Journal* 2 (2010):
69–82, citation p. 69.

77. Sigfried Giedion, *Space, Time and Architecture,* 1st ed. (1941), 406; 3rd enlarged
ed. (1954), 494, 506–8.

78. Jones, "The Form Givers," 10.
79. Thomas Creighton, "Introduction: The Search for Form," *Progressive Architecture* 36 (February 1955): 79.
80. Robert A. M. Stern, *New Directions in American Architecture* (New York: George Braziller, 1969), 8.
81. Niklas Maak, *Le Corbusier: The Architect on the Beach* (Munich: Hirmer, 2011).
82. Originally headed "Housing," the essay was published as "Faith in Your Individuality," *House Beautiful* 98 (November 1955): 270–71, 302, 304. Reprinted in Bruce Brooks Pfeiffer, ed., *Frank Lloyd Wright Collected Writings* (New York: Rizzoli, 1995), 5:131–34. For the context in which the lecture was given, see Pfeiffer's introduction, p. 131. Freya Wigzell has recently discussed Wright's essay in an article about the fascination shells have held for modern architects and reproduced photographs of two of the shells held in the Wright Archives. See Freya Wigzell, "The People Here Think I'm Out of My Mind," *AA Files* 75 (2017): 9–11.

TIMOTHY M. ROHAN

The Meaning of an Anecdote
Wright, Rudolph, and Johnson at the Glass House

Among the most often repeated anecdotes about Frank Lloyd Wright is the one concerning his unexpected visit to Philip Johnson at his Glass House in New Canaan, Connecticut (1945–49) during the mid-1950s (fig. 1). It is usually told with relish by those who enjoy stories about bad behavior as a tale concerning the rivalry between the two architects, culminating with Wright delivering his famous putdown of the house's transparency, "I don't know whether I'm supposed to take my hat off or leave it on!"[1]

The anecdote has been consistently related in this fashion, but there is another, different, and little-known account about Wright visiting the Glass House in April 1956, one that helps us better understand Wright's relationship with postwar American architecture. Fascinatingly, it is an eyewitness, first-person narrative by Paul Rudolph, the architect well remembered for his monumental concrete buildings of the 1960s. It was his contribution to the 1996 *ANY* magazine Festschrift in honor of the ninetieth birthday of Johnson, his longtime friend.[2] Wright probably visited the Glass House several times, but when Rudolph was present the old master behaved differently from the familiar anecdote where he is unremittingly hostile and does not know what to do with his hat. According to Rudolph, the Glass House affected Wright, changing his skepticism about it to appreciation. But there is more to Rudolph's story than that.

The anecdote is really Rudolph's explanation about how complex effects of light and space inspired by Wright's architecture could provide a dramatic, emotionally rich alternative to the uniformly lit and configured spaces associated with the International Style, omnipresent in corporate and institutional work, especially, by 1956, yet criticized as spiritless and conformist at that time by Rudolph, Johnson, and their cohort. It was Rudolph's prescription for how to improve modernism.

Anecdotal histories are often disregarded as self-indulgent and tangential. But they are repeated because they hold lessons, like parables, and therefore deserve serious consideration. Like a punch line in a joke, the narrative

FIG. I. Philip Johnson, Glass House, New Canaan, Connecticut, 1945–49. (Author's photograph, 2018)

trajectory culminates in a specific point that defines the subject of the anecdote's character or tells a truth. Tellers of anecdotes may take liberties when relating a good yarn, but they often base their accounts on a real incident that made a profound impression upon one or more people.

Rudolph's version of this familiar anecdote gets to the heart of an important dilemma. Despite its great success, postwar American modernism doubted itself, continually asking in the mid-1950s if the glass boxes of the International Style merely amounted to a debased functionalism. Compared to the great buildings of the past, did such efforts even constitute architecture? The encounter between Wright, Johnson, and Rudolph concerned such questions, and they found answers to it in a peripatetic fashion that spring day in 1956. Walking and taking in a landscape of great architectural complexity stimulated Rudolph and Johnson to find answers to a fundamental question for architecture posed by Wright at that time about the Glass House: "Is it architecture?"

Anecdotal histories are also often dismissed as unreliable. Therefore, I take into account that Rudolph's memory of the encounter had probably changed over four decades before he wrote it down. Because it was so important to them, Rudolph and Johnson repeated the story to one another

TIMOTHY M. ROHAN

often over the years, probably altering its details and emphasis as they themselves changed and aged. Exemplifying intersubjectivity, this overlapping of storytellers and distance between the event and the published account in this example only adds layers of meaning to it that require interpretation. To accomplish this, I outline Rudolph's development from the early 1940s through the next decade, using him as a case study to show how his generation was drawn to Wright. I then explicate Rudolph's eyewitness account of Wright's visit to the Glass House. Finally, I consider how the encounter advanced the respective developments of Rudolph, Johnson, and even Wright. Hagiographical and usually taken at face value, anecdotes about Wright are numerous and regularly repeated. Our understanding of Wright relies upon such stories to a surprising degree. Reexamining them can deepen our understanding of modernism because the anecdotes reveal as much about the tellers and their concerns as they do about Wright.

Rudolph's development exemplified how postwar American architects cycled through their affinities for the architects whom the discipline was setting up as the masters of Modern architecture, as Cammie McAtee shows in the previous essay: Wright, Ludwig Mies van der Rohe, Le Corbusier, and Walter Gropius.[3] Wright's influence was sometimes celebrated and sometime suppressed, as Neil Levine has explained.[4] In 1956, the ambitious young Rudolph was not known as a follower of Wright, but as one of Gropius's most gifted students. Rudolph emphasized this prestigious relationship with the Bauhaus founder when he was advancing himself in the 1940s and early 1950s, even editing a special issue of *L'Architecture d'aujourd'hui* in 1950 devoted to Gropius and his students' work.[5] But Rudolph had been drawn to Wright since his formative years in Alabama, although he did not always talk much about this fascination at that time.

Born in 1918 and raised in the Deep South of the Great Depression, Rudolph, like Wright, was a minister's son from a rural area far from the centers of architecture and culture. He received Beaux-Arts instruction at Alabama Polytechnic Institute (now Auburn University). Recognizing his talent, Rudolph's teachers encouraged him to apply to Harvard, where he was admitted for graduate studies in 1941. Rudolph later said he never considered studying with Wright, believing that Wright's apprentices at the Taliesin Fellowship only followed in his footsteps. They never matured and became architects with original, creative viewpoints, which is what Rudolph hoped to achieve.[6]

Rudolph nevertheless gravitated to the buildings of Wright. Having made a career comeback with Fallingwater (1935–39) and the S. C. Johnson & Son Administration Building (1936–39), Wright was the most influential

FIG. 2. Frank Lloyd Wright, Rosenbaum house, Florence, Alabama, 1939–40. (Photograph by Robin McDonald, 2022)

practitioner for those Americans engaged with Modern architecture during Rudolph's youth. Rudolph's first encounter with a truly modernist building was a visit to Wright's Rosenbaum house (1939–40) in Florence, Alabama (fig. 2). He later recalled its importance for his development, reminiscing about the Usonian house's cantilevered carport, complex spaces, and especially the way the clerestory windows reflected sunlight across the ceilings in a diffused, changing fashion. Architecture's relationship with light fascinated Rudolph from the earliest years of his development, and he was especially intrigued by Wright's manipulation of natural light.[7]

During a "gap year" Rudolph took before attending Harvard, he was drawn to Wright's Florida Southern College in Lakeland, Florida (1938–58), which made an indelible impression on him. Rudolph recalled its covered walkways, concrete block walls, and oblique axes many times in his own campus plans, such as that for University of Massachusetts at Dartmouth (1963–72). This episode before Harvard also introduced Rudolph to Florida, a place important for his early work and career. In Sarasota, Rudolph gained practical experience when he helped bring Usonian qualities to a house completed in 1941 for the architect Ralph Twitchell (fig. 3). He clad his post-and-beam structure with cypress board-and-batten siding, thus resembling on the surface the treatment by Wright to make self-supporting walls for the Rosenbaum house and other Usonian dwellings.

TIMOTHY M. ROHAN

FIG. 3. Paul Rudolph and Ralph Twitchell, Twitchell house, Sarasota, Florida, 1940–41, dismantled 2007. Sarasota County History Center, photograph by Joseph Steinmetz ca. 1941. (State Archives of Florida/Steinmetz)

Rudolph entered Harvard in the fall of 1941. Though he later praised Gropius for helping him understand modernism, Rudolph seemed uninterested in Gropius's teamwork approach, in contrast to the group of students who later formed The Architects' Collaborative.[8] Instead, Rudolph emphasized individuality, an approach associated with Wright. Joining the camp of students who questioned Gropius's ideas, Rudolph began a friendship with fellow student Philip Johnson, who opposed teamwork, looked to Mies as a model, and knew Wright well.

Rudolph spent little time studying with Gropius. He was actually enrolled at Harvard for only one semester before and one after World War II. When the United States entered the war in December 1941, Rudolph left Harvard, enlisted in the navy, and supervised ship repair in the Brooklyn Navy Yard. Because it offered opportunities to build, Rudolph returned to Sarasota after the war's end and designed a varied series of innovative vacation houses that immediately attracted the attention of the architectural press. In these houses, Rudolph explored idioms beyond what he had learned at Harvard. The first of them further developed the Wrightian qualities of the Twitchell house. In the succeeding houses, Rudolph explored the materials of plastics and plywood, climate, site, regional characteristics, and the examples set by Mies, Le Corbusier, and, again, Wright, whose vocabulary Rudolph circled back to in 1956 with his elegant Burkhardt house, a Wrightian-Japanese villa on the beach (fig. 4).

Though his small office was headquartered in Sarasota, Rudolph regularly attended the architectural discussion groups hosted by Johnson at the Glass House during the 1950s. For Rudolph, the estate complex was readily accessible from Yale University and other northeastern architecture schools where he often taught studios.[9] Begun by Johnson in 1945, the complex consisted of the Glass House, a pellucid, rectangular box, which became one of the most acclaimed buildings of postwar American modernism. Adjacent to it, Johnson built the Brick House, its lesser-recognized, opaque twin. Both lay in a private arcadia of many acres, buildings, and sculpture developed by Johnson over nearly six decades as a retreat and architectural laboratory.

At the Glass House salons, Rudolph joined a resistance camp at the very heart of the modernist architectural establishment.[10] Johnson led discus-

FIG. 4. Paul Rudolph, Burkhardt house, Casey Key, Florida, 1956–57. Photograph by Ezra Stoller, ca. 1957. (© Ezra Stoller/Esto)

TIMOTHY M. ROHAN

sions about alternatives to functionalism and the International Style, which he himself had defined while working as a cocurator of the landmark exhibition and coauthor of the eponymous book in 1932 at the Museum of Modern Art (MoMA). Johnson helped make it the mainstream approach to modernism in the postwar era with buildings like the Glass House—the domestic embodiment of the International Style—only to turn against it by the early 1950s. Johnson positioned himself as something of a rebel, though of course his longtime role as a definer of Modern art and architecture in America made him the ultimate insider and powerbroker. For Rudolph and others in the 1950s the International Style had become a spiritless, mass architecture co-opted by big business, while Wright stood for an emotional, creative, and individualistic architecture. Believing that both were necessary, Henry-Russell Hitchcock had made this distinction quite explicitly in 1947 when he said the International Style was an "architecture of bureaucracy" while Wright's work was an "architecture of genius."[11]

Johnson staged his salons to rally resistance against his own International Style, but beneath this confident agenda ran a deeper vein of uncertainty about the increasingly directionless state of modernism, which raised the question of whether architecture itself could even still exist in the postwar era as a fundamental plank in the platform of high culture. Mass and corporate culture seemed about to overwhelm high culture if the world was not first destroyed by nuclear annihilation.

Rudolph lectured extensively at architecture schools and at national conferences about his developing views on what modernism could become. Published in the architectural journals, these talks expanded upon ideas absorbed from Johnson and his contemporaries such as Eero Saarinen at the Glass House salons. By the mid-1950s, Rudolph arrived at what he called a psychological approach to design where architecture strongly affected individuals, shaping their behavior, moods, thinking, and movement. Such intentionally designed movements through buildings and their settings lay at the basis of modernism, exemplified by Le Corbusier's *promenade architecturale,* also influential for Rudolph. As explained by him in a well-received talk before the American Institute of Architects conference in 1954, Rudolph's own version of such a movement stirred greater emotion. He emphasized, "We need sequences of space which arouse one's curiosity, give a sense of anticipation, which beckon and impel us to rush forward to find that releasing space which dominates, which climaxes, and acts as a magnet, and gives direction."[12]

And yet, though Wright's concept of "compression and release"—an alteration between confined and expansive spaces—was also foundational for this notion of architectural space as choreographed and emotionally compelling movement, Rudolph mentioned Wright relatively little. Despite Wright being the architect best known to most Americans, the mid-1950s leaders of architectural discourse such as Rudolph more frequently referenced European masters, looking to the rationalism of Mies as corporate commissions became seen as the most desirable ones. Wright remained a domestic architect to them. His difficult, confrontational personality also won him few admirers. Rudolph kept his distance from Wright for understandable reasons. Before their memorable encounter in New Canaan, Wright had eviscerated Rudolph when they briefly met at Princeton University in the mid-1950s. Rudolph recalled that Wright asked him what he was doing at the architecture school. Rudolph said, "Well, I'm trying to teach a bit." Wright replied, "Only prostitutes teach."[13]

This returns us to Rudolph's account of 1956 when Wright made his surprise visit to the Glass House. There are several accounts of such visits, but most are casually told and have inconsistencies (even those told by Johnson). Rudolph, however, provided a fuller picture of the encounter and its context, thus his narrative can be seen as a historical document, not just an amusing story. Rudolph's text helps us understand Wright's interactions with his contemporaries, showing that he had a strong presence in the architecture culture of the 1950s even at the age of eighty-nine. Rudolph gave no exact date for the encounter in his narrative, but fortunately he provided a clue, mentioning that Wright ended the visit by remarking that he was leaving for the opening of the New York Coliseum, thus dating the visit close to the building's dedication on 28 April 1956.

Wright was in fact frequently in New York in the 1950s, living at the Plaza Hotel while working on the Guggenheim Museum (1943–59). This important project raised Wright's public profile because he received the attentions of the national media based in New York, and it helped him obtain more commissions in the region, which may explain his presence in Connecticut in April 1956. Wright may have been in the neighborhood to visit Tirranna, his recently completed Rayward house in New Canaan (1954–55).

Such facts confirm that Rudolph's account of Wright's visit to the Glass House in April 1956 is reliable, but Rudolph's anecdote also has the qualities of a myth, suggesting that more profound truths are being told here. Rudolph renders Wright as a dangerous, larger-than-life figure, who the story's other protagonist, the Glass House, must appease. It is significant that it is a building, rather than a human being, that engages in this duel with Wright. After appearing in the introduction, Rudolph and Johnson recede and allow the Glass House to shine, thus embodying Rudolph's belief in architecture as a powerful, emotionally compelling agent with human qualities. Closely parsing this unassuming tale reveals its mythical dimensions and their significance. Modestly beginning his story with the words, "One summer Sunday afternoon," Rudolph writes of peacefully reading a newspaper at the Glass House when suddenly a voice called out: "Is the master of the house at home?" To Rudolph's astonishment, Wright suddenly materialized from out of nowhere on foot and alone. His "mysterious arrival" was itself soon "transformed" by the equally mysterious arrival of at "least a dozen of his acolytes."[14]

In Rudolph's short account, Johnson and Wright transform themselves repeatedly, moving beyond their default, self-appointed roles as the respective upholder and critic of the International Style. They show different sides of themselves in this installment of a rivalry performed in public since the early 1930s. During the mid-1950s, their ongoing road show unfolded with new acts as Wright and Johnson crossed paths at Taliesin West, at Yale University (fig. 5), and most notably at the Glass House. They sparred with one another several times in 1956, a year that marked the apex of their exchanges. That year, they made withering remarks about one another in separate interviews conducted by the journalist Selden Rodman, which he published as sequential, related profiles in a book about postwar American artists and architects for mainstream audiences. Rodman repeated to Wright and Johnson what they said about each other, thus encouraging them to make more extreme remarks for him to report upon, but also creating a running conversation between the two about what constituted architecture, a dialogue that remains instructive today. To provide a more intersubjective analysis here, Rodman's profiles and several of Johnson's own descriptions of

FIG. 5. Wright and Johnson at Yale University, 20 September 1955. Photograph by Austin Cooper, *Yale Daily News*. (Copyright 2010 Yale Daily News Publishing Company, Inc.; all rights reserved; reprinted with permission)

Wright's visits are drawn upon to help corroborate and further explicate Rudolph's narrative.[15]

In Rudolph's story, Wright and Johnson are worthy opponents for one another. Each is like a "trickster"—the archetypal and mischievous breaker of conventional social rules and boundaries in myth and folklore. Tricksters often expose social problems, and yet their mischief also helps to ultimately restore social order.[16] Exemplifying this type of trickster mischief, Rudolph noted that after Wright's arrival and some formulaic pleasantries, Wright began to behave aggressively. In an act that surprised everyone, Wright actually struck the imposing Elie Nadelman sculpture in the living room with his cane and cried out, "I don't like that." At that moment, Wright expressed his power as a dangerous trickster capable of disrupting an ordinary Sunday afternoon. Rudolph remembered that after Wright delivered the blow, "nervous laughter didn't exactly fill the room, but everyone present realized that anything could happen now."[17] Entitled *Two Circus Women* (1930), the object of Wright's attention was a large-scale, papier-mâché sculpture of two standing women joined at the waist, rendered in the modernist sculptor's intentionally naive manner (fig. 6). Even today, it is puzzlingly archaic, almost crude, and seems somewhat incongruous compared to its refined setting. But Johnson had deliberately positioned it there. He intended the sculpture, roughly textured and mottled in color, to be a "foil" to contrast with the house's smooth expanses of glass and steel.[18]

Wright's blow against the *Two Circus Women* can be interpreted as a blow against one of Johnson's prized possessions, as a blow against Modern art, and even as a misogynistic one, but the sculpture's placement in the Glass House living room may have been what disturbed Wright most about it, judging by his other encounters with it. Johnson had positioned it slightly off-kilter in relationship to the door behind it. The door was one of four openings forming a cross-axis within the house. During another perhaps subsequent visit to the Glass House, Wright reportedly made Johnson shift the large sculpture's position (probably with assistance) perhaps to put it in alignment with the cross-axis or to move it further out of this configuration, only to decide that it looked better in its original position.[19] The siting of the sculpture was a matter of great import to Wright. According to Johnson, on still another visit Wright had criticized the placement of a sculpture by Jacques Lipchitz, titled *Figure* (1926–30), which stood outside the Glass House.[20] In keeping with his organic philosophy that all aspects of a building should express an overall, integrated unity, Wright thought that sculptures and objects in and around buildings should be positioned in order to emphasize and reinforce spatial relationships. At Taliesin West, Wright had relocated a boulder covered with Native American petroglyphs in order to mark how

FIG. 6. Glass House living room with Elie Nadelman's *Two Circus Women,* 1930. (Author's photograph, 2018)

the central axis of the complex related to the surrounding mountains. Johnson himself had noted the boulder's pivotal importance when he visited Wright's southwestern headquarters.[21] Johnson used art differently from Wright, often deliberately juxtaposing it with his architecture to dramatize incongruities. Not just a violent act, Wright's blows against the *Two Circus Women* bring to our attention a basic difference between the architects: while Wright emphasized cohesion, Johnson emphasized incongruities, such as difference in scale, in order to give his buildings greater expressive character.

Wright's blow was also symbolic; it was not only a protest against the sculpture's positioning. Wright also struck it because the work embodied the cultural capital that had made Johnson a powerbroker for the world of art and architecture. The sculpture's presence alluded to Johnson's friendship with Lincoln Kirstein, a modernist cultural mandarin who was a leading advocate of Nadelman and modern art at the center of an elite circle of artistic homosexual men to which Johnson also belonged. Such alliances strengthened Johnson's position in the East Coast cultural establishment from which Wright felt excluded. In one of his published conversations with

Rodman, Wright had denigrated Johnson for being a powerful member of the art world and a homosexual in one breath. He said that while he liked Johnson personally, he was "one of that tribe that dominates the art world," by which he probably meant gay men.[22] As was accepted and typical of the era, Wright was openly homophobic as well as casually anti-Semitic, racist, and misogynistic in his remarks. It should be said that Johnson was bigoted as well and could be virulently anti-Semitic despite his friendships with Jews like Kirstein.[23] At times, however, Wright was also surprisingly honest, a teller of truths, again much like a trickster. Wright was unusually frank about Johnson's homosexuality during an era when it was almost never mentioned openly in public, though Johnson's orientation was widely known. Wright understood Johnson well, comprehending that his homosexuality was an important aspect of his character, his power base, and even the way he thought about architecture.

Wright also understood that Johnson's art collection was another way in which he wielded influence, an extension of his position at the Museum of Modern Art. He had been a founding curator of its Architecture and Design Department and had maintained that powerful position into the mid-1950s.[24] Wright had greatly benefited from Johnson's tenure at MoMA. Though Johnson made widely repeated remarks that slighted Wright, memorably calling him the most famous architect of the nineteenth century, he had in fact favored Wright, supporting more exhibitions for him at the museum than for any other architect, but these gestures never satisfied the older man. Wright did not seem able to get over being almost excluded by Johnson from the "Modern Architecture" exhibition at MoMA in 1932. And for that reason the Glass House itself was a tremendous irritant to him because it exemplified the International Style that had threatened to supersede him.

But unlike what occurred in other accounts about his visits to the Glass House, Wright's mood changed in this one according to Rudolph. He was not unrelentingly hostile. Natural light playing across the architecture caused this change. Rudolph stated that after Wright struck the sculpture, the sun came out as if on cue: "Immediately, the sun responded, and the house responded, as always, magnificently to the changing light." Though it is a natural body, the sun in this account behaved mechanically and theatrically. Rudolph makes the sun into a lamp. Such changing natural and artificial lighting effects fascinated Rudolph because he believed that every element in a designed environment could alter moods and behavior. Rudolph was a great believer in the Gesamtkunstwerk. According to him, the Glass House "itself was augmented by its environment, the furnishings, and the art, each contributing to a sense of well-being." Together, all calmed and captivated Wright and everyone present. Rudolph related: "The Glass House had begun

FIG. 7. Glass House bathroom. (Author's photograph, 2018)

to enthrall everyone in it. Seldom has a work of architecture exerted such a powerful influence on its occupants."[25]

And yet Wright was still not completely pacified. He became physical again when the tour moved to the bathroom (fig. 7). Wright struck one of the electric bulbs framing the bathroom mirror with his cane, but amazingly it remained unbroken. It was symbolic that Wright struck a light bulb, for the effects of artificial light were really what was under consideration during this visit, as soon became evident. Rudolph read meaning into the blow itself, seeing it as one that forecast a change of heart by Wright: "This time the blow's meaning was ambivalent—for the gesture was more like a caress, a fond farewell to something that he understood as a work of architecture. The power of the house was made clear by the effect it had upon human behavior."[26]

Wright's blow against the light bulb was a turning point in the narrative. He became calmer, and Rudolph revealed that there was more at stake here than a simple rivalry. As Rudolph saw it, Wright's "caress" of the light bulb was a significant concession by him, indicating the beginning of his acceptance of the Glass House "as a work of architecture." To undermine Johnson and his architecture, Wright had regularly suggested that the Glass House was not original or even architecture, but simply an imitation of Mies's Farnsworth house in Plano, Illinois (1945–51). When asked by Selden Rodman in 1956 what he thought about the Glass House, Wright retorted: "Is it Philip? . . . And is it architecture?"[27] Wright probably also saw the Glass House as a work plagiarized from himself. He frequently complained that other architects, especially European modernists such as Mies, had failed to acknowledge what they had learned from him. The postwar American generation represented by Johnson was no better in his eyes. The Glass House sat on a masonry floor slab warmed by radiant heating much like those found in Wright's Usonian houses. It also related to its hillside site in a fashion recalling how Wright had related Taliesin to the Wisconsin landscape, as Neil Levine has noted.[28]

But Wright's second question—"And is it architecture?"—was the more damning. For Wright, the Glass House's steel framework was so basic and functional that it no longer qualified as architecture. Bare-boned functionalism was an aspect of the European modernism of the 1920s and 1930s railed against by Wright; it had also fallen out of favor. By the mid-1950s, purely utilitarian structures promoted and categorized as modern by developers, but devoid of even the understated aesthetic qualities of the International Style, seemed everywhere to be superseding buildings conceived as architecture as it had been conceived in philosophically informed aesthetic ways by architectural institutions and leading practitioners such as Wright since the Enlightenment. When he subsequently attended the dedication of the New York Coliseum, one of the most banal, large-scale postwar projects undertaken by Robert Moses, Wright remarked dismissively, "It's a great utilitarian achievement, but architecture is something else again."[29]

Wright found the transparency of the Glass House equally problematic because it confused the distinction between interior and exterior. It was that aspect of the house that he criticized in his famed comment: "I don't know whether I'm supposed to take my hat off or leave it on!" In his buildings, Wright always contrasted transparency with opacity. He preferred alternations between darkness and brightness and heaviness and lightness. Traditional architecture often emphasized such juxtapositions, and Wright was as much a conservative as he was a radical.

It is therefore understandable that Wright preferred the more enclosed interior of the nearby, nearly opaque Guest House, also known as the Brick House, which was where the tour advanced to next (fig. 8). Demonstrating his rejection of the ahistoricism and rationalism of the International Style, Johnson remodeled its guest bedroom in 1953 by inserting a mysteriously

FIG. 8. Philip Johnson, Guest House (Brick House), 1945–49, at the Glass House complex. (Author's photograph, 2018)

backlit plaster dome (fig. 9), inspired by the one found in the breakfast room of the London house (1792–1824) of the great Neoclassical architect Sir John Soane. Johnson said the dome signaled his return to historical forms, a direction for Modern architecture he advocated at the Glass House salons.

But it was the bedroom's lighting that most strongly affected Wright. Rudolph recalls how Wright was fascinated by how a rheostat (or dimmer) controlled the concealed lighting behind the dome, an arrangement devised for Johnson by the pioneering lighting designer Richard Kelly, who lit the Glass House, its landscape, and the renovated Guest House interior.[30] Inspired by theatrical lighting, Kelly developed discreet, changeable lighting effects that could rapidly alter the appearance of a building's exterior or its interior. He illuminated many of Johnson's other projects, including, in association with Mies, the Seagram Building in New York (1954–58). Rudolph also knew Kelly and his work. The designer had lit Rudolph's installation for the "Good Design" exhibition at Chicago's Merchandise Mart, organized by MoMA in 1952.

The changing effects of the dimmer in the Guest House bedroom captivated Wright, who transformed the room using the device. Rudolph noted:

"Philip handed Wright the dimmer, which controlled the concealed light that flowed from the overhead canopy and accelerated and decelerated [the] changing light. It was a sheer delight for Wright, who became childlike with a new toy. His sensitivity to the changing light and the time it takes for the eye to adjust to the new conditions were beautiful to behold. Everyone followed the improvised ritual of exploring relationships of space and light. Wright knew he was in command, but Philip knew that it was his creation." At this point, the power balance between Wright and Johnson achieved equilibrium with the two having found mutually engaged and respective roles, at least for the moment.

Rudolph speculated that Wright had never seen a dimmer before. Usually employed for theatrical lighting, the device had not been available for use in the home until a commercially produced version was put on the market in 1953 and did not become widespread until the introduction of further refinements later in that decade. Kelly had probably produced a custom-designed dimmer for the Guest House bedroom featuring the remote control Johnson handed to Wright.[31]

Wright's enchantment with the dimmer was literally the most charged

TIMOTHY M. ROHAN

moment in Rudolph's narrative. The moment is the anecdote's highpoint that reveals an essential truth about the long-standing rivalry between Johnson and Wright: they admired and understood much about one another. It is therefore not surprising that Rudolph elaborated upon the moment in other renditions of this anecdote, including details that he might have thought inappropriate for the account published as a birthday tribute to Johnson in 1996. In these less self-edited versions, Rudolph emphasized how Wright sensed the bedroom's strangely sacred and sensual qualities. In a 1986 interview, Rudolph recalled that Wright "liked the whole thing, although he couldn't quite say that. Wright said that nobody should wear street clothes in such a room. Either there should be special robes you were given to wear in the room or everybody should be in the nude; there was nothing in between."[32] Wright's "special robes" conjured up sacerdotal associations, such as the wearing of vestments in a church, temple, or more ancient place of worship. Wright imbued many of his interior-focused projects with this quasi-religious aura, a characteristic of early twentieth-century architecture, the era when Wright had come of age as an architect. He achieved such effects in part through the manipulation of light, as in the top-lit interiors of Unity Temple in Oak Park, Illinois (1905–8), and the Guggenheim Museum.

By saying that nudity was the only other possible way to inhabit the room, Wright showed that he sensed its sensual qualities, to which he was also highly attuned. Wright frequently made references to sexuality and sexual practices and often used language generally considered profane and unacceptable in conversation. He had practically called Rudolph a prostitute when they first met at Princeton. Rudolph confirmed that Wright understood the room's sensual or sexual qualities in yet another and slightly more salacious version of this encounter. According to Rudolph, Wright had pronounced the Guest House bedroom a "fuck studio" during the April 1956 visit. Wright understood that the contained room was ideal for the type of same-sex activity pursued by Johnson. Unlike the transparent Glass House, the nearly windowless interior of the Guest House bedroom protected its inhabitants from the condemning eyes of homophobic postwar America. Rudolph himself was homosexual and enjoyed repeating Wright's salacious remark for many years after the event, though it was never written down. A former romantic partner of Rudolph's repeated Wright's remark to me in an interview.[33]

For Rudolph, Wright's assessment of the Guest House bedroom as a "fuck studio" was the priceless culmination of the anecdote—a line that revealed a truth, but one hilarious and meaningful to Rudolph because Wright acknowledged what went on in the room at a time when such activities between men were rarely mentioned in print.[34] Always guarded about his homosexuality, Rudolph did not even dare to include the "fuck studio" remark for the version of the anecdote he contributed to the *ANY* Festschrift for Johnson in 1996. The unpublished verbal rendition of this story alerts us to another valuable quality of anecdotes: they record aspects of events that may not have appeared in print, such as the roles of gender, sexuality, or race—dimensions often deliberately left out of the accounts of the past and overlooked by the histories written about them subsequently.

Rudolph concluded the *ANY* version of the anecdote with Wright disappearing almost as suddenly as he had appeared: "The end of this event was as dramatic as the beginning. . . . A spiffy touring car painted Indian red" magically appeared from out of nowhere and bore Wright and his entourage away to the opening of the New York Coliseum whose dedication Wright declared he would outshine. But Rudolph devoted the final line of his account to praising the Glass House's performance, crediting architecture with greater power than any of the remarkable people present. In the last line of his account, Rudolph said, "Clearly the Glass House with its handmaidens (environment, art, and furnishings) had won the day and the century."[35]

How did this encounter with Wright change Rudolph, Johnson, and even the direction of postwar modernism? Following the visit, Rudolph's critique of the International Style became more vocal, and he referred to Wright more frequently in his published work. In October 1956, Rudolph published another article calling for alternatives to the International Style, arguing that much was to be learned about the "psychological demands" of architecture from Wright's treatment of natural light. Always an admirer of Wright's interior spaces, Rudolph accompanied the observation with a photograph of the dramatically lit, inward-looking, practically windowless central office floor of Wright's S. C. Johnson Administration Building in Racine, Wisconsin (1936–39). Washed in a warm, sensual light filtered through a ceiling made of Pyrex tubes, it was another of Wright's sacerdotal interiors, comparable to the columned halls of Egyptian New Kingdom temples. And yet Rudolph was also wryly critical of how Wright and other architects employed sunlight. In the caption he noted: "Wright was born knowing how to manipulate natural light (sometimes without full regard for the use to be made of it). Some other architects have been a longtime learning."[36] By both complementing and criticizing Wright, Rudolph showed that he had learned from his elder without being an acquiescent follower. Rudolph had never wanted to be a mere emulator of Wright, believing that by so doing he would only limit his creative faculties.

Rudolph spent the rest of the 1950s adroitly positioning himself as heir and critic to all those considered the canonical founding figures of Modern architecture—Gropius, Wright, Mies, and Le Corbusier—rather than to any one of them in particular. A talented designer and canny maneuverer through the postwar architectural establishment, Rudolph advanced to its forefront and became chairman of the Yale Architecture Department in 1958. He emphasized the importance of natural light in his studio teaching at Yale, requiring that students draw perspective sections of their projects, like the ones he produced of his own buildings, that showed the effects of natural light upon their interiors, often through clerestories like the ones he had admired in Wright's Rosenbaum house.[37]

Rudolph referred to Wright in his built work as well, though not in ways that were always immediately apparent. Rudolph's famed Yale Art & Architecture Building (1958–64) appears to be inspired by Le Corbusier's monumental postwar concrete buildings, but in terms of plan and massing it also recalled Wright's Larkin Building in Buffalo, New York (1902–6), as was noted by Vincent Scully and Ada Louise Huxtable following the Yale building's completion.[38] Wright continued to inspire Rudolph after his Yale years. In the early 1970s, Rudolph wrote an appraisal of Fallingwater at Mill Run, Pennsylvania (1935–39), admiring its intangible qualities.[39] Then he designed his own version inspired by it, the Bass house in Fort Worth (1970–72), as a series of cantilevered terraces rising above a dry Texas hillside instead of a waterfall.

Rudolph was equally fascinated by artificial lighting, whose powerful, transformative effects were perhaps impressed upon him that day in the Guest House bedroom when Wright manipulated the interior effect using the dimmer. Light itself could be a building material. In the late 1960s, Rudolph experimented with artificial lighting in residential interior spaces, creating effects far more surreal and sensual than those found in Johnson's Guest House for his own apartment in New York (1965–97) and in projects for clients.[40] For Rudolph, the importance of artificial lighting was so great that in 1976 he established Modulightor in New York, a firm selling lighting fixtures he designed with Ernst Wagner.

Johnson, for his part, expertly played up his encounters with Wright as a rivalry to further establish himself as an architectural powerbroker. The fact that Wright chose to visit Johnson at home only added to the aura of the Glass House and luster to Johnson's role as a cultural eminence whom even an old master must visit. Johnson knew a good story, and he spoke about his encounters with Wright more than Wright did. It was Johnson who probably first related Wright's witticism about his hat and the Glass House and thus got it into circulation. In 1956 Johnson told the remark to Selden Rodman, who included it among the provocative exchanges between Johnson and Wright in his 1957 book.[41] Wright uttered the remark, but Johnson "owned" it as well and used it often to great dramatic effect. Most memorably, Johnson repeated the remark publicly in a 1957 talk in Seattle, where it played a part in Johnson's larger reckoning with Wright and his influence as Wright entered his ninth decade. The lecture was published soon after with the title "100 Years, Frank Lloyd Wright, and Us."[42] Like Rudolph's anecdote, the published lecture is worth pursuing: it can be interpreted as Johnson's reply to Wright's visits to the Glass House. After repeating the witticism, Johnson said he was tired of Wright criticizing him and his house for not being architecture. Striking back against Wright, he said Wright's houses were illogical and idiosyncratic.

These remarks at first seemed like the usual performance of the ongoing Johnson-Wright rivalry, but then Johnson changed his tone, grew more serious, and turned to a lengthy account of one of his visits to Taliesin West. Johnson journeyed there several times, but because of the lack of documentation, it is difficult to determine the exact date of this particular tour. In fact, Johnson may even have made this trip up out of the memory of several other visits, reviewed by him after Wright's recent visits to the Glass House. It is significant that Johnson began his Seattle lecture with his account of Wright coming to the Glass House and ended it with himself touring Taliesin West. Johnson structured his lecture symmetrically so that the house tours framed, replied, or reciprocated one another, thus revealing the importance of these moving investigations of architecture for him. In a way that paralleled Wright's tour through the Glass House, Johnson described approaching the desert complex on foot and briefly mentioned encountering a petroglyph boulder (mentioned earlier in this essay). Not just a sculpture, it was a directional object inscribed with "Indian hieroglyphics," which Johnson could not read. Johnson's description of his visit noted several such mysteries that affected the mind, body, and emotions. Johnson said in his introduction to this part of his talk that Wright's greatest achievement was his mastery of "the arrangement of secrets of space."[43] Johnson's account was suspenseful, passionate, and almost dreamlike. It had mytho-poetic tones to it, recalling a hero's journey through a labyrinth to find answers to weighty questions.

Escorted by Wright, Johnson told of how he proceeded through a series of alternately dark and bright courtyards and rooms with views of the desert and gardens, often lit by sunlight filtered in ingenious ways that affected his emotions. Johnson called what was probably the large drafting studio the "most single exciting room that we have in this country" because of the way light shone through its diaphanous, tent-like canvas covering.[44]

No longer a trickster, but now in the role of desert prophet or priest who will reveal truths to an acolyte, Wright led Johnson to a mysterious chamber. Johnson said it was illuminated by a "shaft of light that comes from 12 or 14 feet above." As at the Glass House, light itself was a primary material at Taliesin West, as Johnson evidently understood. Recalling the nearly windowless interior of his own Guest House bedroom, Johnson said of the chamber in his lecture, "It is entirely an inside room, no desert or garden." Again Johnson's visit to Taliesin West resembles Rudolph's description of Wright's visit to the Glass House. Both concluded in a mysteriously lit, self-contained sacerdotal chamber. Wright's presence moved Johnson emotionally. He invited Johnson to sit down and said, "Welcome to Taliesin." With no further commentary, Johnson dramatically ended his lecture by simply telling his Seattle audience, "My friends, that is the essence of architecture."[45]

Johnson's conclusion can be understood as the answer to Wright's query about the Glass House: "Is it architecture?" That question raises a larger one: what should architecture be in the postwar era? One word sums up what the answer was for these protagonists and for many practitioners of Modern architecture in 1950s America: emotional. An emotional, sensuous, and even sensual architecture would be the antidote to the building of the allegedly emotionless International Style or the blandness of utilitarian structures such as the New York Coliseum. In the Seattle lecture, Johnson's answer to Wright's question was a generous one, probably provoked by the dramatic impact of that moment. When Johnson spoke of this experience in an interview with Rodman, his praise for Taliesin West was more measured. Essentially, Johnson said that Taliesin West would not be so moving without Wright himself present. In other words, Wright was the *genius loci,* which is the phrase Rodman used to neatly sum up Johnson's assessment.[46]

Indeed, in part as a result of these encounters with Wright, the "essence of architecture" became for Johnson more than something just material or structural; it was a combined experience of physical movement on foot through space, diffused natural light, and the passage of time. Johnson had also told Rodman that Wright predicated his buildings on "a sort of architecture-in-time."[47] Though he mentioned Wright only briefly in the text, Johnson elaborated upon the concept of "architecture-in-time" in an article that best exemplified his views about such a subjective approach: "Whence and Whither: The Processional Element in Architecture" (1965). Widely cited, the article is considered the best articulation of Johnson's thinking during the postwar era and one of his strongest contributions to its architectural discourse.[48]

Wright's knocks and blows against the Glass House and its contents may have echoed in Johnson's mind in other instructive ways. Perhaps reconsider-

FIG. 10. Philip Johnson, New York State Theater, New York, 1961–64. Photograph by Ezra Stoller, 1964. (© Ezra Stoller/Esto)

ing it as a sculpture whose value was greatest as a directional element, rather than as foil, Johnson fabricated a larger version in marble of *Two Circus Women* by Nadelman that provided a meeting point for theatergoers in the vast marble lobby of his New York State Theater at Lincoln Center (1961–64) (fig. 10). It housed the New York City Ballet, founded by Lincoln Kirstein. The latter had helped Johnson secure the commission for the theater, so again the sculpture was an allusion to their friendship.[49] However, in this case, the sculpture no longer deliberately contrasted with the architecture as it had in the version of it at the Glass House. Instead, Johnson integrated it into the building in terms of both its placement and materials, a lesson perhaps learned from Wright about how objects should be employed in architecture. To enhance the formal qualities of this imposing ceremonial space, Johnson aligned *Two Circus Women* with a second Nadelman sculpture of similar size and proportion, *Two Female Nudes* (1931, fabricated 1962). The dialogue between Wright and Johnson informed the interior and its sculpture. Dramatically lit by Richard Kelly, the theater's immense lobby possessed both the intense, inward-focused qualities of Johnson's Guest House bedroom

TIMOTHY M. ROHAN

and the sacerdotal monumentality of Wright's interior atriums for the Johnson Wax and Larkin buildings.[50]

Analyzing different versions of familiar anecdotes can be a rewarding method of inquiry that reveals overlooked dimensions of events. Rudolph's account of a visit by Wright to the Glass House is a more complex one than the familiar anecdote where the unrelentingly aggressive Wright does not know if he should keep his hat on or take it off. Rudolph's story gives depth and dimension to the complex relationships between Wright and the postwar generation, revealing it to be not simply a rivalry, but a dialogue. Rudolph's story holds several suggestions for us today to think about their relationships. The first is that Rudolph depicted Wright with colleagues, which suggests that Wright was not simply a solitary figure as he often is thought to be but one engaged with the architecture of his time. The second is that many in the postwar generation engaged with Wright in complex ways to suit their own purposes. Their relationships with Wright were not just fraught with either hero worship or disdain. Invoking Wright helped both Rudolph and Johnson advance themselves. Studying Wright's work helped Rudolph develop his own distinctive approach to architecture without becoming an imitator. Wright's work informed Johnson's architecture and not just formally, but in more elusive yet just as important ephemeral ways that attest to the significance of bodily movement and emotion for Johnson.

The third—and most overlooked—is that Wright may have wanted to learn from his younger colleagues. Wright probably visited the Glass House several times to satisfy his curiosity about this much-talked-about building and its additions, not just to berate Johnson once again. Like Rudolph, Johnson thought that Wright could not admit how much he liked the Guest House bedroom, whose every detail he studied.[51] The last house Wright completed before his death, the John Gillin house in Dallas, Texas (1950–58), featured an impressive array of interior lighting effects that could be adjusted by numerous dimmers. Unusual for their time, these features have been credited to the client, who was an electronics enthusiast.[52] But in view of what has been learned here from Rudolph's anecdote, some agency can be returned to Wright for this aspect of the project: perhaps he wanted to achieve interior lighting effects for the Gillin house similar to those he experienced during his visits to Johnson's Glass House complex. It was possible for an old dog to learn new tricks.

Wright's unscheduled April 1956 visit to Johnson in New Canaan can be recognized as an impromptu salon and one of the most consequential, if overlooked, of those held at the Glass House. Most importantly, the very "essence" of what architecture should be was reconsidered that day at the Glass House in a phenomenological fashion that itself suggested how architecture could move beyond the solid verities of structure to more fleeting ephemeral means, as would be explored by the rising avant-garde of the 1960s. The changing plays of light that washed over Wright, Johnson, and Rudolph in both the Glass House and the Guest House bedroom can be seen as something akin to the wordless exchange that passed between them and informed their work in ways that we are only now just beginning to consider.

NOTES

1. For examples of the many versions of the encounter see Mark Lamster, *The Man in the Glass House: Philip Johnson, Architect of the Modern Century* (New York: Little, Brown, 2018), 218; Hugh Howard, *Architecture's Odd Couple: Frank Lloyd Wright and Philip Johnson* (New York: Bloomsbury Press, 2016), 6–7; Franz Schulze, *Philip Johnson: Life and Work* (Chicago: University of Chicago Press, 1996), 223–24; Meryle Secrest, *Frank Lloyd Wright: A Biography* (New York: Alfred A. Knopf, 1992), 394. It may have first been mentioned by Johnson in his article "100 Years, Frank Lloyd Wright and Us," *Pacific Architect and Builder* 62 (March 1957): 3, 13, 35–36, republished in *Philip Johnson Writings* (New York: Oxford University Press, 1979), 193.
2. Paul Rudolph, "A Sunday Afternoon," *ANY: Philip Johnson Festschrift* 90 (1996): 44–45.
3. See also Cammie McAtee, "The 'Search for Form' in Postwar American Architecture" (Ph.D. diss., Harvard University, 2017), 122.
4. Neil Levine, *The Architecture of Frank Lloyd Wright* (Princeton: Princeton University Press, 1996), 424–30.
5. "Walter Gropius et son école: Walter Gropius, the Spread of an Idea," *L'Architecture d'aujourd'hui*, no. 28 (February 1950), special issue edited by Paul Rudolph.
6. Stephanie Williams, "Class of '44," *World Architecture* 19 (September 1992): 20.
7. Rudolph elaborated upon his fascination with Wright from an early age; see Paul Rudolph, "Excerpts from a Conversation," *Perspecta* 22 (1986): 102–7.
8. Williams, "Class of 44," 20.
9. Robert A. M. Stern and Jimmy Stamp, *Pedagogy and Place: 100 Years of Architecture Education at Yale* (New Haven: Yale University Press, 2016), 167. Rudolph was as often in the northeastern United States during the mid-1950s as he was in his Sarasota office. He had also established a small office in 1955 in Cambridge, Massachusetts, to work on his Jewett Arts Center at Wellesley College. In addition to teaching at Yale, Rudolph was frequently in the region because he taught at Harvard, MIT, and Princeton. His ties to the Museum of Modern Art were strong because he designed two exhibitions there: "Good Design" (1952) and "The Family of Man" (1956). For particulars see Timothy M. Rohan, *The Architecture of Paul Rudolph* (New Haven: Yale University Press, 2014), 40–42.
10. For an account of a Glass House salon when Rudolph was present, see Aline B.

Saarinen, "Four Architects Helping to Change the Look of America," *Vogue,* 1 August 1955, 119–21, 149–50, 152.

11. Henry-Russell Hitchcock, "The Architecture of Bureaucracy and the Architecture of Genius," *Architectural Review* 101 (January 1947): 3–6.

12. Paul Rudolph, "The Changing Philosophy of Architecture," *Architectural Forum* 101 (July 1954): 120.

13. Robert Bruegmann, "Interview with Paul Rudolph," 28 February 1986, Chicago Architects Oral History Project, Art Institute of Chicago, 1993, 51.

14. Rudolph, "A Sunday Afternoon," 44.

15. Selden Rodman, *Conversations with Artists* (New York: Devin-Adair, 1957), xx. Rodman said in the introduction that he conducted interviews with Wright and Johnson between January and July 1956. Wright's April 1956 visit to the Glass House occurred within this six-month span.

16. Concerning the longstanding role of the trickster in American culture, see William J. Jackson, *American Tricksters: Thoughts on the Shadow Side of a Culture's Psyche* (Eugene, Ore.: Cascade Books, 2014).

17. Rudolph, "A Sunday Afternoon," 44.

18. Philip Johnson, "House at New Canaan, Connecticut," *Architectural Review* 108 (September 1950): 159.

19. Robert A. M. Stern recalled how Johnson had told him that Wright had had the Nadelman sculpture shifted during another visit (*Philip Johnson Writings,* 192). Hugh Howard dated the incident to spring 1958 in *Architecture's Odd Couple,* 223–24, and noted that not all versions of this incident are in agreement. His account is based upon an interview with Johnson conducted by George Goodwin, 27 July 1992, Archives of American Art, Smithsonian Institution.

20. Rodman, *Conversations with Artists,* 52.

21. Johnson, "100 Years, Frank Lloyd Wright and Us," 193.

22. Rodman, *Conversations with Artists,* 50.

23. For Johnson's anti-Semitism and engagement with fascism, see Lamster, *The Man in the Glass House,* xiii.

24. Rodman, *Conversations with Artists,* 50.

25. Rudolph, "A Sunday Afternoon," 44.

26. Rudolph, "A Sunday Afternoon," 45.

27. Rodman, *Conversations with Artists,* 50.

28. Levine, *The Architecture of Frank Lloyd Wright,* 429.

29. "Visitors Are in a Spending Mood, Dealers Wink at Wear and Tear," *New York Times,* 29 April 2018, 75.

30. Dietrich Neumann, ed., *The Structure of Light: Richard Kelly and the Illumination of Modern Architecture* (New Haven: Yale University Press and Yale School of Architecture, 2010), 152–53.

31. For an account of the dimmer and Richard Kelly's use of it especially for projects by Johnson, see Sandy Isenstadt, "The Invention of Modern Lighting: Richard Kelly and Home Lighting," in Neumann, *The Structure of Light,* 58.

32. Bruegmann, "Interview with Paul Rudolph," 53.

33. Rohan interview with Ellis Ansel Perlswig, 29 October 2009. Perlswig was Rudolph's lover or romantic partner from 1963 to 1967. He remembered Rudolph and Johnson often recounting to one another the story of Wright's visit to the Glass

House. They particularly delighted in repeating Wright's remark about the Guest House bedroom being a "fuck studio." See also Rohan, *The Architecture of Paul Rudolph,* 187.

34. The sexual dimensions of the Glass House were not discussed in print until Alice T. Friedman explained them in her groundbreaking book, *Women and the Making of the Modern House* (New Haven: Yale University Press, 1998), 147–59.

35. Rudolph, "A Sunday Afternoon," 45.

36. Paul Rudolph, "The Six Determinants of Architectural Form," *Architectural Record* 120 (October 1956): 187. For another example of him discussing Wright's manipulation of light, see Paul Rudolph, "Regionalism in Architecture," *Perspecta* 4 (1957): 16.

37. Paul Rudolph, "Excerpts from a Conversation," *Perspecta* 22 (1986): 103.

38. Vincent Scully, "Art and Architecture Building, Yale University," *Architectural Review* 135 (May 1964): 326–32; Ada Louise Huxtable, "Winner at Yale: The New Art and Architecture Building Lives Up to Great Expectations," *New York Times,* 10 November 1963, X19.

39. Paul Rudolph, "Frank Lloyd Wright Kaufmann House, 'Fallingwater,' Bear Run, Pennsylvania, 1936," *Global Architecture* 2 (1970): n.p.

40. For Rudolph's New York interiors, see Rohan, *The Architecture of Paul Rudolph,* 180–205.

41. Rodman, *Conversations with Artists,* 70.

42. Johnson, "100 Years, Frank Lloyd Wright and Us," 192–98. Neil Levine may have been the first to use Johnson's text to analyze Taliesin West; see Levine, *The Architecture of Frank Lloyd Wright,* 255–56.

43. Philip Johnson, "Whence and Whither: The Processional Element in Architecture," *Perspecta* 9/10 (1965):197.

44. Johnson, "Whence and Wither," 198.

45. Johnson, "Whence and Wither," 198.

46. Rodman, *Conversations with Artists,* 53

47. Rodman, *Conversations with Artists,* 54.

48. Johnson, "Whence and Whither, 167–78.

49. Lamster, *The Man in the Glass House,* 292.

50. Cecile Whiting, "Philip Johnson: The Whence and Whither of Art in Architecture," *Journal of the Society of Architectural Historians* 75 (September 2016): 318–38.

51. Howard, "Architecture's Odd Couple," 275; Calvin Tomkins, "Forms under Light," *New Yorker* 53 (23 May 1977): 60; Rodman, *Conversations with Artists,* 54.

52. William Allin Storrer, *The Frank Lloyd Wright Companion* (Chicago: University of Chicago Press, 2006), 358–59. My thanks to Ann Abernathy, who told me about the many dimmers at the Gillin house when I presented this material as a paper at the Frank Lloyd Wright Building Conservancy Conference at MoMA on 15 September 2017. My thanks to Neil Levine for inviting me to speak at the conference. I am also grateful to him and Richard Longstreth for their editing of this essay and completion of this book during difficult times.

JACK QUINAN

Frank Lloyd Wright under the Sign of Phenomenology

Despite the dominance of visual attributes in the practice and study of architecture, compelling evidence indicates that phenomenological methods of inquiry have the potential to deepen our understanding and appreciation of such work. This approach is especially pertinent to the buildings of Frank Lloyd Wright. My essay draws upon the embodied phenomenology of Maurice Merleau-Ponty to explore instances of Wright's attention to vision, sound, touch, taste, smell, and the kinesthetic sense as they occur in selected examples of his architecture. Although such a design strategy may seem to lie outside the organic principles with which Wright strove to create a Gesamtkunstwerk for his clients, the ideas that are the underpinning of phenomenology enable a better comprehension of the sensory-oriented components that Wright employed to create the symphonic architectural experience that he often promised.[1]

Phenomenology originated with Edmund Husserl (1859–1938), a philosopher who explored structures of consciousness and other mental phenomena as they are experienced from the first-person point of view.[2] Husserl's transcendentalist-idealist phenomenology rejected the rationalism of the Western philosophical tradition in favor of a method that examines the individual's lived experience. Intentionality—the idea that consciousness is not solely in the mind but rather of something, such as an object—is central to Husserl's reliance upon an intuitive grasp of knowledge, free of presuppositions and intellectualizing.

In his *Phenomenology of Perception* (1945) Maurice Merleau-Ponty (1908–61) redirected Husserl's thought away from concerns with issues of the intellect to the idea that we inhabit the world through our senses ("all consciousness is perceptual consciousness").[3] Merleau-Ponty created a means for the assessment of architecture with an embodied phenomenology that enfolds the primacy of the visual sense together with concerns for the remaining senses that constitute the complete, experiencing human body. Phenomenology provides a means for examining Wright's architecture, but the possibility that he would have been aware of Husserl's *Logical Investigations* (coincident with Wright's first Prairie houses) is slim, and no documentary evidence of such an awareness has come to light. Nevertheless, significant aspects of Wright's methods have parallels in phenomenology as it was conceived and developed by Husserl and his successors. Wright's intuitive approach to architecture ranks high in this regard.

Wright's attentiveness to the senses is a manifestation of an organic design philosophy that originated with a close observation of nature fostered in the aura of Unitarian and Transcendentalist thought in a childhood further enriched by substantial immersions in music, poetry, and literature.[4] His seminal essay, "In the Cause of Architecture" of 1908, proffered six organic principles extolling simplicity, style grounded in the character of the client, the growth of a building from its site, a color palette drawn from nature, respect for the nature of materials, and the expression of sincerity and integrity in a building.[5] Subsequent iterations of these principles reveal the expression of an increasingly embodied sensibility on Wright's part. In 1914 he wrote of "a *sentient,* rational building . . . and a 'thinking'" as well as '*feeling*' process."[6] In 1939 he declared that "the time is here for architecture to recognize its own nature, to realize that it is out of life itself for life as it is now lived, a *humane and intensely human thing.*" In his statement that "Architecture already favors the reflex, the *natural easy attitude,* the occult symmetry of grace and rhythm affirming the ease, grace, and naturalness of natural life," body and building are merged in Wright's creative imagination.[7]

How then is sensory awareness manifested in Wright's work? Given his ambition to create a Gesamtkunstwerk for each client, the prospect of a super-abundance of instances of sensory awareness among his 350 realized commissions is formidable to contemplate, and with that in mind the following discussion illustrates just some of the ways that Wright attended to the senses in a variety of building types and settings over the course of his long career. The visual sense will dominate, as a matter of course, but among the reasons why Wright's work so captivates is his penchant for synthesizing two or more sensory concerns and his determination to incorporate the sights, sounds, smells, and textures of nature into his clients' lives. The Barton house in Buffalo, New York (1903–4), is a case in point.

VISION, TOUCH, AND KINESTHETIC SENSE AT THE BARTON HOUSE

The Barton house is a seven-room, cross-axially planned, wood-frame, brick-veneer Prairie house similar in scale to the "Small House with Lots of Room

JACK QUINAN

FIG. I. Barton house, Buffalo, New York, 1903–4. Photo Henry Furmann & Sons, ca. 1904. (The Frank Lloyd Wright Foundation Archives [The Museum of Modern Art | Avery Architectural & Fine Arts Library, Columbia University, New York])

in It" that Wright published in the July 1901 issue of the *Ladies Home Journal* (fig. 1). In the absence of documentation pertaining to the Barton's lived experience in the house, evidence of embodied design features can be readily discerned in the house's current, restored state.

As in 1904, visitors to the Barton house today are initially engaged visually and cognitively by certain ambiguities in its design and by its radical departure from the norms of the neighboring houses along Summit Avenue, the majority of which are two and one half stories, rectangular in form, and topped by gable roofs.[8] The Barton house consists of a two-story, oblong block oriented at right angles to the street, with a single-story porch and foyer on one side and kitchen wing on the other, both parallel to the street. Ambiguity is apparent in the two-story portion of the street face owing to the uninterrupted rise of its brick walls from the water table to the second-story windowsill that eliminates any external indication of the actual level of the second floor. This configuration contrasts with that of most of the nearby house fronts along the avenue where either the roofline of a front porch or a belt course clearly delineates the division between the two floors. Darwin Martin, who commissioned the Barton house for his sister, Delta, and her husband, George, inadvertently expressed its ambiguity in a letter to his wife, Isabelle: "My dear: Mr. Lang [the contractor] made his report last night on the Barton House. The bids aggregate at first sight, including the architect's fees,

$10,000. Isn't it awful? Instead of a little house, every man who figured on it referred to it as a big house. Lang constantly reminding them that it was a little house."[9]

The path from the street into and around the Barton house interior is regulated by a 4-foot, 6-inch planning grid that requires numerous right-angle turns, five of which occur from the sidewalk to the front door. Passage along that walk involves pivoting around an 8-foot-high, urn-bearing pier to the 7 steps that lead to a small entry porch. The 5½-foot extension of the eave of the adjacent south porch shelters the doorway, half of the entry porch, and the stairs—a welcome configuration in inclement weather. A powerful sense of envelopment is experienced upon approaching the house as the pier and urn loom, the bottom step is slightly extended toward the street as if in greeting, concrete copings form a continuous horizontal baseline around both porches, the porch eave shelters, and the extra width of the front door (3 feet, 4 inches) welcomes.

In spite of the formality of the grid, the first-floor interior of the Barton house is surprisingly spacious due to the absence of interior walls and doors between the foyer, the living room, and the dining room. These latter two spaces are separated by an expansive hall defined by parallel horizontal oak beams 6½ feet above the floor that are supported by four wooden piers that incorporate three half-scale, built-in cabinets (fig. 2).[10] At their juncture with the north and south walls these beams are transformed into broad moldings that continue around the entirety of the first floor, establishing a reference to human scale that is touchable—either literally (to persons of average height) or visually—and is sensed bodily as the molding wraps the entire space like a belt while continuing the theme of horizontal definition first encountered in the concrete copings of the building's exterior.[11] All the doors, windows, and built-in furniture pieces descend from this molding. The plaster wall and ceiling surfaces are arrayed in soft autumnal colors with a velvety finish and are framed by oak moldings that rigorously delineate the interior spaces.[12]

The moldings and the beams that form the hall introduce an internal spatial ambiguity that further engages visitors cognitively. The cross-axial plan of the house is made visually explicit in the language of the moldings: the north-south axis is articulated by the aforementioned twin beams that cross the east-west axis, while the 52-foot-long axis develops its directional counterthrust through tripartite ceiling moldings that pass over the twin beams to terminate at the extremities of the long space in the form of prows directed toward the surrounding landscape (fig. 3).[13] These beams and moldings contribute to a subtle tension between the semi-discrete quality of the

FIG. 2. Barton house, view of dining room from hall. (Courtesy of Frank Lloyd Wright's Martin House, Buffalo, New York | Photograph by Bill Henrich, IMG_INK)

individual rooms and their participation in the larger space of the long east-west living-room-to-dining-room axis.

The visual experience of the first-floor living spaces is conditioned by solid walls containing four tripartite Chicago windows (4-foot-square panes of clear glass flanked by 19⁵⁄₁₆-inch-by-43⅞-inch operable art-glass panels) on the east, west, and south elevations—there are no windows in the north wall—through which light enters onto the autumnally-hued walls and dark oak moldings.

By contrast, the second floor is accessed by a compact stairway with three angular turns that lead into a partial bay consisting of four art-glass windows—three face north, the fourth west to form a corner—that admits a generous flood of light and views onto the surrounding deciduous canopy. At the summit, the stairway opens onto a narrow, low-ceilinged hallway that extends from the 12-foot-by-18-foot master bedroom in the front of the house to a similarly dimensioned bedroom at the rear.[14] In either direction the sense of compression experienced in the corridor is followed by a palpable sense of release when, at the entrance to either of the end rooms, the ceiling rises 18 inches and the lateral expansion of the space is enhanced by a

panorama of seven art-glass windows, two of which wrap around and partially dissolve the corners of the room (fig. 4).[15]

In contrast to the formality of the first floor, the two end bedrooms offer unique living experiences.[16] All of the seven art-glass windows in each room are 42½-inch-by-36⅓-inch casements that swing open widely to cool the rooms on hot summer nights (fig. 4).[17] The 5-foot projection of the eaves from just above the window frames tempers the sound of rain pelting window glass—an effect that is experienced as sheltering—while in daytime these eaves cast a shadow over the rooms that afforded the Bartons an additional layer of comfort and privacy. The seven front bedroom windows provide a commanding view of Summit Avenue while the rear bedroom, that of the Barton's daughter, Laura, faces a small yard with a maple tree (now lost) that teemed in summer with the sounds of insects, birds, squirrels, and the rustle of its leaves in the wind.[18]

In the absence of evidence documenting how the Bartons furnished the house (beyond their Wright-designed dining table, side chairs, and built-in pieces) or how they experienced the house, its provocative ambiguities, an-

FIG. 4. Barton house, master bedroom window wall. (Author's photograph)

gular paths of movement, spatial freedom, warmth of tactile materials and colors, reposeful horizontal Roman brickwork, and the persistent inscription of the human scale through moldings constitute an enveloping, embodied domestic environment through Wright's attention to the senses.[19]

KINESTHETIC MOBILITY AT THE LAURENT HOUSE

In the 1930s Wright began to investigate new geometries with hemicycles, circles, and triangles as plan forms and with hexagonal, triangular, and diamond-shaped planning grids that injected a new experiential dynamism into his houses. Kenneth Laurent, who was paralyzed from the waist down by a spinal tumor at the age of twenty-seven, approached Wright about designing a house for him in 1949. Wright initially suggested a two-story, concavely curved plan, using the second Jacobs house in Middleton, Wisconsin (1943–49), as a model. But when Laurent found its two-story height problematic owing to his wheelchair-bound condition, Wright designed a single-story house, hemicyclic in plan on a 4-foot planning grid, with two bedrooms, a bath, and a kitchen-dining cove arranged along the outer curve of the east

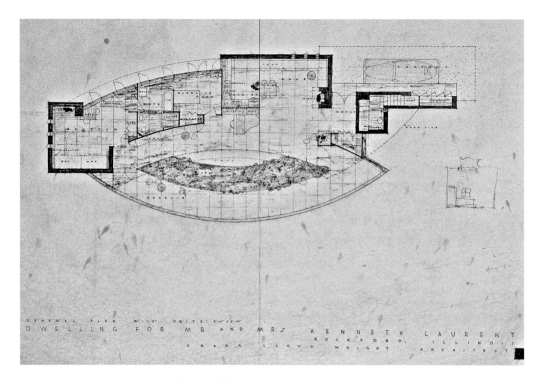

wall (fig. 5). To accommodate Laurent's need for ample room in which to move about, Wright opened the kitchen-dining cove broadly westward into the "garden room" where a concavely curved window-wall faces a small lens-shaped pool, a terraced garden, a stone lantern, and two Japanese maples (fig. 6). The western border of the garden is bounded by a curving, paved pathway enclosed by a concave brick garden wall that inscribes a segment of a continuous indoor-outdoor-indoor elliptical path that freed the occupant from the confines of a conventional house.

Among the many accommodations for Laurent's wheelchair-bound condition were a carport that brought him close to a double-wide main doorway with an easily managed, ¼-inch threshold. Just inside the entrance a broad corridor sweeps along the curved west window wall of the garden room toward the square-in-plan master bedroom where twin beds placed end-to-end along an outer wall facilitated Laurent's access to his wheelchair and to a nearby desk cantilevered to accommodate the wheelchair's dimensions.

Furnishings in the house were scaled to Laurent's seated position in the wheelchair. The chair seats—12 to 13 inches from the floor—are lower than

FIG. 6. Laurent house, corridor to garden room. (Author's photograph)

normal (about 18 inches) so as to elevate Laurent to eye-level with his guests and obviate having to crane his neck back to look up at and converse with them—one of the most difficult kinesthetic aspects of being wheelchair-bound. Wright also designed the ceilings throughout the house to be 7 feet, 2 inches high with smooth surfaces so as to carry Laurent's view out into the garden landscape with a minimum of interruption.

In providing Laurent with a home of curving walls and ready access to nature, Wright intuitively drew upon features that are now widely recognized by environmental psychologists as those most favorably regarded by humans.[20] According to Laurent's friend, Jerry Heinzeroth, "Ken told me that every morning for sixty years he would stop at the bedroom door and look down the curving window wall. The barrier between inside and outside would disappear and nature would flow into nurture. This spirit-lifting beauty would, in his words, 'allow me to forget my disabilities and focus on my capability.'"[21]

SENSORY EXPERIENCES OF WATER AT TALIESIN AND FALLINGWATER

The multitude of sense-oriented design features at both Taliesin in Wisconsin (begun 1911) and Taliesin West in Arizona (begun 1938) are evidence

of Wright's frequent alteration and refinement of the buildings as demonstration projects for the Taliesin Fellows and for his own satisfaction as ongoing "experiments."[22] In 1911, for example, he designed a dam at Taliesin in order to create a pond or "water garden" as a landscape feature, a place of recreation, a source of water to be pumped up to the dwellings and work spaces, and eventually as an electrical power source.[23] Through several iterations, the dam has always been a prominent feature along the access road to Taliesin from State Route 23 for both the spectacle and the sound of its cascading water.[24] In a 1925 rebuilding, the surface of the spillway was rusticated, causing each projecting stone to generate an individual miniature waterfall, a sort of watery veil. Following a flood that washed out the dam in the 1940s, Wright widened the spillway and added a half-pyramid of stones to its left surface to enhance the visual excitement with more vigorous splashing, while creating a medley of two different water sounds that changes subtly as one moves from one side of the dam to the other (fig. 7).[25]

Wright created a variety of water features for his commissions, the majority of which were amenities such as pools or fountains incorporated into the design. In some instances, such as the Pew (1938) and Walker (1948) houses in Shorewood Hills, Wisconsin, and Carmel, California, respectively, he seized the opportunity to engage the building with naturally moving water. In the design of the Kaufmann weekend retreat, Fallingwater, in Mill Run, Pennsylvania (1935–39), the stream played a defining role in his conception of the house.

At Fallingwater, an internal structural core of stone piers and concrete floor slabs supports three floors of living spaces from which smoothly finished, reinforced-concrete terraces are cantilevered over Bear Run in three directions from two floor levels. The cantilevers confer Fallingwater's instant recognizability, but to gain entrance to the house visitors must cross a bridge over the stream and proceed behind the building to an outside entrance corridor of flagstone enclosed by sandstone walls and piers.[26] This pathway is intersected by a secondary spatial axis that crosses near the point of entry through which the sound of the stream is momentarily magnified, reinforcing the significance of its rushing waters to the experience.[27] Within the space people stand in proximity to the blocks and thin slabs of Pottsville sandstone that are laid up with varying levels of projection from deeply raked mortar joints (fig. 8). The texture of the masonry reflects the natural stratigraphy of the stone at its quarry source, but close scrutiny reveals a studied randomness among the thicknesses and projections, particularly in the "stick-outs," Wright's term for the projecting slabs that emulate the building's concrete cantilevers in miniature.[28] Evidences of the quarryman's chisel in the hand-chipped edges of the sandstone slabs encourage an impulse to touch, to make physical contact with the building's distinctive structure.[29]

FIG. 8. Fallingwater, Edgar J. Kaufmann house, Mill Run, Pennsylvania, 1935–39, entry corridor. (Author's photograph, 2017)

The approach to the house presents a compendium of sensory experiences conditioned by a powerful feeling of anticipation and excitement that accrues on the long trek to the site.[30] The quest for the door in the shadowy depths of the entry corridor is accompanied by the crunch of gravel as one crosses from the driveway onto the flagstone. Traces of dampness and the faint odor of moist leaf and plant decay permeates downward from the forest and the stone outcropping above the adjacent driveway. There is a trace of humor in the way the tinkle of a thin stream of water arcing into a stone basin near the door counterpoints the sound of the stream (fig. 9). Within is a small, softly lit foyer replete with a desk, a chair, and an Audubon bird print—hints of a domesticity in a woodland setting.

The photograph that William Hedrich made from the falls below Fallingwater in 1937 may have fixed the *image* of the building indelibly in the world's consciousness, but Wright tied the *experience* of the building inextricably to the sound of the stream. Given his childhood exposure to music under his father's tutelage; his five-year employment under Dankmar Adler,

FIG. 9. Fallingwater, entry area fountain. (Author's photograph, 2017)

a master acoustician, in the office of Adler & Sullivan; and a wealth of experience designing spaces for sound (music halls, theaters, churches, cinemas, and houses) in his own practice prior to 1935, the site conditions at Fallingwater offered Wright an exceptional opportunity to design the house to function with the sound of the stream instrumentally as he had with the water at the Taliesin dam. This was achieved structurally by stepping the three floor levels progressively higher and deeper into the living core and farther away from the sound. Grant Hildebrand has noted that the sound of the stream is "muted by the masses of concrete that intervene between the waterfall and the living spaces," but with the glazed hatch cover over the stairway down to the stream outfitted with three horizontally sliding panels, the sound can be adjusted manually and muted further by closing the terrace doors.[31] The cantilevered terraces—two each on the first and second floors and one on the third—afford views up and down the stream, but the principal cascade remains a tantalizing sound visible only to those willing to lean out over the parapet of the west terrace.

Neil Levine captured the phenomenological essence of Fallingwater definitively in this paragraph on the living room: "The importance of the fireplace and hatch in expressing Fallingwater's relationship to the site makes clear how much the experience of that association depends upon the reaction of all the senses, not just that of sight alone. The response to Fallingwater is multisensory and kinesthetic. The sound and feel of the water permeate everything and are everywhere, but its presence is especially felt underfoot. The connection to the stream is not a disembodied optical one. It is felt though the whole body, through all the senses."[32]

SYNTHESIZING SIGHT AND SOUND AT TALIESIN AND DALLAS

Having been immersed as a child in his father's classical music practice during which he grasped the idea that "a symphony is an edifice of sound," Wright recognized the analogous, mutually enhancing relationship between architecture and music.[33] Consequently, some form of musical ability and participation in regularly scheduled choral and orchestral performances were expected of applicants to the Taliesin Fellowship from its inception in 1932. Following a fire in 1933 at the Hillside Home School gymnasium that Wright had designed for his aunts Nell and Jane Lloyd Jones (1901–3), he created the Hillside Theater by inserting two tiers of six rows of seats in the form of a *V* that tightly embrace the orchestra pit and the stage (fig. 10).[34] There an audience of 180 hears musical performances enhanced by

FIG. 10. Taliesin, Hillside Theater interior, 1933. (Hillside Theater © Mark Hertzberg)

a sounding board over the stage, with a wooden floor over a void that enhances the room's sonic resonance. Owing to the *V* seating layout, each half of the audience observes the performance and the other half of the audience simultaneously—a mutually reinforcing synthesis of sight and sound that is amplified at a cognitive level by the experience of seeing a reflected version of itself.[35]

Sandra Shane-DuBow, an active member of the Taliesin Chorus, has observed: "I think the experience of hearing (and producing) music in the Hillside Theater is memorable because of its design for intimacy and for its quite good acoustics. In a way, those on stage shared the audience—the swiftly rising angle of audience seating brings the audience and the performers physically close and almost encloses the music between them. Having been part of the chorus and of the audience at different times, I can say that for me, the design of the space pulls the audience and the performers into the music. It is magical for both roles . . . both audience and performers are shaped by the space, its angles and its unimpeded and unique sight lines."[36]

Wright's efforts at the Hillside Theater coincided with his design for a "New Theatre" for Woodstock, New York, in 1931, a small, intimate house with 774 seats, some box seats, and a stage mechanized to speed the changing of scenery in order to compete with motion pictures, which had gained in popularity with the introduction of "talkies" in the late 1920s.[37] To en-

JACK QUINAN

hance the sound and the overall experiential quality of his "New Theater" concept, Wright eliminated the proscenium, projected the rounded stage apron well into a fan of three seating tiers separated by two aisles, and extended a prow-shaped sounding board with a flat soffit well out over the audience. The Woodstock project failed to materialize, as did a second version of the design for Hartford, Connecticut, in 1948. The "New Theater" was finally realized as the Kalita Humphreys Theater in Dallas in 1959, for which Wright took measures to ensure the building's acoustical quality (fig. 11). According to restoration architect Ann Abernathy, the exterior shell of the building was constructed of solid reinforced concrete to create an effective mass as a barrier to exterior sound, and most of the interior surfaces were of hard plaster balanced by sound-absorptive plaster for selected surfaces. The ceiling coffers were suspended and slightly sloped to increase the overhead acoustic reflections, thus substantially enhancing the acoustics of the theater. The slope of the floor was kept low to increase volume, and the walls were angled to control reverberation.[38] In the Dallas theater Wright replaced the proposed

FIG. II. Kalita Humphreys Theater, Dallas, Texas, 1955–59, auditorium before alterations. Photo 1960. (The Frank Lloyd Wright Foundation Archives [The Museum of Modern Art | Avery Architectural & Fine Arts Library, Columbia University, New York])

planar sounding board of the Woodstock and Hartford projects with a ceiling of suspended, 4-inch-thick concentric arcs of concrete faced with acoustical plaster that could be accessed from above by service catwalks. These ceiling arcs radiate outward from the stage in the form of a graphic rendition of sound waves—a mutually reinforcing synthesis of sight and sound intended to register on audiences subcognitively.

The effectiveness of Wright's acoustical design in the Kalita Humphreys Theater is difficult to evaluate today because the building has undergone significant alterations since the 1960s. The press notices from the time of opening leaned heavily toward the positive. Abernathy writes, "The Auditorium had an exceptional live acoustic and for the first two decades sound amplification was rarely used, even for children's voices."[39] Joseph Siry unearthed a newspaper article in which Charlton Heston, the film actor, claimed, "This is the most fabulous theater in the world," a comment that might be taken cum grano salis, given Heston's career as a screen actor.[40] Siry also cites an assessment of the theater written by Bernard Rosenblatt that accords well with Shane-DuBow's experience singing in the Hillside Theater: "Actors on Wright's stage felt especially exposed, with the audience curving nearly 270 degrees around the forestage. The cyclorama's rear curve close behind made actors feel that they were projected into the house. Constant awareness of the surrounding audience shaped the style of acting, so that players worked to convey their performances to audience members whose gaze they could see and who were looking at them from different directions. Actors thus felt more compelled to turn in space and to be more mobile on the stage. They and their directors had to work without a demarcating proscenium line. The actors tended to project their speech to other actors out through the audience, which felt itself to be part of the interaction rather than merely observing it."[41] In these few sentences Rosenblatt's (and Wright's) attention to sight, sound, and kinesthetics contribute to an emotional feeling experienced mutually by actors and audience.

ACCOMMODATING THE SENSES IN THE DESERT AT TALIESIN WEST

Wright was drawn to the Southwest by the sensual appeal of its colors, the angular geometries of the mountain and desert landscapes, and an atmosphere infused with the distinctive aromas of the desert flora. Yet the conditions at the Taliesin West site—an inhospitably hot, dry climate, with an abundant variety of spiny cacti, poisonous creatures, and a rubble-rock-strewn desert floor—presented exceptional challenges to Wright's accommodation of the senses through design. Those challenges were met with a complex of ten buildings on eight hundred acres of land on Maricopa Mesa, a swath of desert landscape that rises gradually from Paradise Valley to the foot of the MacDowell Mountain Range northeast of Scottsdale.

The degree to which the plan of Taliesin West, its interweaving of buildings and terraces, and its relationship to the desert, mountain, and valley vistas are attuned to human life is extraordinary, but it should be acknowledged that the complex was designed to be inhabited only from October to April when the average temperatures in central Arizona are in the 60-to-70-degree range, in contrast to the 94-to-105-degree average in the summer months.

Under Wright's direction his apprentices excavated the site to form two parallel terraces along a slightly northeast-by-southwest axis. The upper terrace accommodated the principal living and working spaces—the workshop, Wright's office and study, the drafting studio and drawing vault, the kitchen, dining room, two residential rooms, and the private wing of the Wrights' L-shaped living quarters.[42] The east-west axis is intersected perpendicularly by a north-south axis that includes the social wing of the Wrights' quarters, the "kiva" (here, a single-story rectangular, desert-masonry building for film projection), and one portion of the U-shaped apprentice court that is behind the kiva.[43] The whole complex is situated on a 16-by-16-foot grid that is energized by the 45-degree rotation of three buildings—the workshop, Wright's office, and the apprentice court passageway—and by the triangular form of the sunken garden that defines the lower terrace.

Movement about Taliesin West involves all of the senses working in harmony, heightened by the unfamiliar structural forms and materials, the desert environment, and the brilliance of sunshine approximately 300 days a year on average in central Arizona. Wright's 1938 plan includes 12 flights of stairs on the site comprised of 3 to 15 steps per flight that reflect his manipulation of the 4-foot disparity between the upper and lower terraces and a third plateau above the upper terrace. Because the drafting studio straddles the two main terraces, its principal entrances from the pergola on the upper terrace are 4 feet higher than the lower terrace onto which the adjacent dining and conference rooms project, and the space of the adjoining drafting room opens onto a 12-step, half pyramid bearing petroglyph-covered boulders and overlooking the pool and garden of the lower terrace.

Wright designed the principal access road to Taliesin West to approach from the south in the form of an arc to a point at which the building complex—crowned by the drafting studio—is arrayed in full. Thereafter the road becomes arrow-straight, provides a raking view of the building ensemble, and now terminates at a parking area at the west end of the site where the eastward lean of a 20-foot, 6-inch-high desert masonry light tower directs them toward the point of entry a short distance away—the first of numerous encounters in which the forms, textures, and organization of the buildings, monuments, and artifacts function together with pathways, flights of stairs, and vistas to direct and invigorate the experience of the site.

At the entrance three steps lead down into a small foyer-like space that is open to the sky and defined by battered desert masonry knee walls and the outward-leaning reverse batter of the north wall of Wright's office. Following the long, gradual ascent to Taliesin West by automobile, this short descent onto the surface of its principal terrace conveys a clear sense of having arrived at Wright's oasis domain. Visitors experiencing anticipation and compression in the confined space are quickly impelled forward onto a plaza dominated by the drafting studio (fig. 12). The attached drawing vault and pergola, situated on the two levels of terracing, are enhanced by knee walls and by the horizontal linear scorings of the walls of the drawing vault. The roof pitch of the drafting studio and the playful decorative treatment of its wooden sun shades further stimulate curiosity.

Three pathways fan outward from the entry plaza—one southward to the prow-like point of the lower terrace that overlooks Paradise Valley; a second, westward, offering a telescopic view along the pergola and thoroughfare that represent the site's principal axis; and a third, northward, leading to the plateau of desert contained by the 4-foot retaining wall that forms the north boundary of the living-working terrace. The two principal paths from the

FIG. 12. Taliesin West, Scottsdale, Arizona, begun 1938, entry area terrace. (Author's photograph, 2012)

office onto the site form two sides of the triangle that shapes the lower terrace and provides a perambulatory circuit (akin to Laurent's garden path) that encompasses the working and living core of the site and its sunken garden.

Visitors traversing the long, straight path leading from the office plaza to the prow of the lower terrace experience a bounty of sensations along the way. The path begins on the hard concrete surface of the upper terrace but changes to gravel, a shift that registers as both a crunching sound and as a tactile sensation to the feet, just beyond a flight of three steps with 3¼-inch risers and 17-inch treads that allow an easy, gliding stride.[44] The alignment of these steps at 45 degrees to the path of movement provides greater flexibility to the depth of the treads while subtly directing the visitor's attention to the left toward the sunken grass lawn, triangular pool, and clusters of yucca of the lower terrace—the antithesis of the harsh desert landscape just beyond the retaining wall to the right. While continuing along the gravel path it becomes apparent that the desert is gradually receding as the 16-inch height of the retaining wall at the entrance increases to nearly 5 feet at the vista point as the land slopes downward. There, with Taliesin West behind and the desert below, a visitor is immersed in the expansive valley and mountain vista, the aromatic desert atmosphere, and the occasional sounds of quail, cactus wrens, and flickers. Wright described the site as "like [being] on top of the world looking over the universe at sunrise or sunset," but the experience also evokes Emerson's passage in *Nature,* well known to Wright: "Standing on the bare ground—my head bathed by the blithe air and uplifted into infinite space—all mean egotism vanishes."[45]

The access route from the entrance to the main thoroughfare alongside the drafting room proceeds indirectly, up a flight of six low-rising steps, past a bubbling, circle-in-square water feature (a welcoming reminder of the significance of water to life in the desert), through three turns that include pivoting around a large stone bearing a Hohokam petroglyph, and on into the pergola (fig. 13). In contrast to the transcendental implications of the path to the vista point, the thoroughfare along the axis of the upper terrace is village-like and abounds with carefully considered features—the shelters, paths, walls, doors, steps, water, and artifacts—that begin in the relatively cool confines of the pergola, where the pace of movement is measured by the rhythmic occurrence of the eight pairs of angled wooden brace-beams supporting the horizontal beams overhead.[46]

On the left (north) side of the thoroughfare lies the 4-foot wall that retains the uppermost terrace, a saguaro, a narrow linear garden of desert plants and flowers, a plinth-mounted bronze Chinese dragon, steps leading to the uppermost terrace and to the flat roof of the kiva, and the kiva itself. To the right (south) side, abutting the drafting studio, are the two-story,

FIG. 13. Taliesin West, pergola. (Author's photograph, 2018)

double-battered walls of the kitchen and belvedere, a Chinese ceramic relief, a stairway to the guest balcony, and a doorway to the kitchen, followed by a loggia and a wide breezeway that frames a view across the lower terrace to Paradise Valley. Beyond the breezeway rises the two-story-high north wall of the Wrights' living quarters and the adjoining 23-foot, 4-inch-high water tower that marks the south extremity of the thoroughfare (fig. 14). The pathway between the kiva to the north and the Wrights' quarters to the south is bisected by an elongated hexagonal pool and fountain surmounted by a desert masonry bridge that connects the two buildings (fig. 15).

Here, at the crossroads of Taliesin West, the unifying presence of desert masonry construction warrants attention. Wright's innovative method involved gathering, sorting, and fitting variously sized pieces of sun-baked volcanic talus stone from nearby Maricopa Hill between parallel, upright sheets of wooden formwork in which the stones' outward-facing flat surfaces are surrounded and held in place in a matrix of dry concrete inserted from behind.[47] Smoothly rounded, fist-sized stones were inserted into the formwork to block the downward migration of the newly poured concrete over the surfaces of the talus stones. The process by which the formwork-flattened, ragged-edged smears of concrete frame the rich, earth-hued surfaces of the larger stones and the round stone inserts conveys a crudeness of execution that belies the construction of these agglomerations of

JACK QUINAN

FIG. 14. Taliesin West, main thoroughfare, showing kiva on left and the Wright's quarters and water tower on right. (Author's photograph, 2011)

FIG. 15. Taliesin West, bridge connecting the Wrights' quarters and kiva. (Author's photograph, 2011)

stone and concrete as a tour de force of the engineering of structures that bridge, cantilever, batter, and taper across the site in ways that seem both timeless and modern. These desert masonry structures engage the senses in a particular way: eyes scanning the wall surfaces apprehend the tactile differences between the coarseness of the concrete and the varied textures, colors, and shapes of the stones—a perceptual process called "memory touch" in which the viewer recognizes the tactile quality of the surfaces based upon remembered experiences of similar materials and textures.[48] According to recent neuroscience-based research, an empathetic viewer would "feel" the weight of the larger stones and may even vicariously experience (or wonder about) the struggle to maneuver them into place in the narrow confines of the formwork.[49]

The centrality of the drafting studio to the mission at Taliesin West is apparent in its size as the largest of the original buildings, its central location on the site, its unusual shed-roof design, and its function as a place for maximizing working efficiency in a desert environment. On a 32-by-96-foot plan, the studio was framed up with thirteen "staple-shaped" redwood "trusses," each tilted so that one end bears upon the building's 4-foot-high south wall and its north end bears upon one of the thirteen, 8-foot-high stone piers that elevate the north face to a height of 14 feet (fig. 16).[50] Sloped at a 28-degree angle, the roof was originally enclosed by the insertion of canvas panels in the interstices between the truss beams. The space was further closed partially at its west end where the drawing vault abuts the drawing studio and at the east end by the kitchen wall and fireplace, but it was otherwise open narrowly across the south elevation, broadly to the north, and partially at the building's west end to allow for the free movement of air throughout the space.[51] The north and south openings were originally closed by sheets of canvas while the triangular opening to the west alongside the drawing vault could be manipulated to deflect sunlight by means of an apparatus of colorfully decorated folding wooden panels and stays first seen at the point of entrance to the site.

The drafting studio was designed to take advantage of the location on the slope that rises from Paradise Valley's 1,275-foot elevation to heights among the MacDowell peaks in excess of 3,000 feet, conditions that cause day-to-night fluctuations in the airflow. The daytime warming of the mountain slopes causes air to rise, while in nighttime the slopes cool and the air becomes denser, causing it to flow downslope.[52] By opening the tall north elevation of the drafting room to the cool mountain breeze the space was cooled passively while the thermal mass of the battered desert masonry walls also retained heat for the cool desert evenings, supplemented, when neces-

FIG. 16. Taliesin West, south terminals of original drafting studio trusses. (Carol M. Highsmith Archive, Prints and Photographs Division, Library of Congress)

sary, by the fireplace. Here Wright incorporated the movement of air into the design of the drafting studio much as he incorporated the movement of water into the design of the Kaufmann house.

In contrast to the drafting rooms in the skyscrapers familiar to Wright in Chicago in which the building's structural grid dictated a uniform ceiling height and drafting tables were daylit by tall windows, Wright brought to the drafting studio at Taliesin West a predilection for a Gesamtkunstwerk with particular attention to those senses involved directly in architectural drafting—vision, the kinesthetic sense, and a thermoceptive sensitivity to temperature and humidity. The canvas roof panels admitted a quality of light that was said to be ideal for drafting.[53] The largest expanse of open wall surface faced north, away from direct sunlight most of the day and was further shielded by vertical wooden fins. The interior of the drafting studio opened directly onto the pergola and above that—through a linear sequence of large openings—toward the MacDowell Range. The narrow exposure to the sun on the building's south elevation was shaded by the "fin-like," "C-clamp"-shaped termination of each beam.[54] These elements functioned partially as structure, providing brackets that supported lapped boards that blocked direct sunlight.[55] But they are also a variant form of the "whirling arrow" logo that Wright adapted from a Hohokam petroglyph found near the site.[56]

To allay the pressures of the intense work activity in the drafting studio Wright provided amenities that domesticated the space—a grand piano, the warmth and atmosphere of the fireplace, and the smells and sounds of cooking wafting from the adjacent kitchen. The north-south orientation of the drafting studio offered sites for morning and afternoon tea breaks by and around the pyramid overlooking the pool and lawn in the sunken garden and Paradise Valley to the south, while the building's north elevation provided direct access to the pergola through four sets of double doors above which the large unglazed window openings afforded views of the MacDowell Range constantly shifting under the play of sun and shadow.

Despite the centrality of the drafting studio to the life of several thousand Taliesin Fellows over the twenty-one years with Wright, there is a dearth of experiential written commentary about it; hence we turn to the recollections of Curtis Besinger, the apprentice who supervised construction of the Cabaret at Taliesin West as an experimental proxy.[57]

THE CABARET AT TALIESIN WEST

While Wright's attentiveness to the senses is evident in every commission, the Cabaret Theater is distinguished by a concentration involving *all* of the senses. It was designed in 1950 as a site for the enjoyment of music, film, skits, and dining—a place of multisensory pleasures intended to foster camaraderie among the Taliesin Fellows, to entertain guests, and to provide respite from the rigors of the work routines that reached a high pitch in 1951. Modest in size—94 feet long, 24 feet wide, and 10 feet high—the Cabaret is constructed of desert masonry and is partially submerged into the desert floor (figs. 17, 18). The building's functional zones and connecting features are designated on the plan as the main entrance at the south, which opens into a foyer with adjacent utility spaces that include a small food service area to which dinners for up to seventy-five people were delivered from the main kitchen. Near the north end of the building a dining platform with hexagonal table and chairs for the Wrights and their guests stood near an inglenook and fireplace.[58] A film projection booth terminates the building's north end. Between the dining platform and the foyer and utility spaces there originally were 11 tiers of 88 seats positioned at a 45-degree angle to the stage.[59] These are accessed by a ramp that descends from the dining

FIG. 17. Taliesin West, Cabaret Theater, 1950–51. Photograph by Ezra Stoller, 1950. (© Ezra Stoller/ Esto)

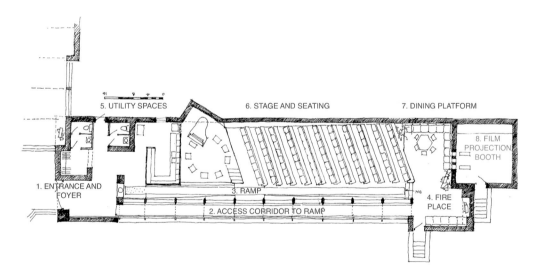

FIG. 18. Cabaret Theater, plan, drawn by Curtis Besinger. (Curtis Besinger Collection, MS 241 D, folder 2.51.a oversize; Kenneth Spencer Research Library, University of Kansas Libraries)

platform level to the stage and film screen. Beyond the stage level the ramp ascends back to the utility area.

On Saturday evenings, following a cocktail party in the Wrights' "Garden Room," the Taliesin apprentices entered through the main door, traversed the gallery leading to the fireplace inglenook and dining platform, made a hair-pin left turn, and descended the ramp to the tiers of seats, the backs of which were equipped with a continuous, narrow counter for dining.

Sensory awareness at the Cabaret began with the sound of a large Chinese gong that signaled the start of an evening's events.[60] Vision takes over at the building's entrance where battered desert-masonry pylons frame bright red double doors with Chinese escutcheon plates—marvels of intricate gold and enamel metalwork—that invite close visual inspection and a firm grasp of the hand. Just inside the foyer a bust of Buddha, encircled in an oculus of desert masonry, radiates serenity amid the sounds and aromas of the adjacent food service area (fig. 19). Just beyond the foyer, a gallery leads toward the rear of the building where the distinctive smell of a mesquite fire sweetens and warms the air. The angled roof braces that line the gallery's inner side define broad openings that allow those entering and those already seated to observe one another, to make an entrance, perhaps, or to locate a friend.

FIG. 19. Cabaret Theater, view from foyer, showing access corridor on right. Photograph by Ezra Stoller, 1950. (© Ezra Stoller/Esto)

FIG. 20. Cabaret Theater, view of auditorium from access ramp. Photograph by Ezra Stoller, 1950. (© Ezra Stoller/Esto)

The 11 tiers of seats, the stage, and the film screen constitute the raison d'être of the Cabaret where Wright intensified the experiential by synthesizing multiple sensory-affecting design features. The seating tiers, for example, are aligned 15 degrees from the building's long axis, affording the audience a clear view of the stage while compelling them slightly to rotate their upper bodies in a modest kinesthetic commitment to the performance. Wright explained the reason for this configuration in a talk to his apprentices: "the ¾ view of a performance, of a person, of anything almost in life is greatly to the good if you take a ¾ view instead of a flat front view. Now the flat front view has characterized all the audience rooms that you know anything about. And here there is no one in the house that has anything more than a ¾ view. And the performance itself is cross the 45."[61]

Sound quality in the Cabaret is intensified by a void excavated beneath a wooden stage floor and an acoustics-enhancing "gash" (Wright's term) in the west wall that housed a baby grand piano.[62] Wright met the acoustical challenge of the building's all-desert-masonry construction intuitively. A latitudinal section of the building shows that the walls lean outward on the west side and fold inward on the east side in order to obviate the standing

FIG. 21. Cabaret Theater, view of auditorium. Photograph by Michael Sutton, ca. 1951. (The Frank Lloyd Wright Foundation Archives [The Museum of Modern Art | Avery Architectural & Fine Arts Library, Columbia University, New York])

sonic waves that occur in a more conventional, shoe-box room configuration (fig. 20). On the east face, the exterior consists of a low, outwardly tilted wall desert masonry from which the inward-leaning structural piers alternate with plywood flaps that can be adjusted to control light, air, and sound in the building.[63]

Besinger noted the Cabaret's "built-in forced perspective. . . . Due to the slope of the side walls the room is wider at the ceiling than it is at the floor. And due to the slope of the floor from the rear toward the front the floor becomes narrower at the front. This built-in convergence augments the normal visual convergence of parallel lines."[64] Thus the unconventional shape of the room made sight and sound mutually enhancing (fig. 21).[65]

With the completion of the Cabaret in 1951 Wright directed that six Chinese paintings on silk be mounted on wooden panels and attached to the ceiling with wooden dowels and brackets, which were taken down in the 1960s.[66] Wright described his treatment of the Cabaret ceiling "like putting tension in the head of a drum" and added, "the ceiling was a little hard and a little bare so I put those free-standing strips running across the ceiling— across the sound, much as you'd tighten a violin string on a fiddle. Now, just what they do, I don't know. But they do something. Because the sound was very much more resonant after that."[67] In this instance Wright, again seeking a synthesis, employed pictorial art objects in the manipulation of sound.

Classic European, Russian, and American films became an integral part of the Saturday evenings at Taliesin beginning in the early 1930s. When the Cabaret was completed, Wright, fascinated by the idea that sound could be made visible, had the film projector altered so that the audience would see the soundtrack along with the film. What was the experience of the Cabaret like? Besinger characterized it as "simple, but not uninteresting, . . . a clear architectural lesson in how a building that did not have an interesting exterior—could be made into a place that was deeply satisfying to be in."[68] As Besinger implied, the Cabaret is modest in comparison to Wright's many more prominent commissions, but in its evident attention to all the senses and the frequency with which two or more senses are synthesized, it, along with the other examples treated here, suggests that there is more to discover in Wright's work through the methods of phenomenology.

NOTES

1. Frank Lloyd Wright to Darwin D. Martin, letter of 13 October 1905: "No quarter, no! not until D.D.M. [Darwin D. Martin] has the most perfect thing of its kind in the world,—a domestic symphony, true, vital, comfortable." Wright-Martin Papers, University at Buffalo Archives, Buffalo, New York.

   When Wright visited the Hanna house just after they had moved in, he said, "Why, it's more beautiful than I had imagined; we have created a symphony here." Paul and Jean Hanna, *Frank Lloyd Wright's Hanna House: The Clients' Report* (New York: Architectural History Foundation, and Cambridge, Mass.: MIT Press, 1981), 84.

2. Edmund Husserl, *Logische Untersuchungen* [Logical Investigations], 2 vols. (Halle, Germany: M. Niemeyer, 1900, 1901). Phenomenology was introduced into the history and theory of architecture by Christian Norberg-Schulz in *Intentions in Architecture* (Cambridge, Mass.: MIT Press, 1967).

3. Maurice Merleau-Ponty, *Phenomenology of Perception* (London: Routledge & Keegan Paul, 1962), 459.

4. Wright wrote about the impact of his mother, his father, and his mother's family on him in *An Autobiography* (New York: Duell, Sloan & Pearce, 1943), 3–60. Through the extensive archival research of biographers Robert C. Twombly (*Frank Lloyd Wright: His Life and His Architecture*); Brendan Gill (*Many Masks: A Life of Frank Lloyd Wright*), Meryle Secrest (*Frank Lloyd Wright: A Biography*), and others, the record of Wright's formative years has been expanded and clarified.

5. Frank Lloyd Wright, "In the Cause of Architecture," *Architectural Record* 23 (March 1908): 156–57.

6. Wright, "In the Cause of Architecture—Second Paper," *Architectural Record* 35 (May 1914): 406.

7. Frank Lloyd Wright, "An Organic Architecture," in Bruce Brooks Pfeiffer, ed., *Frank Lloyd Wright: Collected Writings* (New York: Rizzoli, 1993), 3:302.

8. The twenty-five houses on the block of Summit Avenue with the Barton house are rectangular in plan with their long axes aligned to fit 25-by-100-foot lots. The majority of these houses are accessed by a front walk that leads directly from the street to steps, a porch, and a front door. Typically the porch roof coincides with the line demarking the second floor of the house. The Barton house differs in that it occupies two lots and is accessed by a walk that leads toward the porch extended to the south and requires a right-angle turn to the stairs that lead to a landing where another right-angle turn brings one to, and through, the front door.

9. Darwin D. Martin to Isabelle R. Martin, letter of 14 August 1903, Wright-Martin Papers.

10. Two of the built-in cabinets contain a combination of radiators and shelves front and back.

11. Paul Rodaway, in *Sensuous Geographies: Body, Sense, and Place* (Abingdon-on-Thames, U.K.: Routledge, 1994), 48–54, wrote of "Global Touch," which is generally passive, as in the movement of the body through space or water; "Reach Touch," such as the everyday intentional uses of hands, arms, and fingers; and "Imagined Touch," which involves experience rooted in memory.

12. The horizontal wall molding is repeated throughout the second floor of the Barton house.

13. From a seated position facing west in the living room the line of the north-south beams that define the hall can be seen through the south-facing living room window to continue in the line of the edge of the porch roof. The corresponding line of the kitchen roof is not visible from within the house, however.

14. The second-floor corridor opens onto two small bedrooms on the south side and a bathroom and the stairwell on the north.

15. The second-floor corner casement windows swing open left and right away from a structural post.

16. These observations are based upon the year (1994–95) that the author lived in the house.

17. The house was originally outfitted with a fan in the attic and a trap door in the master bedroom closet ceiling that drew warm air out of the house during the summer.

18. The author moved into the Barton house during a hot August day in 1994. The house was not air-conditioned, but when all the casement windows in Laura's bedroom were swung fully open, cool air filled the room late in the evening.

19. Wright designed a built-in sideboard and shelving, light sconces, and radiator enclosures for the house. A freestanding dining table and eight side chairs are now in the collections of the Minneapolis Institute of Art.

    The author contacted Barton descendants by mail during the 1990s in search of some insight as to their or their parents' experience of living in the house, which they rented from Darwin Martin. The respondents rebuffed the inquiry with a vague generalization to the effect that the Bartons were nice, simple people.

20. Regarding human favorability toward curved forms in architecture see Oshin Vartanian et al., "Impact of Contour on Aesthetic Judgments and Approach-Avoidance Decisions in Architecture," *Proceedings of the National Academy of Sciences of the United States of America* 110, suppl. 2 (18 June 2013): 10446–53.

Concerning the impact of nature on humans see Rachel Kaplan, Stephen Kaplan, and Robert L. Ryan, *With People in Mind: Design and Management of Everyday Nature* (New York: Island Press, 1998). See also Rachel Kaplan and Stephen Kaplan, *The Experience of Nature: A Psychological Perspective* (Cambridge: Cambridge University Press, 1999).

21. The author is grateful for an interview with Jerry Heinzcroth at the Laurent house on 5 October 2015 and follow-up correspondence. He graciously agreed to take me about the house in Laurent's wheelchair.

22. Wright stated: "These are all experiments, and everything that goes around on this place ought to be an experiment," in a talk to the Taliesin Fellowship about the design of the Hillside Theater, transcribed from a recording made 25 July 1954, reel #103, Frank Lloyd Wright Foundation Archives, Avery Architectural & Fine Arts Library, Columbia University, and Museum of Modern Art, New York (hereafter FLWFA).

23. Kathryn A. Smith and Donald G. Kalec, "Fuermann Photographs Taliesin," *Journal of Organic Architecture and Design* 6:1 (2018); pls. 15 and 16 illustrate the Taliesin dam as built in 1911; pl. 38 illustrates the dam as rebuilt ca. 1926–28. Smith has also written incisively about the dam at Taliesin in the context of Wright's landscape and in the larger context of Wright's frequent uses of waterfalls in his work in "A Beat of the Rhythmic Clock of Nature: Wright's Waterfall Buildings," in Robert McCarter, ed., *On and By Frank Lloyd Wright: A Primer of Architectural Principles* (London: Phaidon, 2005), 216–31.

24. Jian Kang addresses the positive impact of water on humans in "Soundscape and Movement," in Peter Blundell Jones and Mark Meagher, eds, *Architecture and Movement: The Dynamic Experience of Buildings and Landscapes* (London: Routledge, 2014), 124.

25. The author showed a photograph of the dam to Liz Phillips, a sound artist based in New York, who immediately recognized its aural implications. To verify and experience what Phillips observed, the author listened to the sound of the dam at Taliesin at various positions from its left to its right side in October 2018.

26. During their occupancy of the house, the Kaufmanns drove to it on an access road leading to the driveway alongside the entrance corridor where they disembarked.

27. The pathway to Fallingwater's entrance comprises an irregular arrangement of walls that form the 20-foot-long space. The north wall is 8½ feet long, and the south expanse is 24 feet long; they are staggered so that the north opening onto the driveway is narrow, while the south opening onto the terrace is twice as wide, with the result that the corridor feels airy until it narrows near the door.

28. Wright referred to the protruding slabs of sandstone as "stick-outs," according to Donald Hoffmann in *Frank Lloyd Wright's Fallingwater: The House and Its History* (New York: Dover, 1993), 33.

29. Harry Francis Mallgrave, *Architecture and Embodiment: The Implications of the New Sciences and Humanities for Design* (London: Routledge, 2013), 121–39, recounts how the discovery of mirror neurons by Vittorio Gallese and his associates at the University of Parma in the 1990s provided a scientific basis to the pioneering empathy theories of Robert Vischer, Theodor Lipps, and others.

30. Grant Hildebrand, *Origins of Architectural Pleasure* (Berkeley: University of California Press, 1999), 51–88, examines the psychological characteristics of exploration, enticement, and peril that make architecture pleasurable. Included

among an international selection of examples are Wright's Kaufmann, Hanna, Melvin Maxwell Smith, and Tracey houses.

31. Grant Hildebrand, *The Wright Space: Pattern & Meaning in Frank Lloyd Wright's Houses* (Seattle: University of Washington Press, 1991), 104.

32. Neil Levine, *The Architecture of Frank Lloyd Wright* (Princeton: Princeton University Press, 1996), 249. His chapter on Fallingwater in that volume and his "To Hear Fallingwater Is to See It in Time," in Lynda Waggoner, ed., *Fallingwater* (New York: Rizzoli, 2011), 188–215, reflect an unsurpassed knowledge of Wright and modernism with a phenomenological reading of Fallingwater that rivals and enhances the firsthand experience of the building.

33. Wright, *An Autobiography,* 13.

34. For an eyewitness account of the fire and reconstruction of the Hillside Theater, see Frances Nemtin, "The Hillside Theater at Taliesin," in *3 by Wright* (by the author, 2008), unpaginated. The *V* of the seating tiers is not symmetrical; there are six rows of seats on the north side of the space and three on the south.

35. Mallgrave, *Architecture and Embodiment,* 121–39.

36. Sandra Shane-DuBow to author, email, 19 April 2019.

37. Joseph M. Siry, "Modern Architecture for Dramatic Art: Frank Lloyd Wright's 'New Theater,' 1931–2009," *Art Bulletin* 96 (June 2014), 213–37.

38. Ann Abernathy to author, email and attachment, 23 February 2015, "Notes on the Kalita Humphreys Theater (KHT)—Sound Quality."

39. Abernathy email.

40. Charlton Heston quoted in "New Dallas Theatre Center Praised for Design, Ideas," *San Angelo Standard-Times,* 27 December 1959. According to Joseph M. Siry, "Modern Architecture for Dramatic Art," 232.

41. Siry, "Modern Architecture for Dramatic Art," n. 126, cites Bernard Sheldon Rosenblatt, *The Dallas Theater Center of the Kalita Humphreys Theater: A Frank Lloyd Wright Theater in Theory and Practice* (Stanford, Calif.: Department of Speech and Drama, Stanford University, 1962).

42. Wright's office and study building straddles two terrace levels: the office proper is three steps below the point of entry and six steps below the level of the upper terrace while the attached study maintains that same floor level because its foundation was excavated into the upper terrace level. By having a visitor walk *down* to the office level Wright inverts the then commonplace western pattern of entry that involves mounting steps to a front door. This, together with the sense of envelopment by desert masonry walls, engages the visitor with an unusual combination of spectacle and intimacy.

43. Curtis Besinger, *Working with Mr. Wright: What It Was Like* (New York: Cambridge University Press, 1995), 76, wrote of visiting the Hopi villages of Walpi and Oraibi, where kivas were numerous, on the annual migration of the Taliesin Fellowship from Arizona to Wisconsin.

44. For an excellent analysis of a landscape designed for perambulation, see Robin Veder, "Walking through Dumbarton Oaks: Early Twentieth-Century Bourgeois Bodily Techniques and Kinesthetic Experience of Landscape," *Journal of the Society of Architectural Historians* 72 (March 2013): 5–27.

45. Wright, *An Autobiography,* 453; Ralph Waldo Emerson, *Nature* (Boston: James Munroe, 1836), 13.

46. James J. Gibson, *The Ecological Approach to Visual Perception* (Hillsdale, N.J.: Lawrence Erlbaum, 1986).

47. The wooden forms that comprised either side of the formwork were parallel but were canted inward or outward to create battered walls. Small round stones were often inserted into the desert masonry molds to block the flow of concrete over the colorful flat outer faces of the talus stones.

48. Rodaway, *Sensuous Geographies,* 54, defines "imagined touch" as "a haptic experience rooted in the memory and expectation."

49. In *Architecture and Embodiment*, Mallgrave traces the development of empathy theory from Robert Fischer's intuitive dissertation, "On the Optical Sense of Form" (1873), in which he coined the term *einfuhlung* (empathy or, more literally, "feeling itself into") to the scientific studies of the brain in the 1990s by a group of neurophysiologists at the University of Parma led by Leonardo Fugazzi that have revealed the role of mirror neurons in animal and human behavior.

50. Besinger, *Working with Mr. Wright,* wrote, "the wood trusses (they were not trusses although we did call them that!)" (47).

51. Unlike a drafting space in a tall urban building in which the floor and ceiling are parallel and the air is static, the sloping north-south section of the drafting studio captured the naturally occurring air movement of the site enhanced by the movement of air from the low to the higher regions within the space.

52. Anthony Puttnam, who joined the Taliesin Fellowship in the early 1950s, spoke to the author in 2010 of the sound of an air mass that formed at the base of the MacDowell Range and moved down the hillslope over Taliesin West and on down to Scottsdale. He said you could hear it moving. It was not a sand spout. He was not sure what caused it.

53. John Howe, "Reflections of Taliesin," *Northwest Architect,* July–August, 1969, 26–30, 63.

54. Donald Aitken pointed out in a presentation at Taliesin West in March 1987 that the location of these windows high on the north side of the drafting studio carried light deeper into its southern side. Neil Levine employs the terms "fin-like" and "C-clamps" to describe the drafting studio beam-ends in *The Architecture of Frank Lloyd Wright,* 270.

55. The "C-clamps" that terminate the lower end of each beam are formed of two right-angled members, the second of which is carved to fit against the contours of the masonry wall. The weight of the truss at the lower end is carried internally by a secondary angled beam.

56. Levine, *The Architecture of Frank Lloyd Wright,* 279–80. These squared beam ends continue a theme derived from a petroglyph found near the site and incorporated into the Taliesin West logo in the form of a metal sign on Shea Boulevard pointing toward Taliesin West and affixed to the leaning entrance pylon that points toward the entrance to the site. Although the "C-clamps" appear to grasp the foundation wall, the beams are supported by interior angled braces.

57. Besinger, *Working with Mr. Wright,* 208–10.

58. The Wrights and their guests entered the Cabaret by way of stairs and a doorway adjacent to the inglenook and fireplace.

59. Although the plan drawn by Curtis Besinger (fig. 5.18) depicts 88 seats in the tiered section of the Cabaret, in a photograph from the 1960s (fig. 5.21), there are

69 seats. Subsequently every other tier of seats was removed to create spaces for wooden tables and metal chairs.

60. Wright spoke about the gong during a talk to the Taliesin Fellowship recorded as "F.LL.W. Reel #18A (1 April 1951), 4, FLWFA: " the only things you haven't seen here are those Chinese things. . . . And we got a gong in San Francisco that just about hangs between those two posts . . . You don't have to hit it with anything but your fist. You strike it with your fist and it will roar like no lion could ever roar."

61. See Wright's talk to the Taliesin Fellowship recorded on 25 July 1954, FLWFA, concerning the V-shape seating of the Hillside Theater, but also applicable to the Cabaret.

62. Wright, talk to the Taliesin Fellowship, 25 July 1954: "Now another feature of the house [the Hillside Theater] you have wondered why we made the wooden floor over the stage. THAT wooden floor is like the top of this table, . . . [Wright raps on it] In other words, it's a drum-head. Now we found that so successful out at the Cabaret theater at Taliesin West, that I resolved to try it here on a larger scale. So this whole theater floor is as sensitive as a drumhead. Now when you play the piano, when you play the cello, when you speak, it has the quality that the cello itself has—a musical instrument itself has, you see. It has resonance without reverberation."

63. The flaps were originally of canvas that dried out quickly in the desert climate.

64. Besinger, *Working with Mr. Wright,* 210.

65. Wright, "Talks to the Fellowship," F.L.L.W. Reel #18A (1 April 1951), 5, FLWFA: Wright explained the design of the Cabaret by harking back to his experience with Adler & Sullivan in the 1880s: "Dankmar Adler's theory was that the trumpet was good for the pattern of the house [theater auditorium]. And all his houses, if you'll remember, were just like this [the Cabaret], you see. The stage and where you spoke were exactly like putting your voice at the nexus of the trumpet."

66. The dowels, brackets, and mounted Chinese paintings have been replaced by strings of tiny white light bulbs.

67. Wright, "Talks to the Fellowship," 1 April 1951, 8.

68. Besinger, *Working with Mr. Wright,* 210.

RICHARD LONGSTRETH

The Impact of the Work of Frank Lloyd Wright (and Louis Sullivan) on Historic Preservation Practice in the United States, 1950–1980

The buildings of the nation's most celebrated architect, who helped lay the essential foundations for Modern architecture worldwide, and the rise of a coherent national movement to preserve valued historic buildings and landscapes in a systematic fashion may seem like an unlikely coupling. Wright disparaged most of the architecture that preservationists strove to protect up into the mid-twentieth century. Like many architects, he even regarded buildings that he admired, especially his own, as work to be modified, sometimes transformed, with changing conditions over time, not necessarily as things to be conserved for future generations to appreciate. Ironically, under the circumstances, a number of the buildings Wright designed played key roles in the struggle to propel historic preservation as a substantial and widespread practice between 1950, when the need for this endeavor was beginning to be understood in ever-broadening circles, and 1980, by which time a national program was firmly established, involving myriad parties in the public and private sectors alike.[1]

Efforts to save examples of Wright's work helped define the scope of this movement in terms of its embrace of architectural design as an important attribute of historical significance, as well as preservationists' concern for Modern architecture and work of the recent past more broadly.[2] Wright's buildings also had an impact on strategies for protection, methods of interpretation, and the conceptual parameters for restoration in this realm. Finally, the stature of Wright and his work helped define a distinctive American architectural heritage. Although Wright's legacy is the principal focus of this study, I include several buildings by Adler & Sullivan, two of them occupied by Wright in early stages of his career, to offer a more complete picture of how what was heralded as Modern architecture affected both outlook and practice in the preservation field.

While Wright's views might seem antithetical to the objectives of the historic preservation movement, the relationship is more complex. He certainly had no interest in preservation as it was practiced during most of his lifetime—as a pursuit to safeguard antiquities and in many cases to restore them to a state they had not known for a century or more. Wright does not seem to have shared preservationists' concerns for safeguarding the salient physical characteristics of historic buildings. Even with some of his own works Wright's remarks could seem callous from a preservation perspective. When he learned of the impending demise of his Midway Gardens on Chicago's South Side (1913–14) a mere fifteen years after it opened, Wright apparently remarked that the complex had been so denatured by alterations that it was not worth saving. Some twenty years later the threat to the Larkin Company Administration Building in Buffalo (1902–6), one of his most important nonresidential projects, caused Wright to respond that it had had a useful life and deserved a respectable death.[3]

As with most architects, when Wright was asked to do new work on one of his existing buildings, his approach was to design in his current manner. This was manifested in the remodeling of the Moore house in Oak Park (1895), an unusually historicizing scheme for Wright even at that early date. The alterations he designed in 1923 after a fire destroyed many portions of the dwelling were idiosyncratic, acknowledging its original Tudor-inspired character but reflecting at least a few of the profound changes that had occurred in his work over the intervening quarter century. An even longer time period had elapsed when he drew plans for altering the interior of the house he designed for Isabel Roberts in River Forest, Illinois (1908), in 1955— a remodeling that is generally considered to have had a detrimental effect on the original.[4] Wright's offers to work on adapting the Robie house, discussed in Daniel Bluestone's contribution to this volume, and to restore the theater in the Auditorium Building, discussed in the text below, might well have entailed modernization as much as retrieval of their original designs.[5]

Wright's own residences in Oak Park, Illinois; Spring Green, Wisconsin; and Scottsdale, Arizona, were, of course, subjected to continual changes, in part to address new requirements, but also to test new ideas not necessarily tied to programmatic needs. The addition of Wright's office ("studio") in Oak Park (1897–98) provided a striking, even jarring, contrast to the adjacent family residence in part owing to its substantially different function, but also because it came at a time when the architect was pursuing a radically new direction in his work. The changes made at the many iterations of Taliesin and at Taliesin West, on the other hand, are far less obvious as such to the point that the overall appearance of both is far more one of a coherent entity than an accretive one.[6] Wright's Research Tower (1943, 1947–50)

RICHARD LONGSTRETH

addition to the S. C. Johnson Company Administration Building in Racine, Wisconsin (1936–39), offers a brilliant counterpoint to the original edifice, achieving a clear sense of differentiation and an arresting contrast in form, structure, and appearance of transparency, on one hand, while seeming to be an integral, indeed essential, component of the greater whole. In the challenging world of adding creatively and sympathetically to an existing building of note, the Racine complex remains exemplary.[7] And, while Wright was notorious for the way his designs ignored, even turned their backs on, urban and suburban environments alike, his unrealized scheme for the Masieri Memorial in Venice (1951–55), discussed by Alice Thomine-Berrada in this volume, entered a new frontier in exploring how Modern architecture could complement venerated historic settings. His solution remains as poignant for practitioners today as it did over sixty years ago.

The international attention that was fomented due to the threat of demolishing the Robie house in Chicago (1908–10) during the late 1950s had little precedent in the United States (fig. 1). A century before, Mount Vernon had been the focus of a national, private-sector campaign to rescue the hallowed property from oblivion, and the reconstruction-restoration of the core of Williamsburg, Virginia, to its late eighteenth-century state beginning in the late 1920s attracted national renown within a few years.[8] But even in the immediate post–World War II period preservation endeavors in the United States remained primarily local affairs. The fact that architects and others interested in architecture from across the country and abroad would express outrage over the planned destruction of the Robie house was a new manifestation of a public sentiment that had been steadily coalescing since the war's end.

The plight of the Larkin Building (1902–6), which was demolished in 1950, reveals how much the situation had changed in less than a decade. The company sold what had once been the showpiece of its large mail-order complex in 1943 to an out-of-town speculator who soon abandoned his acquisition when the tax benefits he anticipated could not be realized. Two years later the City of Buffalo foreclosed on the property owing to unpaid taxes. Repeated attempts to sell and even to find new uses for the building failed. Sacked and stripped by vandals, the derelict hulk was finally sold for the paltry sum of $5,000 in 1949. Demolition ensued, but plans to replace it with a truck terminal soon dissolved, and the site was relegated to serve as a parking lot (fig. 2). Local papers covered these events, but there was little protest until after the great pile had gone. The significance of the building was then recognized. In 1949 the *Buffalo Evening News* issued an editorial

House & Home

MAY 1957 SIX DOLLARS A YEAR — ONE DOLLAR A COPY

ARCHITECTS · APPRAISERS · BUILDERS · CONTRACTORS · DECORATORS · DEALERS · DISTRIBUTORS · FHA-VA · MANUFACTURERS · MORTGAGEES · PREFABRICATORS · REALTORS

HOUSE OF THE CENTURY: Since 1857 no house has had more influence

■ How FHA is scrapping the MPR's to write a whole new set of rules

Round Table: Three new plans to make trade-in finance easy

How to help your baths sell your house

The inside story of 1957's biggest housing tract

NEWS BEGINS ON PAGE 37 / NEW WAYS TO BUILD BETTER, PAGE 175 / COMPLETE CONTENTS, PAGE 109

FIG. I. Robie house as "House of the Century," *House & Home,* May 1956, cover. (Author's collection)

titled "The Shame of Our City," lamenting the neglected state of "one of the great examples of the genius of Frank Lloyd Wright" and arguing for a continued search for new uses. But as in so many cases, efforts to save the Larkin Building remained localized. Andrew C. Ritchie, former director of Buffalo's Albright Art Gallery (now Albright-Knox Art Gallery) and subse-

quently director of the department of painting and sculpture at New York's
Museum of Modern Art, wrote an impassioned protest that appeared in the
New York Herald Tribune. Prophetically, he called for a "federal commission"
to be established to inventory and protect such great architectural works, but
his plea remained a cry in the dark.[9] Even with a building that had become
well recognized as exceptionally significant—a building designed by someone
who was finally becoming seen as a master in his field—the lament of its loss
was little more than a whimper.

But during the ensuing years, a growing contingent of practitioners,
critics, scholars, and others who cared for architectural heritage began to
believe that the loss of important examples in the United States should not
be considered an inevitable result of progress. At a time of prosperity and
optimism, great cultural works could surely be saved, and now many Americans grew more confident that they had an architectural heritage worth
saving. While most of this concern was channeled toward buildings erected
before the Civil War, the Wright legacy was starting to defy age prejudices.[10]
As Cammie McAtee explains elsewhere in this volume, Wright's reputation
continued to grow during the 1950s. He came to be seen not only as an im-

portant Modern architect, but the greatest architect ever to work in this country—an international luminary whose designs at the same time represented a quintessentially American culture and values.[11] With the loss of the Larkin Building still fresh in people's minds, the imminent threat to the Robie house afforded opportune circumstances for a groundswell of grassroots outrage. Several years before the impending doom of New York's Pennsylvania Station (1902–11) the Robie house became a nascent national movement's cause célèbre.[12]

At the onset of efforts to preserve the building, the ad-hoc Committee to Preserve the Robie House had requested the secretary of the interior to designate the building a historic monument under the provisions of the Historic Sites Act of 1935. The National Park Service rejected the initiative, probably at least in part since such designation was reserved for properties deemed suitable for future national park units. However, the increasing demand for federal recognition of places that would never become part of the national park system led to the creation of the Registry of National Landmarks in October 1960.[13] Less than three years later, and one year after William Zeckendorf's highly publicized rescue of the Robie house, the dwelling was awarded national historic landmark status, a move initiated by local supporters of the property anxious to raise the funds necessary for its restoration. Designation was considered a momentous event not only by Chicago preservationists but also by federal officials. In April 1964 Secretary of the Interior Stewart Udall came to the site to preside over ceremonies.[14] The Robie house was indeed one of the first national historic landmarks chosen for its physical (i.e., architectural) attributes rather than for such historical associations as the residence of a famous figure or the scene of a major event. In addition, it was the first work of Modern architecture to be so recognized. Over the next half-century, twenty-two additional Wright buildings would receive the designation as well, almost equaling the total number of Modern, post-1930 buildings by other architects listed, and far exceeding the number by any other single architect.[15]

The Robie house case was at once catalytic and symptomatic of a major shift in preservationists' attitudes. Efforts to rescue the dwelling put Modern architecture on the preservation map. The campaign implanted the notion that addressing work of the recent past—work less than half a century old, or created within living memory—was important to understanding America's architectural legacy. That notion was quick to take root in both the national and local conscience even if decades would pass before it became firmly cemented in preservation practice.

The perilous saga of the Robie house and what was increasingly seen as a widespread threat to Wright's work generally was perhaps a factor in the timing of Edgar Kaufmann jr.'s deeding of Fallingwater (1935–39) to the Western Pennsylvania Conservancy in October 1963, a gift that attracted national attention. Though Kaufmann had for some years given thought to the long-term protection of the place he had inherited from his parents— one that he had been instrumental in convincing them to commission—the transfer may well have related to a broader sense of urgency. In covering the event, *New York Times* architecture critic Ada Louis Huxtable observed, with some exaggeration, that "the decision . . . comes at a time of crisis for other important Frank Lloyd Wright buildings. Wright's houses have been mutilated by remodeling; some have burned, others stand derelict and empty. This accelerated loss is becoming a matter of increasing alarm." The next month, the writer of an article in London's *Architectural Review* opined: "An unhappy fact today is that crucial [Modern] buildings of the past have become expendable. It is becoming increasingly difficult to assess the work of some of the most important architects as their buildings disappear— often with only the sketchiest documentation left to justify earlier critics' excitement. Frank Lloyd Wright is a case in point."[16]

Kaufmann's strategy to protect his beloved family retreat, which he had used as a weekend getaway since the mid-1950s, was innovative in several respects. While long world-renowned as a work of architecture, the house occupied but a tiny fraction of the five hundred acres entailed in the gift. Kaufmann selected a nature conservancy, which until then had only held open space, rather than an organization such as the National Trust for Historic Preservation, to ensure the presentation of "powerful art and powerful nature into something beyond the sum of their separate powers" (fig. 3).[17] His viewpoint not only reflected Wright's belief in nature as the source for creativity in the arts. The decision was also a pioneering venture in the pursuit of unity, as well as reconciliation, in the often still fractious relationship between the protection of culture and nature.[18] At the transfer ceremony he remarked: "What are these grounds and this house? Acres of rock and acid earth, second-growth trees and icy streams . . . and something more: a place of vigorous beauty, of self-renewing enchantment, of adventuresome picturesqueness that answer perfectly the romantic need in modern hearts, the need to be natural, to experience nature not as grist for our mills but as the habitat that has formed us." He continued: "conservation is not preservation; preservation is stopping life to serve a future contingency; conservation is keeping life going."[19] While one might quibble with the semantics, Kaufmann's perspective broke new ground. Fallingwater was living history, not in the then usual sense of being a period piece with costumed docents, but a place where visitors could contemplate the conceptual relationships between artifice and nature.

FIG. 3. Fallingwater, Mill Run, Pennsylvania, 1936–39. Aerial view, showing the house (bottom center) and some of the extent of the surrounding forested landscape. (Christopher Little, courtesy of the Western Pennsylvania Conservancy, 2010)

Kaufmann was thus adamant that Fallingwater not become a house museum in the way that phenomenon had evolved during the first half of the twentieth century—a place frozen in time and generally the result of a carefully crafted (and often inaccurate) exposition of domestic life in some distant past. Instead, it should be, in Kaufmann's words, "a recreational and cultural center to stimulate and encourage man in his march for the beautiful and the lovely in nature and in architecture, music, painting and the arts." But the greatest demand came from people wishing to see the house.[20] Unlike most such properties, which were then presented to the public primarily due to their antiquity, their association with a famous person or event, or their Gilded Age extravagances, Fallingwater was shown as a work of art, with guides recruited from the school of architecture at Carnegie Institute of Technology (now Carnegie-Mellon University) and the fine arts department at the University of Pittsburgh taking small numbers of visitors at a time to explain the intricacies of its arresting design and site. At an early date the decision was made to leave the interior in a state that still appeared to be inhabited, as if the family had just stepped out for a walk. At that time, a few nineteenth-century houses had been acquired as museums with their furnishings more or less intact, but their presentation was gener-

RICHARD LONGSTRETH

ally cast in a traditional vein, with visitors gazing through thresholds or behind ropes into spaces that appeared more arrested in time than inhabited.[21]

Finally, Fallingwater was strikingly new. The house had been completed only twenty-five years earlier, making it the youngest building to receive such protection in the United States and probably across the globe at a time when few preservationists were interested in much that was under a century old. Pushing further the beachhead established by the Robie house campaign, Kaufmann's preemptive move had a decisive impact on what was considered worthy of preservation in the United States, just as it broke new ground in interpretation and relating natural and cultural resources. Unlike the Robie house, Fallingwater looked brand new, as if it had just been constructed. On the other hand, as with the Robie house, the case for preserving Fallingwater was a strong one. Few people publicly questioned the value of protecting a building that ranked among the most venerated works of twentieth-century architecture virtually from the time of its completion.[22] Kaufmann's act also entailed measures to ensure economic viability. His generous gift of property was matched by one of supporting funds—an endowment of $500,000 and an annual $30,000 education grant for five years from a foundation established by his father.[23]

A third noteworthy achievement in preserving work of the recent past and an equally important precedent-setting case unfolded the same year as Fallingwater's opening, 1964, with Wright's Pope-Leighey house in Falls Church, Virginia (1939–40). Unlike the Kaufmann residence, that built for Loren Pope and his family was an early Usonian house—modest in size and appearance and then little known as a work of architecture beyond a cadre of specialists. And while, irrespective of age, houses that caught the attention of preservationists tended to be ones constructed for people of considerable means, the Pope-Leighey residence was erected on a tight budget for a family that was comfortably off, yet with limited resources.[24] So rather than representing the rarefied world of cultivated wealth, the dwelling was emblematic of a key objective in Modern architecture: to provide shelter for the mass market.

The threat of demolition for an interstate highway was a source of consternation for its second owner, widow Marjorie Leighey, who, with her husband, had purchased the house in 1947. Through a series of fortunate, serendipitous circumstances the case caught the attention of the National Trust's executive director, Robert Garvey Jr., and some National Park Service officials, who now recognized Wright's importance for the preservation field. After the house's fate seemed sealed and attempts by the trust failed to alter the situation, Leighey wrote to Secretary of the Interior Udall offering to deed her dwelling to the Park Service. Udall, who had a keen interest in Wright and was already involved in efforts to protect the Robie house as well as the Imperial Hotel in Tokyo, threw himself into the situation. In March 1964, Udall convened a meeting with the federal highway administrator, Virginia highway department and Fairfax County officials, the chairman of the National Capital Planning Commission, the director of the Park Service, and the chairman and the executive director of the National Trust in the Leighey living room. While this "tour" was intended to achieve accord, highway representatives insisted that their project had gone too far to reroute. The session, however, did lead to a commitment by the National Trust to reconstitute the house at another, compatible location and open it to the public.[25]

Udall's inclination toward personal diplomacy in this case helped lay the conceptual framework for an important provision in the National Historic Preservation Act of 1966. Section 106 of the act stipulated that all federally sponsored or licensed undertakings affecting properties listed on the National Register of Historic Places, which the act created, be subject to review by the Advisory Council on Historic Preservation, a body comprised of federal agency heads that the act also established. Since its implementation over a half century ago, the 106 review process, as it is known, has had an enormous impact, resulting in the preservation of countless historic resources nationwide.[26] The case also was significant in that the National Trust took a house even younger than Fallingwater at a time when that organization remained rather conservative in its outlook. The trust was gradually becoming more activist in its orientation and was playing an ever more important role in the transformation of preservation into a strong national movement. On the other hand, the seven other historic properties it held in 1964 dated almost entirely to the late eighteenth and early nineteenth centuries, and all of them were ambitious works for their respective periods and places.[27]

The trust was the leading private-sector group in the preservation field, and its embrace of the Pope-Leighey house was a conspicuous step in advancing the historical significance of Modern architecture (fig. 4). The initiative was not without controversy, however. After considering a number of sites, the grounds of Woodlawn plantation in southern Fairfax County, Virginia, were deemed most suitable by all parties involved. The trust took care to have the process of disassembly and reconstitution undertaken in what was then considered to be an exemplary manner, contracting with Wright's successor firm, Taliesin Associated Architects, for plans and with a master carpenter who had worked on the original house.[28] At the same time, objections by some of the organization's trustees to having the dwelling sited too close to the Federal-period plantation house, necessitated using land

RICHARD LONGSTRETH

FIG. 4. Pope-Leighey house, Fairfax County, Virginia, 1939–40; reconstituted 1964–65. View of living room during Marjorie Leighey's occupancy. (Author's photograph, 1967)

that differed from the original site in its topography and giving the house a new orientation, which markedly changed the effects of natural light in the rooms. The trust took pains to showcase its new acquisition, including issuing a booklet on the house and its preservation several years after it opened. Still, the project remained the subject of debate among some visitors, area residents, and even trustees over subsequent decades.[29] In retrospect, of course, the trust's actions can be seen as a pioneering embrace of the mid-twentieth century in the long-rarefied world of house museums.[30]

The successes of Fallingwater and the Pope-Leighey house were predicated on ample funds to ensure their long-term preservation. The Robie house, on the other hand, reminded advocates that the monies needed to safeguard and use even so renowned a work of architecture could be difficult to attain. Once the Robie house was in the hands of the University of Chicago, which did not have dedicated funding for restoration, a special committee was formed, chaired by Ira J. Bach, the city's planning commissioner. Its goal was to raise $250,000 for the work needed to make the house a viable component of its institution. Launched in 1962, the national campaign received no small amount of publicity, but a year and a half later only about $40,000 had been raised. The fund continued to increase slowly, and some dollars were allocated for emergency repairs, but four years after its inception, the committee had to settle for a much more modest restoration endeavor than it had originally envisioned.[31]

The problems incurred in ensuring a sustainable future for the Robie house even after it had been "saved" by Zeckendorf paled in comparison to those entailing much larger public and commercial buildings during the 1960s and 1970s. Those problems were epitomized by the nearly decade-long and ultimately futile effort to save Wright's Imperial Hotel in Tokyo (1913–23). The international campaign to rescue the sprawling compound was among the most widespread and well publicized of the era. And while far from American shores, the building became a poster child for issues that preservationists in the United States regarded as particularly acute and challenging.

Few buildings have enjoyed, and suffered, so colorful a history as the Imperial Hotel. Opening on the day of the Kanto earthquake, which devastated large swaths of the Japanese capital, the building temporarily served as a staging ground for rescue efforts. Once stability returned to the city, the hotel served its intended purpose as a luxurious center for Tokyo residents and visitors alike, earning the reputation as one of the world's finest establishments of its kind. Yet plans to demolish the building for a larger facility were announced in 1936, a mere thirteen years after its completion. The proposal was aborted due to public opposition and Japan's subsequent Asian territorial advances. The demands of military aggression imposed severe rationing on the home front, rendering the Imperial "a dreary place" by the latter months of 1941, well after foreign patronage (save German officials) had plummeted.[32] The building suffered some damage from American firebombing in 1945, and after the war's end it was taken over by occupation forces to house senior U.S. officers and visiting dignitaries. The imperial family, which held majority stock in the enterprise, relinquished its holdings in 1947, placing the property on the tax rolls. Restored to Japanese ownership as an entirely commercial enterprise in 1952, the Imperial began to retrieve its old luster as a social magnet.[33] But the building's fabric had suffered from the settling of its various parts due to makeshift repairs from war damage, earthquakes, and, later, construction of an adjacent subway and nearby multistory commercial buildings.

Japan's remarkable postwar recovery led not only to a booming economy and a radical transformation of the Marumouchi district in which the Imperial lay, but also a surge in tourism. Scarcely a year after reassuming control, the hotel's management announced plans to construct an annex that would increase capacity by 200 rooms. The project soon expanded into a two-phase scheme, with 650 rooms, completed in 1958. The ten-story concrete structures were rendered in a slick modernist vein that Americans had been instrumental in positing as the new gold standard for hostelries abroad.[34] Wright, not surprisingly, rebuked the trend, snapping that the annex was an "outrageous insult to the character of the original building," adding that "westernization" had achieved what earthquake and war could not. The annex's architect, Teitaro Takahashi, retorted: "Wright's building is not at all Japanese, as he claims. . . . It was nicely designed for its period—but that was the Rickshaw Age." Somewhat later, Kenzo Tange, by then considered Japan's foremost practicing architect and a major figure internationally, was even more condescending: the design "reflects a kind of orientalism with which the Japanese no longer identify."[35] To many eyes, the building did indeed look anachronistic. It had been erected in a Tokyo comprised largely of one- and two-story wood-frame buildings so that the taller sections of the hotel initially loomed above most neighbors. Moreover, its configuration departed markedly from major urban hotels of the 1920s and earlier across the globe. The low-slung, multisectioned mass was more suggestive of a posh resort than a great hostelry in the metropolitan core (fig. 5). Tokyo's transformation into a major world city since the 1910s made the Imperial seem all the more out of place.

The embrace of newness carried the day. The Imperial's owners considered the annex to be their flagship and the Wright building a white elephant. Less than a year after the second annex opened, the company announced that the original complex, still not forty years old, would be demolished. Structural problems, soaring land values, exorbitant maintenance costs, and guest complaints of "low ceilings, small rooms and maze-like corridors" were cited as justification.[36] Still, the hotel's general manager, Tetsuzo Inumaru, who joined the staff shortly before the Wright building's completion, hoped much of that edifice could actually remain and a new, high-rise addition be incorporated.[37] The absence of a concrete plan amid the uproar generated by the announcement led to an abeyance, but only for a few years. The intent to demolish the hotel in its entirely before the decade's end was made public in August 1964; that decision was finalized in January 1967.[38] Protests erupted in Japan and around the world. An international Committee for the Preservation of the Imperial Hotel was inaugurated, growing to some 1,350 members. A petition to the Diet, signed by twenty thousand persons, and an untold number of communiqués were sent to the hotel's management and to government officials, including the prime minister.[39]

But in the end the building was lost. The Imperial had indeed suffered serious structural damage over the years, and the porous Oya stone that comprised many of its lively decorative surfaces had absorbed so much pollution that it was beyond long-term preservation.[40] No party was willing or able to commit the many millions of dollars it would have taken to purchase

FIG. 5. Imperial Hotel, Tokyo, 1913–23; demolished 1967–68. Aerial view showing postwar development of surrounding commercial district. Photograph ca. late 1950s. (Author's collection; Imperial Hotel, Tokyo)

and restore the building, let alone operate it as a viable commercial enterprise. Funds were raised to dismantle the entrance section and move it to Meji Mura, a museum village of late nineteenth- and early twentieth-century buildings near Nagoya. When the monies for reassembly became available, however, the rescued fabric proved to be almost entirely unsalvageable, and the work was one of reconstruction more than reconstitution.[41]

The Imperial's storied past, including exaggerated claims of its structural innovations and of its being the sole Tokyo building to survive the 1923 earthquake, combined with the assessment that it was one of Wright's greatest buildings, contributed to a number of American preservationists seeing the loss as one of their own.[42] Fresh on the heels of the protracted, painfully public demolition of New York's Pennsylvania Station, the Imperial's fate seemed symptomatic of a fundamental problem in protecting architecture erected over the previous hundred years. The case also underscored the challenges with saving large commercial buildings, especially those that lay

RICHARD LONGSTRETH

on land that had greatly increased in value, were considered functionally obsolete, and were beset with structural and other physical deficiencies. As demolition commenced, Ada Louise Huxtable captured the sense of frustration. The hotel, "one of the masterworks of the century," she asserted, "focused world attention on one of the major problems of our time—the loss of the heritage of the 20th century." She opined that the building "is the victim not of natural forces or cataclysmic events, but of the two most powerful instruments of destruction of our time: progress and obsolescence." The prospect was gloomy: "the course of preservation today is largely a series of losing battles." She lamented that "the devastation of our monuments, the scuttling of the arts that are peculiarly and greatly our own, are primarily the result of a value system that puts civilization at the bottom of the pile. The price of a disposable culture is the right to call ourselves a civilization at all."[43]

The plight of the Imperial also resonated with Americans concerned about architectural heritage because it was symptomatic of circumstances far more common in this country than in many places abroad during the third quarter of the twentieth century: a large commercial building old enough to be cast as outmoded in business circles, requiring considerable monetary outlay for needed improvements, and occupying land that was sharply increasing in value. These challenges, endemic to the architecturally rich cores of the largest U.S. cities, were seen as particularly acute by the 1960s, as the demand for new urban development rose to a degree not seen for more than three decades. Awareness of the significance of nineteenth- and early twentieth-century commercial architecture likewise was ascending. As Chicago had been the focus of historical studies of that subject since the 1930s, so it now became the center of attempts to address the preservation of such work. What became known as the Chicago School of Architecture was cast as an essential foundation for Modern architecture. The preservation campaigns in this realm did not, of course, entail the work of Wright, whose extant buildings were primarily residential and in outlying areas, but rather that of his *Liebermeister,* Louis Sullivan, and Sullivan's partner, Dankmar Adler.[44]

The future of one of Adler & Sullivan's greatest projects, the Auditorium Building (1886–90) seemed ominous immediately after World War II. The Civic Opera had vacated the premises in 1929, and the great theater itself closed twelve years later. However, Roosevelt University's purchase of the building in 1947 bestowed the pile with a sympathetic owner. University officials viewed the design of the building as an asset and gradually sought to revitalize its spaces—a pioneering instance of adaptive use undertaken in the cause of preservation.[45] Nearly a decade later Wright, who, of course, had worked on the building and had spent the most formative stage of his early career as Sullivan's lieutenant in the Auditorium office tower, decried the neglect of the theater as "Chicago's shame and a universal disgrace," offering his services to "restore" the facility, but he also lauded the university's efforts to rehabilitate the former hotel banquet room in a sympathetic manner.[46] In 1959 the university allowed a private, nonprofit group, comprised of many prominent Chicagoans, to undertake retrieval of the theater as a performing arts center. Four years later the newly appointed head of the building committee, architect Harry Weese, advanced the then unusual proposition actually to restore, rather than modernize, the spaces, claiming that contrary to prior assessments the structure was physically sound and that its preservation would substantially reduce the project cost. Work proceeded on an incremental basis. With a grand, much publicized opening in October 1967, the project was heralded as one of the most stunning preservation triumphs of the era. Ada Louis Huxtable remarked on the work done on this "anchor-point of architectural history," emphasizing the theater's superiority to many far more expensive new performing arts centers. Costing "just over $2 million," the venture, she cautioned, "raises a healthy skepticism about . . . it-can't-be-done preservation studies"[47]

The transformation over two decades of the Auditorium Building into an exemplar of adaptive use and preservation occurred only because its owner was willing, indeed often eager, to support that agenda. The importance of Roosevelt University in the project's success was driven home by the sequential battles to save two nearby Adler & Sullivan buildings with owners who were determined to secure higher profits from the land that their edifices occupied.

The Garrick Building (1890–92), where Wright had occupied an office early in his independent career, was put up for sale in 1960 by the famous Chicago movie circuit, Balaban & Katz. Efforts to block demolition, for a parking garage, were rejected by the landmarks commission. While the owners' attorney claimed the facility could no longer be used, two arts groups went on record as willing to locate there even though they did not have the money to acquire the property. A county superior court judge refused to grant the demolition permit, arguing that "esthetic, artistic, and cultural value" could be considered not only in clearance for urban renewal, but also in preserving landmarks—an important precedent for the later, decisive Supreme Court ruling in the Grand Central Station case. Three months later the state appellate court overturned the ruling. Before the building was demolished in 1961 all preservationists could do was scramble to save ornamental fragments, of interest in their own right but a poor substitute for the entire work.[48]

However, the Garrick's loss and the broader threat it embodied were instrumental in enacting a local landmarks ordinance that offered protection for listed buildings. Endorsed by Mayor Richard Daley, who had formed a committee to address a situation that Huxtable described as "the biggest, noisiest, most dedicated and desperate campaign waged by any American city on behalf of the great old buildings that are being knocked down like tenpins," the ordinance was signed into law in early August 1963.[49] Unlike New York's ordinance, enacted a year later and to a substantial degree as a result of the loss of Pennsylvania Station, the Chicago law required owner consent and set a high bar for monetary compensation, but it was still considered a major step in the ongoing effort to protect the city's heritage. Preservationists soon learned that the central issue was far from resolved, however. In 1968 Adler & Sullivan's Meyer Building (1892) was summarily demolished even though it was on the pre-ordinance list of properties maintained by the city landmarks commission since its founding in 1957. The mayor had yet to appoint new commission members to oversee the ordinance, and thus no petition had been made to the city council to include those listings.[50]

Even when a revamped landmarks commission began the process of proposing worthy properties, most owners objected. Sullivan's Carson Pirie Scott & Company department store (1898–99, 1902–03) was a major exception.[51] More or less concurrently, however, the owner of Adler & Sullivan's Chicago Stock Exchange Building (1893–94) refused to cooperate. Although the building was operating at nearly full occupancy, its owner claimed obsolescence and the intention to erect a much taller building on its prime location in the financial district. A yearlong campaign as intense as that to save the Garrick failed to alter the situation, and as at the Garrick, saving fragments was all preservationists could do when demolition commenced in 1971.[52]

Such losses, coupled with the growing veneration of the work of Wright, Sullivan, and their followers, led the National Park Service to consider the possibility of collaborating with the City of Chicago and other area municipalities to create a "national cultural park," consisting of multiple properties that embodied the best examples of architecture created in the metropolitan region during the late nineteenth and early twentieth centuries. In a publication devoted to advancing the idea, Park Service historical architect Hugh C. Miller opined: "The Chicago School movement [both tall commercial buildings and smaller-scale work of the Prairie School] prompted an architectural revolution, wholly American in origin, that anticipated by several decades a similar development in Europe." This "movement," he intoned, was "as consequential in world cultural history as the development in twelfth-century France that produced Gothic architecture and in fifteenth-century Italy that produced Renaissance architecture. Of these three equally significant nodal points in the history of western man, only the consequences of the Chicago school were truly global in scope." Secretary of the Interior Rogers C. B. Morton noted in the book's introduction: "I have always been impressed by the great landmark buildings of Chicago. . . . Economic pressures engendered by urban growth are relentlessly destroying them one after another. Ways must be found to ease these pressures. . . . The Department of the Interior stands ready to participate."[53] The proposal never advanced beyond a broad conceptual framework, but the initiative revealed how important such work had become to those concerned with protecting American culture.

At least as important as efforts to provide safeguards for individual properties of historical significance during the 1960s and 1970s was the increase in the creation of historic districts. Designating such places enabled preservationists to address many more buildings and other components of the landscape than individual landmark listings. But behind the creation of historic districts lay the even more consequential concept that the whole could be more important than the sum of its parts, that the physical setting in which historic properties existed could be a vital contributor to understanding their significance. This idea underlay thinking when the first two historic districts—in Charleston, South Carolina, and the Vieux Carré in New Orleans—were created during the 1930s and remained an underpinning of the growth in historic districts after World War II. The spread of this practice accelerated greatly in the 1960s and 1970s, especially after the creation of the National Register of Historic Places. But for most of that period the districts so recognized experienced their primary development during the eighteenth or early nineteenth centuries. Focusing on precincts defined during the Gilded Age was still a relatively new concern; the twentieth century remained all but ignored.

A major precedent was set in expanding the temporal scope of consideration for historic districts by the Village of Oak Park, Illinois, around 1970, when its Citizens Action Committee commissioned two specialists to survey the community to identify the work of Wright and his Prairie School colleagues. University of Chicago professor Paul Sprague, an architectural historian who devoted much of his career to the study of Wright and Sullivan, and Wilbert Hasbrouck, executive director of the Chicago Chapter of the American Institute of Architects and founder of the *Prairie School Review,* a pathbreaking journal devoted to the subject, were commissioned to undertake the project. As a result of their findings an ordinance was crafted and a seven-person landmarks commission established to oversee the venture, which the Village Board approved in February 1972. Twenty-two buildings by Wright and thirty-five by kindred spirits formed the basis for the district, occupying an area one and one-half miles square. The ordinance had no police power; the commission was intended to promote community pride in this legacy and advise property owners when requested.[54] Even though scant attention was initially paid to the many other buildings that gave the historic district much of its character, the endeavor was nonetheless a momentous step in equating what was considered "modern" with what was considered "historic."

Oak Park residents also took action to save the house and studio that Wright had designed, beginning in 1889, for himself and his growing family and where he did his professional work for a decade. When the property went up for sale in October 1972, two nonprofit organizations were formed, one to hold the acquisition in trust until a preservation plan could be developed; the other, the Frank Lloyd Wright Home and Studio Foundation (now Frank Lloyd Wright Trust), to undertake management and restoration. When the latter group had difficulty raising the $190,000 purchase price, it struck a precedent-setting partnership with the National Trust, which bought the building in April 1975. Under the terms of the agreement the foundation paid the trust roughly half of the acquisition cost. The National Trust, in turn, leased the property to the foundation for a nominal fee over a period of up to forty years.[55] This cooperative venture allowed the foundation to get on its financial feet and benefit from the National Trust's strategic and technical expertise as well as its national standing. The venture also enabled the National Trust to expand its portfolio of properties at a fraction of the cost that would otherwise be incurred. Such an exchange never became a widespread practice; however, it was a harbinger of the new entrepreneurial ventures that were increasingly becoming a part of preservationists' efforts to expand their parameters of operation and their success record.

Within three years, the Home and Studio Foundation also developed a restoration strategy that would establish a new level of sophistication in preservation practice. Wright had constantly modified as well as added to his quarters. The last major changes were made in 1911 when the studio was recast as his estranged family's residence and the house as income-generating apartments. Documenting the sequence of changes and then deciding to what state the complex should be restored was seen as a major challenge from the start. Since its inception in the United States during the latter decades of the nineteenth century, restoration practice almost always focused on returning the property to what was thought to be its original state. This tendency could strip a building of accretions that were significant in their own right. Sometimes such restoration resulted in historical incongruities. Paul Revere's house in Boston, for example, was brought back to a seventeenth-century state that was hardly what its namesake would have known when he occupied the premises.[56]

By the 1970s a growing contingent of American preservationists were advocating methods long championed by the English: allowing a property to reveal significant changes over time. The Oak Park house became an important exemplar of this shift. After two years of study, the report, issued early in 1979, carefully examined all the options and provided a detailed rationale for restoring the building as a palimpsest, but only spanning the years prior to Wright's departure for Europe in 1909, years when the household was intact and the studio was a working office (fig. 6). "Probably no residence in the nation has ever been restored [actually, prepared for restoration] with so much advanced planning, research and attention to complicated details," wrote Paul Gapp, architecture critic for the *Chicago Tribune,* in 1979, adding that the project had already become a national model for similar endeavors. Published by the University of Chicago Press, the report was indeed a benchmark in the growing level of sophistication toward the treatment of

FIG. 6. Frank Lloyd Wright studio, Oak Park, Illinois, 1897–98. View from Chicago Avenue during restoration. (Author's photograph, 1984)

RICHARD LONGSTRETH

historic buildings at a time when practices in the United States often were still more elementary in nature than those of European countries.[57]

By the 1980s, taking steps to protect significant examples of Modern architecture became less unusual and less controversial as the preservation movement itself had grown in participants, become more professional, had greatly increased the scope of resources deemed worth saving, and had marshaled an array of tools to forge an impressive record of successes.[58] The fate of individual buildings as renowned as the Imperial Hotel and Chicago Stock Exchange was no longer so problematic. Adler & Sullivan's Wainwright Building in St. Louis (1890–91) and Guaranty Building in Buffalo (1894–96), both considered among the foremost examples of tall commercial building design in the United States, were probably the last cases where the threat of loss was substantial. Impending demolition for a parking lot in 1974 led the National Trust to purchase the Wainwright as a holding action. Subsequently, Missouri's governor stepped in, acquiring the building for use as state offices. A national competition was held for the rehabilitation and new construction on an adjacent lot, with first prize accorded to the then much-celebrated architectural firm of Mitchell/Giurgola.[59] Events surrounding the Guaranty were less dramatic but extended over a seven-year period before the building's future was secure.[60]

If the Wainwright and Guaranty's outcomes were a fitting end to the problem of retaining world-famous buildings, many other significant examples of twentieth-century architecture, including works by Wright, continued to be lost during the 1970s. No fierce campaigns were launched to rescue Wright's Francis Apartments on Chicago's South Side (1895), which was demolished after a long vacancy in 1971. A similar fate befell Francisco Terrace (1895), on the city's West Side, three years later, its locally pioneering role as a philanthropic project to address the need of low-income households and distinctive design notwithstanding (fig. 7).[61] At the opposite end of the economic spectrum, Wright's summer house for the Littles in Deephaven, Minnesota (1912–14), one of the architect's largest and then least-known residential designs of the early twentieth century, generated concern locally and elsewhere as well but attracted no buyers when the elderly Little heirs tried to sell it. Prohibited by zoning restrictions from adaptation to other uses and even from property subdivision, the grand house seemed doomed. Only the unusual purchase in 1972 by the Metropolitan Museum of Art, which reconstituted the living hall in its American Wing, saved a fragment of the sprawling manse.[62] The Little house had remained with few changes over the years. On

FIG. 7. Francisco Terrace, Chicago, 1895; demolished 1974. (Author's photograph, 1966)

the other hand, the Lake Geneva Hotel at Lake Geneva, Wisconsin (1911–12), had never been a financial success and experienced numerous alterations, although its salient characteristics remained discernible. Following a major fire, it was demolished in 1970.[63]

Such buildings would likely fare better today. The economic obstacles so forcefully present with the Adler & Sullivan commercial blocks and even the challenges faced by retaining the much smaller Wright apartment buildings in Chicago and hotel at Lake Geneva have been substantially mitigated by revisions to the federal tax code that offer monetary incentives for the re-habilitation of listed, income-producing properties. First implemented as part of the Tax Reform Act of 1976, the provisions of which were bolstered in 1980 and also soon began to be complemented by similar legislation in many states and some localities, this strategy has had an enormous impact on preservation efforts nationwide ever since.[64] Public appreciation for such work has also greatly expanded. And numerous special-focus, nonprofit organizations—most pertinent in this case, the Frank Lloyd Wright Build-ing Conservancy—have been formed.[65] Without the coalescence of these phenomena, rescuing and giving new vitality to otherwise economically problematic edifices such as Wright's Park Inn and City National Bank com-plex in Mason City, Iowa (1908–10), would never have occurred.[66]

Awareness and advocacy have also helped safeguard many Modern houses

FIG. 8. Storer House, Los Angeles, 1923–24. (Author's photograph, 1966)

not protected by historic landmark or district ordinances and not privy to national tax incentives. The obstacles may seem just as daunting as with large commercial properties. Houses that are decades old can incur hefty costs just to put them in good repair and bring them up to code. Such dwellings are now often considered modest in size and lacking in desirable amenities. Finally, land values may well exceed the normally assessed value of the dwelling. What has rescued many such places has entailed a change in outlook: the house is not merely shelter or an emblem of attainment; it is a work of art and as such worth considerably more than residences comparable in their dimensions and location. Wright's Storer house in Los Angeles (1923–24) (fig. 8) was a catalyst in this realm. After purchasing the building in 1984 the celebrated Hollywood producer Joel Silver undertook a meticulous and very expensive restoration. This much-publicized enterprise induced others in the film industry to similarly partake in the rich stock of Modern domestic architecture found in southern California.[67] Within a decade the phenomenon broadened to a national one, with some real estate brokers even specializing in significant Modern work. Still, the remarkable house Wright designed for son David and his wife Gladys in Phoenix, Arizona (1950–52), was almost lost in 2012 (fig. 9).[68]

No architect's legacy more than Wright's has figured so prominently in shaping preservation practice regarding twentieth-century buildings in the

FIG. 9. David and Gladys Wright house, Phoenix. (Bob.Hassett@russlyon.com)

United States. Yet as that legacy reveals many gains in the field since 1950, it also demonstrates the challenges that persist.

NOTES

I am grateful to David De Long, Lisa D. Schrenk, John Sprinkle, de Teel Patterson Tiller, and Michael Tomlan for reviewing a draft of this piece and offering numerous useful suggestions. Neil Levine's comments were enormously helpful as well. John Fowler, Morrison Heckscher, James Jacobs, Keirnan Murphy, Susan West Montgomery, Jack Quinan, Carol Shull, John Sprinkle, and John Waters supplied me with much useful information. My investigation of the topic began with a modest essay: "Frank Lloyd Wright and Historic Preservation in the United States, 1950–1975," *Save Wright,* Frank Lloyd Wright Building Conservancy, 5 (spring 2014): 4–10.

1. A thoughtful overview of changes in preservationists' outlook and practices during this period is afforded by Michael A. Tomlan, *Historic Preservation: Caring for Our Expanding Legacy* (New York: Springer, 2015), chapter 2. See also United States Conference of Mayors, Special Committee on Historic Preservation, *With Heritage So Rich* (New York: Random House, 1966). A good sense of the expanding scope of architecture considered by preservationists during the late 1960s and 1970s can be gleaned from a two-volume series: Constance M. Greiff, ed., *Lost*

America: From the Atlantic to the Mississippi and *Lost America: From the Mississippi to the Pacific* (Princeton, N.J.: Pyne Press, 1971 and 1972, respectively). Both volumes have revealing forewords by James Biddle, then president of the National Trust for Historic Preservation, and both prominently feature buildings by Wright. See also Tony P. Wren and Elizabeth D. Mulloy, *America's Forgotten Architecture* (Washington, D.C.: National Trust for Historic Preservation, and New York: Pantheon, 1976).

2. In the essay that follows, Daniel Bluestone argues this impact can be seen as a mixed blessing. On the other hand, preserving architecture from the post–World War II period and even of more recent vintage has become a major thrust of preservation in the last several decades and has spawned a substantial amount of literature. See the "Historic Preservation" section in Richard Longstreth, comp., "A Historical Bibliography of Architecture, Landscape Architecture, and Urbanism in the United States since World War II," 2002, revised May 2020, Society of Architectural Historians, https://www.sah.org/docs/default-source/bibliographies/recent-past-bibliography.pdf?sfvrsn=a4f5539b_9.

3. "Old Midway Gardens to Be Auto Laundry," *Chicago Daily News,* 20 July 1929, 19; Jack Quinan, *Frank Lloyd Wright's Larkin Building: Myth and Fact* (New York: Architectural History Foundation, and Cambridge, Mass.: MIT Press, 1987), 128. With the loss of the Larkin Building, especially, Wright may have felt personal regret but wished to avoid any overtones of sentimentality in the public realm.

4. For illustration, see William Allin Storrer, *The Frank Lloyd Wright Companion,* 1993; revised ed. (Chicago: University of Chicago Press, 2006), 32–33, 153, 423; Bruce Brooks Pfeiffer, ed., *Frank Lloyd Wright: The Complete Works, 1885–1916* (Los Angeles: Taschen, 2011), 62–64; Bruce Brooks Pfeiffer, *Frank Lloyd Wright: The Complete Works, 1917–1942* (Los Angeles: Taschen: 2010), 104–05; and Bruce Brooks Pfeiffer, *Frank Lloyd Wright: The Complete Works, 1943–1959* (Los Angeles: Taschen, 2009), 424.

5. While in the preservation field "restoration" entails the accurate retrieval of a work to some previous state, the term has also long been used to refer to a much broader scope of treatments that can give a work a renewed lease on life.

6. The Oak Park complex is discussed in the text below. Synoptic descriptions of the Taliesins over time can be found in *The 20th-Century Architecture of Frank Lloyd Wright: Nomination to the World Heritage List by the United States of America (2018), Revised 2019* (Chicago: Frank Lloyd Wright Building Conservancy, 2019), 143–48, 167–74. A detailed analysis of the evolving nature of the Arizona compound is found in "Taliesin West: Preservation Master Plan," Harboe Architects, Chicago, for the Frank Lloyd Wright Foundation, https://franklloydwright.org/preservation/.

7. For background, see Mark Hertzberg, "Adding the Research Tower: A Coda to the S. C. Johnson Administration Building," in Richard Longstreth, ed., *Frank Lloyd Wright: Preservation, Design, and Adding to Iconic Buildings* (Charlottesville: University of Virginia Press, 2014), 86–105. Other essays in that volume address aspects of the broader issue. Some preservationists concerned with compatibility in design believe that work rendered in so strong a personal style as Wright's should not have additions by others. Yet William Wesley Peters of Taliesin Associated Architects designed seamless, complementary additions to several

Wright buildings, including the First Unitarian Society of Madison Meeting House in Shorewood Hills, Wisconsin (1946–52), in 1963–65; and the Hoffman house in Rye, New York (1955), in 1972.

8. Two recent analyses of preserving Mount Vernon over the past century and a half are Lydia Mattice Brandt, *First in the Homes of His Countrymen: George Washington's Mount Vernon in the American Imagination* (Charlottesville: University of Virginia Press, 2016); and Carol Borchert Cadou, ed., with Luke J. Pecoraro and Thomas A. Reinhart, *Stewards of Memory: The Past, Present, and Future of Historic Preservation at George Washington's Mount Vernon* (Charlottesville: University of Virginia Press, 2018). Concerning Williamsburg, see Charles B. Hosmer Jr., *Preservation Comes of Age: From Williamsburg to the National Trust* (Washington, D.C.: Preservation Press, and Charlottesville: University Press of Virginia, 1981), chapter 1; and Richard Handler and Eric Gable, *Creating the Past at Colonial Williamsburg* (Durham, N.C.: Duke University Press, 1997).

9. "The Shame of Our City," *Buffalo Evening News,* 15 April 1949, 24; Andrew C. Ritchie, "The Famous Larkin Building Goes to the Wreckers," *New York Herald Tribune,* 23 October 1949, D1, D4. For synopses of the case, see Jerome Puma, "The Larkin Building, Buffalo, New York: History of the Demolition," *Frank Lloyd Wright Newsletter* 1 (September–October 1978): 2–6; and Quinan, *The Larkin Building,* chapter 7.

   Ritchie's call for a federal commission presaged the revival of the Historic American Buildings Survey in the late 1950s and the establishment of the National Register of Historic Places following passage of the National Historic Preservation Act of 1966.

10. See, for example, Aline B. Louchheim, "To Save the Houses of Our Heritage," *New York Times Magazine,* 28 June 1953, 16–17, 22–23.

11. The historiographical groundwork for this view extends back to the 1920s. Fiske Kimball devoted a chapter to Wright in his pioneering volume, *American Architecture* (1928), discussing his early twentieth-century work and its international impact. Only Kimball's beloved Thomas Jefferson received comparable attention in the text. Four years earlier, in *Sticks and Stones: A Study of American Architecture and Civilization,* critic Lewis Mumford had posited Wright's work as the humane and American antidote for what he saw as the European over-infatuation with the machine. Sheldon Cheney introduced the Larkin Building as the "first specific example of creative architectural treatment in response to the machine challenge" in his widely read volume, *The New World Architecture* (New York: Tudor, 1930 (92). Probably the most influential survey of Modern architecture published in the United States before Siegfried Giedion's *Space, Time and Architecture* (1941), the text devoted a substantial amount of attention to Wright's residential, institutional, and commercial designs, placing them in the broader context of North American and European modernism during the previous four decades. Nikolaus Pevsner's *Pioneers of the Modern Movement* (1936) featured Wright in a more concise and conceptually narrower framework. With its reissuance in 1949 by the Museum of Modern Art as *Pioneers of Modern Design,* the volume gained a large American audience. After World War II, Wright also figured prominently in Wayne Andrews's *Architecture, Ambition and Americans* and James Marston Fitch's *American Building: The Historical Forces That Shaped It* (both 1947).

12. Concerning the demolition of Pennsylvania Station, which occurred between 1961

and 1966, and its aftermath, see Hilary Ballon, *New York's Pennsylvania Stations* (New York: W. W. Norton, 2002), 101–7.

13. John H. Sprinkle Jr., "'Of Exceptional Importance': The Origins of the 'Fifty-Year Rule' in Historic Preservation," *Public Historian* 29 (Spring 2007): 86–91. See also John H. Sprinkle Jr., *Crafting Preservation Criteria: The Origins of the National Register of Historic Places* (New York: Routledge, 2014), 116–19.

14. Sprinkle, "'Of Exceptional Importance,'" 93–94. See also Bluestone, this volume. For a short, but insightful piece revealing Udall's outlook on preservation, see Stewart Udall, "'The Future Is too Much with Us . . .,'" *Historic Preservation* 16:4 (1964): 126–27.

   John Sprinkle noted to me that circumstances had markedly changed by the 1960s, with an interior secretary, and an administration, more partial to twentieth-century architectural design. Furthermore, part of the Park Service's initial rejection may also have been because Wright was still alive at that time, a factor that officials believed could prejudice granting national historic landmark status. Communication from John Sprinkle to author, 22 January 2019.

15. I am grateful to James Jacobs, formerly of the National Historic Landmarks office of the National Park Service, for supplying me with this information. The architects with the next closest numbers of listed work are Henry Hobson Richardson with thirteen and Louis Sullivan with ten.

16. Ada Louis Huxtable, "Wright House at Bear Run, Pa., Will Be Given Away to Save It," *New York Times,* 7 September 1963, 21; Alan M. Fern, "The Midway Gardens of Frank Lloyd Wright," *Architectural Review* 134 (August 1963): 113–16, quote p. 113.

17. Charles F. Lewis, "Doors Open at Fallingwater," *Carnegie Magazine* 38 (September 1964): 237–40, quote pp. 237–38. David De Long, who knew Kaufmann for many years, informed me that Kaufmann told him that the National Trust was not chosen out of fear the house would become frozen in time. Communication with the author, 15 January 2019.

18. Concerning the subject, see William Cronon, "The Trouble with Wilderness; or, Getting Back to the Wrong Nature," in Cronon, ed., *Uncommon Ground: Rethinking the Human Place in Nature* (New York: W. W. Norton, 1996), 69–90, 479–82; William Cronon, "The Riddle of the Apostle Islands: How Do You Manage a Wilderness Filled with Human Stories?," *Orion* 22 (May–June 2003): 36–42; Loretta Neumann and Kathleen M. Reinburg, "Cultural Resources and Wilderness: The White Hats versus the White Hats," *Journal of Forestry* 87 (October 1989): 10–16; and Richard Longstreth, "Protecting Artifice amid Nature: Camp Santanoni and the Adirondack Forest Preserve," in Ethan Carr et al., eds., *Public Nature: Scenery, History, and Park Design* (Charlottesville: University of Virginia Press, 2013), 197–215.

19. Lewis, "Doors Open," 238; Edgar Kaufmann jr., *Fallingwater: A Frank Lloyd Wright Country House* (New York: Abbeville, 1986), 65, 66.

20. "Fallingwater Is Saved Before It Is Imperiled," *Architectural Record* 34 (October 1963): 24; Lewis, "Doors Open;" David R. Jones, "The Pennsylvania House That Wright Built," *New York Times,* 13 June 1965, XX18.

21. A good example is the Morse-Libby house in Portland, Maine (1857–60), which is a remarkable survival of a lavish mid-nineteenth-century interior. It was given to the Society of Maine Women in 1943 and subsequently opened as a museum. See John

Cornforth, "The Victorian Mansion, Portland, Maine," *Country Life* 167 (27 March 1980): 926–29 and (3 April 1980): 1014–17.

22. For a dissenting view, see "Mail: Frank Lloyd Wright," *New York Times,* 4 July 1963, XX3.

23. The elder Kaufmann's foundation was also instrumental in establishing the Western Pennsylvania Conservancy.

24. This phenomenon held true even for many seventeenth- and eighteenth-century houses that were then considered "typical" examples of their time, but, benefiting from research of recent decades, are now known to represent close to the uppermost tier of domestic architecture when they were erected.

25. For discussion, see Steven M. Reiss, *Frank Lloyd Wright's Pope Leighey House* (Charlottesville: University of Virginia Press, 2014), 84–96. Useful period accounts include Peter S. Diggins, "Rte. 66 Perils 'Haven' on Earth," *Washington Post,* 3 October 1962, C1; Lon Tuck, "Virginia Is Aiming a Rte. 66 Bulldozer Right at a Frank Lloyd Wright Home," *Washington Post,* 25 February 1964, B1; Wolf Von Eckardt, "Wright Would Chuckle at the Irony," *Washington Post,* 8 March 1964, G8; Ben A. Franklin, "House by Wright Faces Demolition," *New York Times,* 20 March 1964, 26; Lon Tuck, "Udall Acts on Wright House Fate," *Washington Post,* 21 March 1964, B1; Ben A. Franklin, "Udall Will Fight on Wright House," *New York Times,* 22 March 1964, 80; "Udall Drive to Save Wright House Gains," *New York Times,* 4 May 1964, 13. Marjorie Leighey retained the right of occupancy until her death, so that for some years the house was open to the public on a limited basis.

26. No synopsis or overall evaluation of the impact of the Section 106 process exists; however, dozens of case studies are posted on the Advisory Council on Historic Preservation's website. Perhaps it was not entirely coincidental that in 1967 Robert Garvey went from his position at the National Trust to serving as executive director of the Advisory Council, in which capacity he would organize meetings among agency heads to resolve conflicted cases.

27. Namely: Casa Amesti (1827; acquired 1953) in Monterey, California; Woodlawn (1800–1806; acquired 1954), located near Mount Vernon in Fairfax County, Virginia; Decatur House (1817–19; acquired 1956) in Washington, D.C.; Shadows-on-the-Teche (1831–34; acquired 1958) in New Iberia, Louisiana; Oatlands (1804, 1827; acquired 1964) near Leesburg, Virginia; and Belle Grove (1794–97; acquired 1964) in the Shenandoah Valley. Only Woodrow Wilson's house (1915–16, 1922; acquired 1963) in Washington dates to a later period, and it was brought into the fold for its close association with a famous president and his sizable collection of furnishings and papers. The addition of Lyndhurst (1838–42, 1865; acquired 1965), a major example of a Gothic Revival villa by Alexander Jackson Davis in Tarrytown, New York, also expanded the scope of the Trust's property holdings. For a period account, see Nona Brown, "Stately Homes of America," *New York Times,* 14 February 1965, XX1, 15. See also Elizabeth D. Mulloy, *The History of the National Trust for Historic Preservation, 1963–1973* (Washington, D.C.: Preservation Press, 1976), 14–16, 28, 53–58.

28. Reiss, *Frank Lloyd Wright's Pope Leighey House,* 96–108; "Ceremony Assures Future of Home Designed by Frank Lloyd Wright," *Washington Post,* 31 July 1964, B1; "A Wright House in Virginia Is Saved," *New York Times,* 31 July 1964, 20; Meryle Secrest, "U-Turn Preserves House for History," *Washington Post,* 18 June 1965, C2; Sprinkle, *Crafting Preservation Criteria,* 189–90.

29. Helen Duprey Bullock et al., eds., *The Pope-Leighey House* (Washington, D.C.: National Trust for Historic Preservation, 1969); Terry Brust Morton, "Visitors React to Controversial Trust House," *Preservation News,* February 1967, 5. Some twenty years later, William J. Murtagh, then special assistant to the president at the National Trust, asked me to speak informally to the trustees, who were meeting at Woodlawn, about the significance of the Pope-Leighey house because some of them still questioned the wisdom of having the house at all.

30. Thirty-eight Wright houses now serve as museums or are otherwise open to the public; see Joel Hoglund, ed., *Wright Sites: A Guide to Frank Lloyd Wright's Public Places,* 4th ed. (Chicago: Frank Lloyd Wright Building Conservancy, and New York: Princeton Architectural Press, 2017). The National Trust has more recently acquired two later icons of Modern architecture: Ludwig Mies van der Rohe's Farnsworth house in Plano, Illinois; and Philip Johnson's estate in New Canaan, Connecticut.

31. "Drive Begun to Restore Robie House," *Chicago Tribune,* 21 August 1962, A6; Mary Huff, "Restoration of Robie House Is Drive Goal," *Chicago Tribune,* 9 September 1962, A3; "Committee Plans Restoration of Robie House," *Architectural Record* 133 (April 1963): 29; "Robie House Unit Asks Aid in Fund Drive," *Chicago Tribune,* 8 October 1963, B18; Thomas Buck, "Robie House Restoration Fund Is Short $210,000," *Chicago Tribune,* 5 January 1964, B10; "Robie House Still Imperiled," *Progressive Architecture* 46 (March 1965): 53; "Doom Haunts Wright's Robie House," *Chicago Tribune,* 21 March 1965, B1; "Robie House Restoration to Commence in Month," *Chicago Tribune,* 18 April 1965, SA2; "Robie House Job Waits for Money," *Chicago Tribune,* 5 June 1966, P4.

32. Henry C. Wolfe, "Tokyo, Capital of Shadows," *New York Times Magazine,* 26 October 1941, 6. A detailed and very useful company history was issued for the hotel's centenary: *The Imperial: The First Hundred Years* (Tokyo: Imperial Hotel, 1990).

33. Mac R. Johnson, "Army in Tokyo Will Hand Back Imperial Hotel," *New York Herald Tribune,* 25 January 1952, 4; Murray Shumach, "Army Exits Sadly from Tokyo Hotel," *New York Times,* 2 April 1952, 3; Shinjiro Kirishiki, "The Story of the Imperial Hotel, Tokyo," *Japan Architect,* no. 138 (January–February 1968): 137. Bruce Goff recalled that in the immediate postwar years Wright was asked to come to Tokyo to oversee work that needed to be done, but he declined. See Robert Kostka, "Frank Lloyd Wright in Japan," *Prairie School Review* 3:3 (1966): 18.

34. For background, see Annabel Jane Wharton, *Building the Cold War: Hilton International Hotels and Modern Architecture* (Chicago: University of Chicago Press, 2001).

35. "It Isn't Right According to Wright," *Engineering News Record* 161 (14 August 1958): 25; Kostka, "Frank Lloyd Wright in Japan," 5. See also "Tokyo's Imperial Hotel to Get 200 Room Annex," *Chicago Tribune,* 3 May 1953, 20; "Imperial Hotel Getting Giant New Wing," *New York Herald Tribune,* 2 March 1958, H54; and "An Annex Dwarfs Wright's Imperial Hotel in Tokyo," *Chicago Tribune,* 2 August 1958, 14.

36. Robert Trumbull, "Imperial Hotel in Tokyo Periled," *New York Times,* 4 May 1959, 12. See also "Wright's Imperial Hotel," *Architectural Forum* 110 (June 1959): 11.

37. A. T. Steele, "The Years Catch Tokyo's Old Imperial Hotel," *New York Herald Tribune,* 13 August 1960, 8.

38. "Tokyo Hotel Designed by Wright Is Doomed," *New York Times,* 9 August 1964, 2;

"Imperial Hotel Now Due to Be Razed This Year," *Chicago Tribune,* 22 January 1967, A1; Robert Trumbull, "Tokyo to Replace Hotel by Wright," *New York Times,* 29 January 1967, 278; Don Shannon, "Tokyo to Raze Imperial Hotel Starting Dec. 1," *Los Angeles Times,* 8 November 1967, 20. See also "The Imperial Hotel Problem Again," *Japan Architect,* no. 108 (May 1965): 9–10.

39. "Imperial in Tokyo Needs a Miracle," *New York Times,* 29 October 1967, 21; Karen Kamrath, "The Stubborn Hotel Is Shaking," *AIA Journal* 48 (November 1967): 70–72; Samuel Jameson, "Imperial Hotel, Survivor of 2 Disasters, to Be Destroyed," *Chicago Tribune,* 8 November 1967, C8; "Committee for the Preservation of the Imperial Hotel," *Inland Architect* 11 (December 1967), 12–13; Kirishiki, "The Story of the Imperial Hotel," 138; "Tokio: Imperial Hotel, 1922–1967," *Domus,* no. 459 (1968): 5; Bunji Kobayashi, "Frank Lloyd Wright's Imperial Hotel in Tokyo," *Historic Preservation* 20 (April–June 1968): 62–68. See also Chioyda Ward, "The Imperial Hotel," *Japan Architect,* no. 138 (January–February 1968): 113–31.

40. Shindo Akashi, "The Imperial Comes Tumbling Down," *AIA Journal* 50 (December 1968): 42–48, affords an insightful examination of the building's structural problems at the time of its demise.

41. "Japanese May Save Old Wright Hotel," *New York Times,* 5 November 1967, 12; "'Japan's Williamsburg' Gets Part of Wright's Imperial," *AIA Journal* 66 (August 1976): 8–9; "Preservation—Restoration: Imperial Hotel, Tokyo, Japan," *Frank Lloyd Wright Newsletter* 1 (January–February 1978): 6–9; Sam Hall Kaplan, "Tokyo's Imperial Hotel Façade Preserved," *Los Angeles Times,* 6 May 1984, VII:1, 24. Additional information was obtained during a site visit in November 2018.

   In the preservation field "reconstruction" refers to creating anew a work that no longer exists or is in total state of ruin, as with the Stare Meastro in Warsaw or the Frauenkirche in Dresden. Generally, reconstructions are performed on or close to the site of the original, as with the Governor's Palace at Williamsburg, although some such as George Washington's polygonal barn complex at Mount Vernon or the Imperial Hotel fragment are done at an entirely different location. "Reconstitution" refers to the accurate reassembly of a work on a different site. In some cases, portions of a building cannot be disassembled and reconstituted, as was the case with the concrete floor slab at the Pope-Leighey house.

42. Recent assessments of the building's structure include Robert King Reiterman, "The Seismic Legend of the Imperial Hotel," *AIA Journal* 69 (June 1980): 42–47, 70; Joseph M. Siry, "The Architecture of Earthquake Resistance: Julius Kahn's Truscon Company and Frank Lloyd Wright's Imperial Hotel," *Journal of the Society of Architectural Historians* 67 (March 2008): 78–105; and Kathryn A. Smith, "Materials and Structure in Frank Lloyd Wright's Imperial Hotel: Failure and Success," *OAD: Journal of Organic Architecture + Design* 6:3 (2018): 4–35.

43. Ada Louise Huxtable, "The Imperial: Going, Going, Gone?" *New York Times,* 10 December 1967, 200. See also Priscilla Dunhill, "Requiem for a Masterpiece," *Architectural Forum* 128 (May 1968): 70–75.

44. Sullivan was heralded as a "prophet of Modern architecture," to borrow the subtitle of Hugh Morrison's pathbreaking monograph on him first published in 1935 by W. W. Norton in conjunction with the Museum of Modern Art. Sullivan gained that distinction not only because of the praise Wright accorded him, but also as a key figure in the Chicago School. After Morrison's monograph Sigfried Giedion's

Space, Time and Architecture (Cambridge, Mass.: Harvard University Press, 1941) played a profound role in furthering the importance of this phenomenon in tall commercial building design. It was expanded in Carl Condit's *The Chicago School of Architecture* (Chicago: University of Chicago Press, 1964), which made a direct connection between work of the late nineteenth century and contemporary skyscrapers by Ludwig Mies van der Rohe, C. F. Murphy, and Skidmore, Owings & Merrill.

45. While repurposing buildings has occurred since antiquity, the practice was generally employed due to lack of adequate funds for new construction. Exceptions existed such as Glenn Brown's rescue in the 1890s of the Octagon as the new headquarters of the American Institute of Architects in Washington, D.C. But for the most part it was not until the 1960s that preservationists began to promote adaptive use in a positive light as a means of saving valued historic buildings.

46. Shirley Lowry, "Wright Urges Restoration of the Auditorium," *Chicago Tribune,* 20 October 1956, 20; Shirley Lowry, "Work to Renew Ornate Room at Roosevelt," *Chicago Tribune,* 12 February 1957, A10. Subsequently, Roosevelt secured money to restore the second-floor lounge; see "For New Lounge," *Chicago Tribune,* 24 April 1957, 7. These efforts soon attracted national attention; see "The Auditorium Building," *Historic Preservation* 10:2 (1958): 60–62.

47. "Chicagoans May Restore Old Theater," *New York Herald Tribune,* 3 April 1959, 13; Austin C. Wehrwein, "Chicago Patching Noted Auditorium," *New York Times,* 1 March 1964, 55; "The Auditorium: A Restoration," *Architectural & Engineering News* 8 (January 1966): 42–43; Betty J. Ritter, "Rebirth of Chicago's Auditorium," *AIA Journal* 47 (June 1967): 65–68; Ridgely Hunt, "Resurrection of a Masterpiece," *Chicago Tribune Magazine,* 20 October 1967, 26–31, 34, 36, 38, 40; Wilbert R. Hasbrouck, "Chicago's Auditorium Theater," *Prairie School Review* 4:3 (1967): 7–19; Ada Louise Huxtable, "Culture Is as Culture Does," *New York Times,* 2 June 1968, D25. See also "Harry Weese, a Landmark Man," *Preservation News,* November 1975, 3; reprinted from *Time.*

48. "Judge Prevents Garrick Razing," *Chicago Tribune,* 24 August 1960, C9; "Change: Veto Demolition on Esthetic Grounds," *Architectural Forum* 113 (October 1960): 9, 11; "Sullivan-Adler Reprieved in Chicago," *Progressive Architecture* 41 (October 1960): 51; "Court Backs Razing of Garrick Theatre," *New York Times,* 23 November 1960, 18; Robert Kotulak, "Friends of the Garrick Building Rally to Save Its Art Work," *Chicago Tribune,* 22 January 1961, 28; "Garrick Art Works to Be Distributed," *Chicago Tribune,* 27 June 1963, D10; Jim G. Indreika, "The History of the Schiller (Garrick) Theatre: Chicago's Handsomest Playhouse," *Marquee,* Journal of the Theatre Historical Society, 30:3 (1998): 4–9. For detailed accounts of the preservation campaign, see Daniel Bluestone, "'Desecration of the Highest Magnitude': Demolishing the Garrick, 1960–1961," in John Vinci et al., eds., *Reconstructing the Garrick: Adler & Sullivan's Lost Masterpiece* (Chicago: Applewood Foundation; Minneapolis: University of Minnesota Press, 2021), 114–97; and Theodore W. Hild, "The Destruction of the Garrick Theater and the Birth of the Preservation Movement in Chicago," *Illinois Historical Journal* 88 (Summer 1995): 79–100.

49. Ada Louise Huxtable, "Chicago Saves Its Past," *New York Times,* 14 August 1963, 30.

50. "Struggle Continues to Preserve Buildings of Past Importance," *Chicago Tribune,* 11 February 1968, D1.

51. "Carson's Named Landmark," *Chicago Tribune,* 7 November 1970, 15; Ada Louise Huxtable, "The Chicago Style—On Its Way Out?" *New York Times,* 29 November 1970, 145.

52. "Chicago Stock Exchange Threatened," *Preservation News,* February 1970, 3; "Old Building Denied Status as Landmark," *Chicago Tribune,* 1 July 1970, B7; Diane Maddex, "Chicago Stock Exchange Reaches 11th Hour," *Preservation News,* August 1970, 1, 3; "Stock Exchange Fall Probable," *Preservation News,* September 1970, 1, 2; "Old Exchange Building Set for Wrecking," *Chicago Tribune,* 12 February 1971, C9; Donald Yabush, "Landmarks Unit Bids for Survival of Stock Exchange," *Chicago Tribune,* 21 March 1971, W9; "Stock Exchange Gets Reprieve," *Preservation News,* March 1971, 1, 6; Jack Houston, "Save Old Exchange: Historians, Architects," *Chicago Tribune,* 15 April 1971, W4; "Landmark Hearing Scheduled," *Chicago Tribune,* 13 May 1971, N17; "Stock Exchange Razing Barred Temporarily by Chicago Mayor," *Preservation News,* May 1971, 1, 6; "Chicago Council Given New Plea to Protect Old Stock Exchange," *Preservation News,* July 1971, 1, 3; "Save Old Exchange, State Court Asked," *Chicago Tribune,* 5 October 1971, 3; "Clear Way to Raze Landmark," *Chicago Tribune,* 8 October 1971, D14; Seth S. King, "12th-Hour Drive Is Made for a Chicago Landmark," *New York Times,* 15 October 1971, 28; Jack Houston, "Sentiment Can't Buy Any Landmarks," *Chicago Tribune,* 31 October 1971, 20; Joan W. Saltzstein, "Requiem for a Masterpiece," *Wisconsin Architect* 12 (December 1971): 10–13; Ada Louise Huxtable, "A Bad End, and a Good Idea," *New York Times,* 26 December 1971, D24; Alan G. Artner, "$520,000 Art Institute Gift to Remake Stock Exchange," *Chicago Tribune,* 3 April 1974, 6; Gary Washburn, "Sullivan-Adler 'Landmarks' to Rise Again," *Chicago Tribune,* 11 August 1974, A1.

53. Hugh C. Miller, *The Chicago School of Architecture: A Plan for Preserving a Significant Remnant of America's Architectural Heritage* (Washington, D.C.: U.S. Department of the Interior, National Park Service, 1973), v, 1, ii.

54. David Schneidman, "Meeting to Discuss Historic Status of Oak Park Portion," *Chicago Tribune,* 19 September 1971, W_A4; "Village Makes 'Wright Move,'" *Chicago Tribune,* 13 January 1972, W2; David Schneider, "Oak Park Approves Frank Lloyd Wright Landmark District," *Chicago Tribune,* 13 February 1972, W9; Aggie Fowles, "Oak Park's Unique Heritage," *Nation's Cities* 12 (May 1974): 22–23. The district was entered on the National Register in December 1973.

55. Alvin Nagelberg, "Wright Landmark for Sale," *Chicago Tribune,* 5 October 1972, C9; Paul Gapp, "Historic Wright Home Purchased for Preservation," *Chicago Tribune,* 14 July 1974, 34; Paul Gapp, "U.S. Foundation to Buy Wright Home," *Chicago Tribune,* 20 April 1975, 41; "Trust Acquires Wright Home," *Preservation News,* October 1975, 1, 6.

56. For background, see James M. Lindgren, *Preserving Historic New England: Preservation, Progressivism, and the Remaking of Memory* (New York: Oxford University Press, 1995), 37–40.

57. Paul Gapp, "Restoration Rolls Along," *Chicago Tribune,* 4 March 1979, D4; Restoration Committee of the Frank Lloyd Wright Home and Studio Foundation, *The Plan for Restoration and Adaptive Use of the Frank Lloyd Wright Home and Studio* (Chicago: University of Chicago Press, 1978). The process of determining the nature of treatment and of restoration itself was further presented, now to a broader audience, in Zarine Weil, ed., *Building a Legacy: The Restoration of Frank Lloyd Wright's Oak Park Home and Studio* (Oak Park, Ill.: Frank Lloyd Wright

Preservation Trust, and San Francisco: Pomegranate, 2001). See also Paul Sprague, "Frank Lloyd Wright Home and Studio: Homeward Bound," *Historic Preservation* 28 (July–September 1976): 4–8. The restoration committee consisted of twenty-seven people, representing a variety of professional expertise. It was chaired by architect John G. Thorpe, who became well known for his work on Wright houses. A valuable recent study is Lisa D. Schrenk, *The Oak Park Studio of Frank Lloyd Wright* (Chicago: University of Chicago Press, 2021).

58. I have made some attempt to examine this phenomenon; see Richard Longstreth, "20th-Century Heritage Conservation in the United States of America," in Bruno Reichlin and Roberta Grignolo, eds., *Conservation of 20th-Century Heritage: A Historical-Critical Encyclopedia,* vol. 1 (Basel: Colmna, forthcoming), 431–38.

59. "Trust Buys Option on Wainwright," *Preservation News,* December 1973, 1, 6; "St. Louis Parking Lot?" *New York Times,* 29 January 1974, 32; Ada Louise Huxtable, "In St. Louis, the News Is Better," *New York Times,* 10 March 1974, 129; "3 St. Louis Landmarks Saved by New Owners," *New York Times,* 31 July 1974, 34; Paul E. Sprague, "The Wainwright—Landmark Built and Saved," *Historic Preservation* 28 (October–December 1974): 5–11; Ada Louis Huxtable, "New York Can Learn a Lot from St. Louis," *New York Times,* 26 January 1975, 122; "Winning Design for Wainwright Restoration," *Architectural Record* 157 (January 1975): 37. By later standards, the rehabilitation was far too interventional, and the new building complex necessitated the demolition of an eight-story, turn-of-the-twentieth-century office block that was an important contributor to the historic urban context.

60. "Buffalo Building Saved," *Preservation News,* April 1974, 8; "Buffalo Citizens Fight for Sullivan Landmark in Danger of Demolition," *AIA Journal* 66 (June 1977): 8; "Saving Sullivan's Prudential Building," *Progressive Architecture* 60 (March 1979): 30, 35, 37; Susan Doubilet, "In the Empire State," *Progressive Architecture* 65 (November 1984): 88–94. Major spaces in the Guaranty's lower floors have been restored, while the whole interior of the Wainwright was gutted—a treatment that would likely not occur today.

61. Pfeiffer, *Frank Lloyd Wright: The Complete Works, 1885–1916,* 57–59, 65; Storrer, *Frank Lloyd Wright Companion,* 28–30; Carla Lind, *Lost Wright: Frank Lloyd Wright's Vanished Masterpieces* (New York: Simon & Schuster, 1996), 76–79. Francisco Terrace's entrance arch was reconstituted in a middle-class residential development that replicated the general form, if not the character, of the original. See Devereaux Bowley Jr., "Saving the Idea of Wright's 1895 'Model Tenement,'" *Inland Architect* 20 (February 1976): 18–20.

62. "Owners to Raze Wright House," *Preservation News,* February 1972, 3; "Metropolitan Acquires Wright's F. W. Little House," *Preservation News,* June 1972, 3; Tom Martinson, "A Loss of Consequence," *Northwest Architect* 37 (March–April 1973): 83–85; Morrison H. Heckscher, "Collecting Period Rooms: Frank Lloyd Wright's Francis W. Little House," in Thomas Hoving, ed., *The Chase, the Capture: Collecting at the Metropolitan* (New York: Metropolitan Museum of Art, 1975), 207–17; Morrison Heckscher, "Frank Lloyd Wright's Furniture for Francis W. Little," *Burlingtonian Magazine* 117 (December 1975): 871–75; Paul Goldberger, "Making Room for Wright," *New York Times Magazine,* 5 December 1982, 162–63; Edgar Kaufmann jr., *Frank Lloyd Wright at the Metropolitan Museum of Art* (New York: Metropolitan Museum of Art, 1982), 26–33

63. *Preservation News,* September 1970, 2; P. J. Meehan, "Frank Lloyd Wright's Lake

Geneva Hotel," *Frank Lloyd Wright Newsletter* 4:2 (1981): 6–10; Lind, *Lost Wright,* 118–19; Pfeiffer, *Frank Lloyd Wright: The Complete Works, 1885–1916,* 310–11.

64. For background discussion of economic incentives in historic preservation, see J. Mark Schuster, with John de Monchaux and Charles A. Riley, eds., *Preserving the Built Heritage: Tools for Implementation* (Hanover, N.H.: University Press of New England, 1997), chapter 4; and Tomlan, *Historic Preservation,* chapter 5.

65. For background, see Jack Quinan, "The Origins of the Frank Lloyd Wright Building Conservancy," and Ron Scherubel, "The 'Saves' in SaveWright," *Save Wright* 5 (Spring 2014): 11–16, and 22–27, respectively; and Ron Scherubel, guest ed., "Strategic Interventions," *Save Wright* 3 (Spring 2012): whole issue.

66. The prolonged grassroots initiative to preserve the complex is discussed in *The Historic Park Inn Hotel and City National Bank* (Mason City, Iowa: Wright on the Park, 2007).

67. "Storer House for Sale for $1 Million," *Los Angeles Times,* 6 June 1981, B1; Paul Goldberger, "A Lasting Wright Legacy," *New York Times Magazine,* 16 June 1985, 54, 56, 72; Daniel Cohen, "Wrighting Past Wrongs," *Washington Post,* 28 November 1985, Home Sect., 15–16; Robert Goff, "Modernism Is Modern Again," *Forbes,* 7 September 1998, 256, 258. Silver undertook an even more extravagant restoration of Wright's Auldbrass plantation near Yemessee, South Carolina (1938–41, which also entailed constructing portions of the compound that had never been realized, using Wright's drawings as the basis for the work. See David G. De Long, *Auldbrass: Frank Lloyd Wright's Southern Plantation* (New York: Rizzoli, 2003).

68. For background, see Neil Levine, "The Importance of the David and Gladys Wright House," and Janet Halsted, "Saving the David and Gladys Wright House," *Save Wright* 5 (Spring 2014): 28–29, and 30–37, respectively.

DANIEL BLUESTONE

Wright Saving Wright

Preserving the Robie House, 1957

Advocates of demolition nearly always lurk around major preservation campaigns. This was certainly the case on 6 June 1957 when the board of directors of the Chicago Theological Seminary gathered in Frank Lloyd Wright's Robie house (1908–10) for their semiannual meeting. The seminary had purchased the dwelling in 1926 and had used it variously as a classroom, a refectory, a temporary dormitory, and, most recently, a conference center for meetings of the board and other seminary gatherings. The board now envisioned a new use for the property, which occupies the northeast corner of Chicago's Woodlawn Avenue and 58th Street. It would become the site for the seminary's proposed forty-two-unit married student dormitory and refectory.[1] When the seminary announced its plan to demolish the Robie house in February 1957, it spurred an international preservation campaign.[2]

Letters, petitions, newspaper and journal editorials, and personal appeals by Chicago residents, professionals, the city's mayor, aldermen, members of the just established Commission on Chicago Landmarks, and by Frank Lloyd Wright himself aimed to save the Robie house. At the June 1957 board meeting director Graham J. Morgan, chair of the Seminary Building Committee, updated the board on the meetings that seminary officials attended with preservation advocates. Then, sitting in their places in the Robie house, the board voted to move forward with demolition. They settled on a time schedule for their project; a request for demolition bids would be made on 15 July; demolition would begin on 1 September; and construction of the new dormitory, designed by Holabird, Root & Burgee, would commence during the last ten days of October.[3] The directors of the seminary had heard a great deal about the significance of the Robie house's dramatic horizontal lines; its sweeping, low-slung roof; its art glass windows; and its dominant central chimney. They knew that the house essentially codified Wright's Prairie School designs and helped revolutionize Modern architecture. For the board of directors the 10,800 square feet of land that the house sat on was much more important than its architectural significance; the site nicely aligned with the seminary's main building located on the adjacent block, just west of Woodlawn Avenue. Nevertheless, this architectural and institutional vision, these plans, and the board's vote and determination all came to naught. The successful 1957 campaign to preserve the Robie house soon loomed nearly as large in preservation history as the building did in architectural history; the campaign became a landmark in the making of landmarks. With crucial assistance from Wright himself, the preservation campaign helped transform the very nature of the preservation movement, both for better and for worse.

The debates over the fate of the Robie house and the competing claims made on its site exposed shifting cultural, legal, and economic tensions within the preservation movement—tensions that still roil heritage efforts over a half century later. This essay explores the competing visions for demolition and preservation of the Robie house. These visions were framed by different assumptions about the responsibility for, and the meaning of, heritage stewardship in the context of contemporary programs of urban renewal and institutional revitalization.

Frank Lloyd Wright was eighty-nine years old when he learned of the Chicago Theological Seminary's plan to demolish the Robie house. Leon Despres, the Chicago alderman for the ward where the building stood, sent Wright the newspaper article about the proposed demolition and asked that Wright get involved in the campaign to save the house. Despres implored: "I would hope very much that you could say or write something about this. If you care to send any comment to me, I will be glad to undertake to disseminate it."[4] Wright did much more than Despres requested. He got into the middle of the fray. Within two weeks of learning about the seminary's plan, Wright traveled to Chicago to meet with the people who were organizing to preserve the house. A Committee to Save Robie House had already been formed and included television producer William B. McDonald, architect George Fred Keck, *Chicago Tribune* religion reporter Richard Philbrick and his wife Ruth Rowe Philbrick, University of Chicago professors of art Harold Haydon and Francis H. Dowley, *Hyde Park Herald* publisher Bruce Sagan, Alderman Despres, and Thomas Stauffer, a teacher of history and philosophy in the Chicago city college system.

On 18 March 1957, with fanfare, flair, and newspaper and television reporters following in his wake, Wright, walking with his cane in hand and his pork pie hat on his head, toured the Robie house. Wright expressed outrage over the demolition plan, and he deployed a certain verbal outrageousness to be sure that people learned about the crisis. The architect dismissed the seminary's estimates that the house needed $100,000 in rehabilitation work.

He pronounced the house to be in excellent condition, with only the kitchen needing updating. He then gleefully turned his verbal barbs on the seminary leadership, declaring, "This is a cornerstone of American architecture. To wreck it would be like destroying a fine piece of sculpture or a beautiful painting. The destruction of a thing like this could only happen in America, and it is particularly sad that professional religionists should be the executioners. It all goes to show the danger of entrusting anything spiritual to the clergy."[5] He worked to verbally push seminary officials back on their heels, insisting that they had "never spent a dollar to keep it up." Wright complained that "janitorship" had been lacking and that "the students came in there and made whoopee, too, you know." He later insisted that the proposed dormitory would be little more than a "rooming house where diapers would be changed and where people would be making whoopee."[6]

Wright's visit was widely reported, and his presence helped galvanize the preservation coalition, building crucial momentum for the cause (fig. 1). But Wright did more than create a public relations bonanza. He raised the possibility that the Frank Lloyd Wright Foundation would purchase the house and establish it as an architectural museum and a meeting place for discussions and debates about American architecture. In 1958 when there were active discussions about the National Trust for Historic Preservation taking ownership of the house, Wright entered direct negotiations with the Trust to become the primary tenant for the house. What he sought was to "assure the life of the Robie House as a culture center of Organic-Architecture: a place

FIG. I. Newspaper coverage of Frank Lloyd Wright's visit to a threatened Robie house. *Chicago Tribune*, 19 March 1957, III:10. (*Hyde Park Herald*)

where a new society of Architecture *itself* (instead of architects themselves) may find a meeting place for assurance and instruction in architecture by way of models, drawings and literature upon that subject." Wright wanted to name the organization FFAA, or Foundation for American Architecture, with the Frank Lloyd Wright Foundation providing the initial support and promotion. All this would be done "free of all expense to the National Trust."[7] Wright's idea for establishing a new use for the Robie house seemed refreshingly forward thinking, but it also followed a well-established preservation strategy to save historic buildings by founding a museum and community gathering place. In April 1957 *Architectural Forum* editorialized: "A hundred years may have to pass before the educated public will know that Robie house is worth more than Mount Vernon as an expression of the genius of the American People. Robie House is needed of and for itself as one of the wellsprings of the eternal human spirit."[8] Wright's own proposals for an architectural museum and center underscored the debt he seemingly owed to long-established preservation practice and to George Washington's manse, preserved in the 1850s by the Mount Vernon Ladies Association and operated as a house museum and national shrine.[9]

At a fundamental and quite local level, leading advocates of the Robie house's preservation had settled upon a vision of what they felt their neighborhood should look like. In their view the house added beauty and distinction to Hyde Park, the community of which the seminary and the University of Chicago were a part. Writing to the University of Chicago's chancellor, Lawrence A. Kimpton, a law student declared: "You, sir, perhaps better than any other person in the city, know the value of preserving Hyde Park as a handsome neighborhood. Many of us have admired your efforts in that direction. Certainly few buildings can give Hyde Park the distinction lent it by the Robie House. In fact, it is not extravagant to describe it as the most distinguished building in Chicago. Why, if this is true, should the University not make efforts to save it?"[10] This appeal to Kimpton's sense of the neighborhood life and beauty was rooted not only in his leadership of the university but also in his service as president of the South East Chicago Commission, established by the university to oversee urban renewal in adjacent neighborhoods. Trained at Cornell University in philosophy and a scholar of Immanuel Kant, Kimpton had served as dean of students and vice president for development before becoming the chancellor in 1951, succeeding Robert Maynard Hutchins.

The pleas to Kimpton were important because they showed the extent to which preservationists had ensnared the university in their campaign. The institution maintained a cooperative agreement, sharing courses, students, and faculty with the adjacent Chicago Theological Seminary. Preservationists wielded this connection as a cudgel, insisting in public appeals that the "Chicago Theological Seminary at the University of Chicago" planned on demolishing the Robie house. This rhetorical construction brought tremendous pressure on the university, and it ended up working as the university eventually played a central role in resolving the threat to the house. Another preservationist, Allen P. Golden, of the American Artists Group, argued for the Robie house as part of the neighborhood context. He wrote to Kimpton, "Even the casual visitor to Chicago is well aware that many parts of the South Side can be profited by wise re-development. Make way for progress by destroying valueless bits of the past, not by destroying its greatest monuments."[11] In arguing for the importance of the Robie house, University of Chicago sociologist David Riesman bemoaned the absence of "cultivation of aesthetic senses" and the lack of awareness of architectural "monuments" among undergraduates; he then forecast that "the world ahead could be very monstrous in terms of the objects around us, and we need anything in our visual environment which offers another model."[12]

John M. Shlien, an assistant professor of clinical psychology at the University of Chicago, cast the local argument for the Robie house in even more personal terms. He wrote Kimpton that he had taken to heart the chancellor's advice to faculty that they resist the temptation to move to the suburbs, fleeing neighborhood decline and deterioration in Hyde Park. Kimpton wanted the faculty to stay and help maintain a tight residential enclave. Shlien declared that he had stayed and purchased a house against financial advice and had taken a "gamble" on the future of the neighborhood. The plans to demolish the Robie house seemed to work in the opposite direction, diminishing the quality and character of the neighborhood. Shlien insisted: "As for Robie House, it seems to me that there would be nothing upward and onward about destroying it and plac[ing] a dormitory there. It would simply be a mistake."[13] He also predicted that demolition would cause "world-wide damage to our reputation."[14]

The insistence on the Robie house's significance in defining and protecting the neighborhood's character bears comparison with ideas from a half century earlier that had influenced the house's original creation. The early debates about what should stand on the site took place between adjacent property owners; this contrasted sharply with the Robie preservation effort, which was between a single property owner and a broader public that lacked any direct financial or ownership stake in the property. This distinction is central to coming to terms with how preservation often operates in the United States. Despite the still frequent belief that Wright's early twentieth-century houses rose amid open prairie, the Robie house was actually among the last constructed on the urban block. In the decade and a half before the dwelling was built, the adjacent lots were developed for residences, filled with blocky, freestanding, single-family houses generally two and one-half to three stories high. The houses all observed a deed covenant that had been established by the initial developers who subdivided the property for residential construction. The covenant provided for a building line setback from the western property line of thirty-five feet. A quasi-suburban landscaped character was thus established on the block.

In 1897 Charles L. Hunter constructed the large brick residence immediately north of what later became the Robie house lot. Eight years later Herbert and Jennie Goodman purchased the Hunter house. Herbert Goodman was a wealthy manufacturer of mining equipment and mineshaft locomotives and a member of the board of the University of Chicago. In 1906 John H. Gray purchased the future Robie house site for $12,900 with plans to build a two-flat apartment building. A deed restriction limited residential construction to single-family houses, and Gray sought the permission of Goodman to build his apartments. Goodman balked at the idea. Gray then, partly out of spite, started cutting down elm trees on the property and preparing the site for the construction of a taxpayer block consisting of seven, one-story store units, which were neither anticipated nor explicitly prohibited by his property deed. In order to protect the residential character of his house and block, Goodman bought the lot from Gray for $17,500. In May 1908 when Goodman sold the lot to Robie for $13,500, he put a more detailed set of restrictions on the land that would establish and bind the residential character of the parcel and mandate a mutual "protection of the property . . . for the benefit of the property owned by the other" for the foreseeable future. The legal agreement prohibited "the erection upon the whole or any part of the said premises, of any hotel, flat building, apartment building, livery stable, store, or warehouse or any building except buildings devoted wholly and exclusively to residence purposes."[15] The agreement dissipated the threat of a commercialized corner or higher-density residential development.

Zoning, which regulated the character and type of buildings constructed on Chicago parcels, did not originate until the 1920s. Prior to then, although there were codes regulating building form and the fire regulation of building materials by zone, covenants were the most important means of establishing and maintaining building and neighborhood character. Covenants bound people buying property with their neighbors around a shared vision of the neighborhood that extended for generations. It is notable that in 1957 as preservationists scrambled to find some leverage with the Chicago Theological Seminary, they failed to argue that the covenants placed on the Robie property by Goodman made a dormitory on the site illegal. Seminary officials may have assumed that they could skirt the covenants since they owned the Goodman property as well, but the covenants were modeled on and reflected restrictions on other properties along the block. This was never put to the test. It is notable that when historic preservation laws developed in the United States, like covenants, they tended to emphasize harmoniousness and compatibility in historic districts and compelled owners to abide by established character.

In retrospect, there is no small irony in the fact that preservationists advocated for the preservation of the Robie house—a dwelling that was notable for its inharmoniousness and incompatibility with the surrounding residences. Yes, it was a single-family house, like other residences on the block. However, its dominant lines were horizontal, while the neighbors were vertical. The Robie house technically observed the building line of adjacent houses, but Wright used a loophole in the covenants, which permitted verandas beyond the building line, to extend the house's distinctive prow-like porch prominently into the ribbon of greensward that fronted adjacent houses. Its form violated the decorum and established character of the block on which it was built. It is significant that if modern preservation ordinances had been in place in 1908 when the Robie house was designed, those regulations would very likely have barred its construction. The preservationists' penchant for harmony and compatibility in new design in historic districts often frustrates precisely the architectural inventiveness that they celebrate in their preservation campaigns.

Beyond competing visions of neighborhood character stood another fundamental question: Who should be responsible for stewarding architectural heritage? People and institutions affiliated with organizations like the Frank Lloyd Wright Building Conservancy and the Frank Lloyd Wright Trust generally assume that individuals and private foundations should shoulder the responsibility of preserving Wright's architectural heritage. Wright designed many extraordinary buildings. He occasionally railed against his former clients for not taking proper care of the buildings he had designed. But, here, the assumption was that, in the first instance, the people who built Wright houses would take care of them as well. And, beyond that, the people who later came to own the houses should take care of them. Owners were viewed as primarily responsible for the architectural heritage. This was obviously not the case after 1926 when the seminary purchased the Robie house. The institution was interested in the land and had no interest at all in being the stewards of architectural heritage.

Both seminary and university administrations bridled at the suggestion that ownership of the Robie house necessitated stewardship and responsibility for heritage. Indeed, both institutions rejected the claim, insisting that their educational missions were such that maintaining the house would actually constitute fiduciary *irresponsibility*. Just as the controversy got started, the seminary's leadership insisted that the Robie house was not "suited for any productive use in the Seminary's educational program." Seminary officials quoted private engineering estimates that the house required approximately $100,000 in repairs to make it safe and bring it up to current codes, declaring that "with its limited funds, derived entirely from contributions, [the seminary] finds it economically impossible to maintain the Frank Lloyd Wright house as an architectural monument."[16] Albert R. Hauser, an obscure figure and one of the few architects to publicly support the seminary's position, underscored the issue of institutional resources and purpose: "The Seminary's responsibility is not to preserve the Robie House but to provide needed facilities for its students on the only suitable property available."[17]

The university was even more pointed in its effort to shift responsibility for heritage away from the seminary and itself. Chancellor Kimpton wrote to Alderman Despres and Barnet Hodes, a member of the Chicago Commission on Chicago Landmarks: "Of course the University of Chicago would like to see the Robie House preserved. In this connection, however, as lawyers you must both appreciate that there are very real moral and legal limitations as to how the Trustees of the University of Chicago may expend its funds. Donors whose generosity have made possible the University of Chicago have given their funds for the purpose of furthering education and research. Unless special funds are obtained for the purpose of acquiring the Robie House and for its rehabilitation and maintenance, we do not have either the legal or the moral right to encumber education funds for the preservation of this historical monument."[18] Responding to a letter from faculty and staff at Pomona College, Emery T. Filbey, vice president of the university, wrote: "Your letter indicates that the preservation of the Robie House as an architectural monument is an obligation of C.T.S., and, failing this, there is the thought that the University of Chicago must intervene. There is just one way in which this could be done, since this University has no funds for the purchase or maintenance of architectural monuments. We could either discharge or fail to appoint two professors. I have been informed that C.T.S. has no funds for the preservation of monuments. Is it not possible that the public of which you are a part has a responsibility for the service about which you are concerned?"[19] The previous day, writing to another Robie house advocate, Filbey had not even bothered to put the matter of responsibility in the form of a question. He wrote to Arthur Rissman: "We are all in agreement that our cultural heritage must be preserved. The responsibility rests upon the public rather than upon a single individual or upon a single institution. So far the individuals who have written to this office on behalf of Robie House have not suggested that their personal funds would be made available for the protection of Robie House. There has been the inference that we should discharge enough professors to make funds available for this purpose. I am not impressed."[20] Filbey could be even more acerbic in response to suggestions of outsiders. A graduate of Harvard cited the example of Harvard moving historic houses in the context of a modern building project. Filbey responded: "It is unnecessary to remind you that neither of the institutions to which you assign responsibility for the preservation of Robie House enjoys the luxury of underlying financing in the amounts available to Harvard, whose example you would have us emulate."[21] Another Harvard-affiliated advocate drew a curt response: "To hell with Robie House. Why doesn't Harvard buy it?"[22]

Filbey was actually wrong. In the United States, with the exception of civic buildings, responsibility for architectural heritage had very rarely rested with the public. The Robie house campaign simply underscored this fact. Abner J. Mikva, who represented Chicago in the Illinois General Assembly, pointed this out to Alderman Despres in May 1957: "It is absolutely not feasible to seek an appropriation for the Conservation Department to purchase Robie House as a memorial. I have sounded out some sentiment in Springfield [the state capital] and it is all negative."[23] What was true for Illinois was also true for the federal government. When television producer William McDonald contacted the National Park Service proposing that the house be declared a national historic site and purchased by the federal government, Park Service officials refused to consider the request seriously.[24] Private-sector owners had long taken care of the architectural heritage; difficulties arose when they decided not to take care of their buildings or planned to raze them; in such situations there was really no backup mechanism for preservation. In other words, there was no established legal or cultural strategy for heritage when it fell into the wrong private hands.

Robie house advocates did not suggest laying off professors to steward architectural heritage. However, they were not shy in asserting that the seminary and the university actually had a unique responsibility to the building as part of their broader mission to steward culture and civilization. This assertion even came from academics in other institutions. Leopold Arnaud, dean of Columbia University's School of Architecture, wrote that his faculty understood that "it is sometimes inconvenient to possess historic monuments but nevertheless, there is a moral, sentimental and national responsibility involved and we feel that every effort should be made to preserve historic and outstanding examples of our past. . . . preserve it as an important example of our contribution to the development of architecture."[25] Professor John H. Mackin, of the University of Illinois and a member of the Session of the First Presbyterian Church, wrote to the president of the seminary that "when a man buys a work of art he assumes a responsibility to preserve it for his whole community." Not to take care of work of art would seem to violate the very principles at the foundation of seminary pedagogy. He continued: "The Seminary has a responsibility to preserve and maintain the Robie House if it can. If it cannot, it must find the men who can. To do nothing and then to claim that the only alternative is to destroy it is a violation of Christian stewardship."[26] Allen S. Weller, the dean of Fine and Applied Arts at the University of Illinois, suggested to Kimpton that universities had a unique responsibility when it came to heritage preservation: "It is particularly sad to think that its destruction could be contemplated by a great institution of learning—the very place which must evaluate our debt to the past and cherish the enduring elements in it."[27]

Just beyond the ideas that the seminary should have a sense of stewardship and that the university should exemplify a commitment to culture and beauty across the generations stood another important cultural vision. Advocates of the Robie house's preservation believed that both institutions should represent a different set of ideals than the bottom line calculus of modern business. Here, again, stewardship of knowledge and beauty provided the foundation for this vision. Some people drew a direct comparison with the business community in insisting that the university and seminary needed to preserve the Robie house. Peter Selz, the chair of the Pomona College Art Department and soon-to-be curator of New York's Museum of Modern Art, for example, wrote to Kimpton, arguing: "We know that in the past fine architectural monuments have been destroyed by real estate interests. But we hope that the Chicago Theological Seminary will not fall into that category. The Robie House is a monument of the greatest significance and its demolition would indeed appear to be an act of barbarism."[28] The seminary and university, it was asserted, needed to behave differently from ostensibly crass real estate developers. Indeed, they needed to affirm a higher state of culture and promote things beyond the materialism and consumption of modern times. Robert F. Bishop wrote to Kimpton insisting that the university be guided by the more eternal ideals of beauty, declaring: "It is unthinkable that a society which produces so many motor cars, television sets, etc. cannot afford the luxury of saving the most worthwhile monuments of its culture. Perhaps the City of Chicago together with the University of Chicago, dedicated as it presumably is to the culture of our times, could together find the financial wherewithal to preserve this building. In fact, it seems to me incredible that a great University would not jump at the chance."[29] This very drama between spirit and mammon had played a significant role in the founding of the University of Chicago and the Chicago Theological Seminary. The cultural question, or critique, that hovered over Chicago was whether a city with shallow historical roots, booming demographic and economic growth, and massive accumulations of both wealth and poverty could produce anything of enduring value. The university and the seminary were part of the answer; in Chicago, it was often asserted, wealth was not an end in itself, it was the means to achieve a higher and more refined civilization and culture; the university and the seminary were examples of this, and they needed to uphold a higher standard than economic calculus and convenience.

The charge that both institutions had seemingly patterned their actions toward the Robie house on those of business or real estate development was one directed at the heart of their identity. The criticism was that in pursuing, or not preventing, demolition of the Robie house they were doing the opposite of what such institutions might be expected to do. Peter Selz was not the only one to suggest that the proposed demolition amounted to "barbarism." The celebrated architectural historian and critic Sigfried Giedion, of the Zurich Federal Institute of Technology and Harvard, called demolition "a crime, an act of barbarism."[30] Similarly, Peter H. von Blankenhagen, a professor in the University of Chicago Committee on Social Thought, declared: "To raze Robie house is an act of barbarism."[31] Warner A. Wick, a University of Chicago professor of philosophy, drew on Plato: "the plans to destroy it are what Plato would have called impiety; and this impiety is being committed by theologians."[32] Poet Carl Sandburg toured the Robie house in August 1957 and turned to verse in condemning the demolition plan, comparing it to Nazi book burning, only worse: "To tear it down would be an irrevocable loss, like smoke on the horizon with wind blowing it away never to have it again . . . Most of the books the Nazis burned had copies elsewhere, they were not irrevocably lost; In a sense this is a book rare and fine, To tear it down would be equivalent to the Nazis burning entire editions of books, so there would be no copy."[33] The chair of the University of Chicago art department called the plans "inexcusable vandalism."[34] Yale architectural historian Vincent Scully organized a campaign for the Robie house by coordinating outreach to forty-five colleges and universities. To raze the house involved ignoring the highest aspirations of American culture; for Scully the building was "an intrinsic expression of a peculiarly American culture. It is the culmination of a full century of American attempts to find symbolic expression for some of the most deeply felt American myths and urgings."[35] For institutions of education, culture, and religion, these charges had to be taken seriously.

The seminary tried to parry the criticism of its plans by offering to give the Robie house to anybody who would move it off of the site. Indeed, the seminary even offered to donate the amount of money that it would take to demolish the building to any fund established to move the house. The institution further suggested that the Robie house could be moved to nearby public parkland—Jackson Park or the Midway Plainance—where it could be maintained as a "great civic asset."[36] With its concrete foundation slab and its heavy masonry construction, the move did not strike most people as economically feasible. Still, the *Sun-Times* editorialized in favor of the move, which it did not view as "an insurmountable task for an age of wonders. The Robie House merits the same veneration, we believe, as does a French chateau, and like a chateau could be taken apart brick by brick and reassembled in an appropriate setting somewhere out of the traffic lane of progress."[37] For his part, Wright "roared in indignation" when he heard the suggestion to move the house: "It would be no more cricket to move it than to move Mt. Vernon."[38] Here, again, George Washington's home was evoked in thoughts of and plans for the Robie house.

Seminary and university officials did make modest efforts to call into question arguments related to the particular significance and accomplishment of the Robie house. In justifying its plans, the seminary declared: "Chicago is fortunate in having many other examples of the work of this architect."[39] In pointing this out the seminary was suggesting that the loss of the Robie house would not be as catastrophic a loss to local culture as Robie advocates suggested. Both institutions also sought to question the merits of the building by insisting that the house's initial design and subsequent deterioration made its architectural quality very much an open question. Filbey articulated this sentiment most clearly in a letter to architect Percival Goodman: "I cannot feel moved to suggest that the present owners divert funds available for theological education to the protection and maintenance of an 'architectural monument' which, because of faulty architectural design or engineering, is reported to be at the point of falling apart."[40]

Filbey wrote to another preservation advocate: "You may be surprised to know that correspondence received at this office is not all favorable to the retention of this house as an architectural monument. Architects and members of the public refer to the house as a monstrosity and feel that wrecking it is long overdue."[41] He crafted a similar argument in dismissing out of hand a suggestion from an alumnus that the house could be used as a residence for the chancellor himself: "your suggestion that the Chancellor would undertake to live in the Frank Lloyd Wright house must mean that you are unaware of the building in relation to a place to live. Wright did a wonderful job in the rendering of live drawings and in space relationship, but he was unaware of or disregarded the business of designing a house for people to live in, particularly in Chicago. The end result of the designation of Robie House as the official residence of our Chancellors would be the early loss of the Kimpton family and a long waiting period before another could be appointed."[42] When asked whether the seminary planned to demolish the dwelling, Kenneth R. Hougland, the institution's business manager, declared: "it may fall down . . . the walls are leaning out. It's not constructed properly . . . and it is badly designed. . . . We are in business to educate ministers not to support a national shrine."[43] The strategy to countering the Robie house preservation campaign by questioning the design and the quality of the construction was literally swamped by the local, national, and international insistence on the precedent-setting place of the design in Modern architecture. It might have made seminary and university officials feel better about their resistance, but it obviously failed to change the dominant view of the building's central place in the modern world and the imperative for its preservation.

An underlying reason why both institutions balked at calls not to demolish the Robie house was that in the 1950s they came to view demolition as an essential investment in their survival. They conceived of, and did everything in their power to support, the demolition of hundreds of buildings in the area. The university, the seminary, the South East Chicago Commission, the Chicago Land Clearance Commission, and local civic organizations assumed that without expansive demolition of deteriorated and "blighted" commercial and residential properties neither the institutions nor the surrounding middle-class housing areas would remain viable. Both institutions turned a deaf ear to the pleas from renters and owners who were among the thousands of residents displaced through urban renewal. Officials of the seminary and university alike stubbornly adhered to demolition plans that seemed the only hope for institutional renewal and growth. In August 1954 the *Chicago Tribune* published a long account of the difficulties presented by a deteriorating neighborhood for the university, with the headline: "U. of Chicago Opens Critical Fight for Life." One of the world's "greatest centers of learning" was confronting the possibility that it could "fade into mediocrity." Money was short because student enrollment had declined precipitously from 14,000 in the pre-Depression and post–World War II eras to just 4,800 in 1954. The most important problem being confronted was the need for "improvement and stabilizing of the neighborhood in which it [the university] lives. A university, whose scientists have measured the speed of light, ushered in the atomic age, and studied galaxies thousands of light years from the earth suddenly have found its neighborhood in danger of being engulfed by slums."[44]

Hyde Park had experienced a spate of apartment and house subdivisions in the years after World War II that brought poorer people into the neighborhood. The university under its previous chancellor, Robert Maynard Hutchins, had supported racially restrictive covenants that excluded African Americans, except for domestic servants, from living in, leasing, or owning property in the area bounded by 55th Street on the north, 59th Street on the south, Cottage Grove Avenue on the west, and Stony Island Avenue on the east, an area that included the university campus, the seminary, and the Robie house. In 1948 the United States Supreme Court decided in the *Shelley vs. Kramer* case that such covenants violated the constitution and could not be enforced by courts. With legal barriers removed, Hyde Park became much more racially mixed, and university officials' concerns over neighborhood deterioration, crime, and their ability to attract students, faculty, and staff rose dramatically.[45] In 1952, just a year after Kimpton became chancellor, the university established the South East Chicago Commission, a community planning and development organization charged with coordinating initiatives related to urban renewal, housing, code enforcement, community policing, and development. Kimpton became president of the commission, and planners were soon working closely with the Chicago Land Clearance Commission, which had the power to seize land by eminent domain, demolish buildings, and turn the land over to developers for new construction. The plans targeted areas in which houses and apartments had been subdivided and in which poor and minority residents resided at considerable density. University officials quickly became inured to criticism of the demolition of residences and business buildings pursued as part of neighborhood rehabilitation. For the university, demolition did not look like "barbarism" or "vandalism"; it looked like its best hope for neighborhood and institutional salvation and renewal.

For the seminary, demolition had been central to its campus building since it relocated to Hyde Park from Ashland Avenue, on the West Side of Chicago, after World War I. Unlike the university, which built its original campus quadrangle in the 1890s on undeveloped land, the seminary moved into a settled neighborhood, first occupying and then demolishing three houses built in the 1890s and early 1900s to make room for its main building. Designed in 1923 by Herbert Hugh Riddle on 58th Street, between University and Woodlawn avenues, the seminary building had a shallow street-facing courtyard that opened south toward the university's monumental Rockefeller Chapel, designed by Bertram Goodhue, then under construction. The chapel was one of several university buildings that extended the campus away from the original quadrangle to sites facing the landscaped Midway Plaisance that connected Jackson Park to Washington Park. Even before the completion of its main building, the seminary was planning to develop a linear campus along 58th Street, one block north of, and parallel to, the Midway extension of the University of Chicago. The Robie house purchase was a step toward this vision of extending the seminary campus east along 58th Street to Kimbark Avenue (fig. 2). The logic of urban renewal demolition simply advanced to embrace the logic of demolition and re-development that the seminary had pursued since the 1920s.

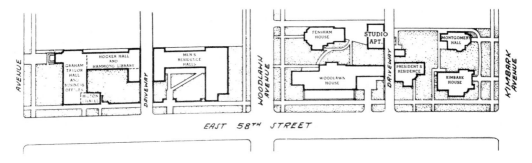

FIG. 2. Site plan of Chicago Theological Seminary, showing the Robie house on third block from left, ca. 1950. (Chicago Theological Seminary Archives)

Part of the sense of urgency to construct married student housing at the seminary derived from the concern that students had been forced to reside in precisely the same kind of makeshift accommodations that seemed to be propelling Hyde Park toward slum conditions. In 1958 when the dormitory was finally under construction, the seminary published an article that had a perspective view of the new building juxtaposed with images of the student's current accommodations—nineteenth- and early twentieth-century houses that been subdivided (figs. 3–4). The caption read: "As many as 9 families have lived in these single-family residences sharing bathrooms, kitchen, etc." The photographs of the houses had large "X"s across the images to demonstrate their unworthiness for such uses.[46] An earlier representation of the married student housing condition showed families sharing kitchen and dining spaces, noting: "The present converted residences for married students provide quarters for several families in houses intended for single family living, wiring is inadequate, baths and kitchens must be shared, remodeling these structures to conform with the Chicago housing code is impractical because of their age and condition."[47] These visual representations of a makeshift and obsolescent environment paralleled similar graphic treatment of buildings planned for destruction under neighborhood urban renewal.

In September 1957, as he continued to be prodded to find a way to resolve the Robie house crisis, Kimpton wrote an unpublished essay titled "Education and Demolition," in which he expanded his experience of Hyde Park and the university into a broader argument about the decline of American cities and the attendant crisis of higher education. Kimpton observed: "The American city over the past quarter century—even the past half century in the case of the older ones—has had a bad time. Increasingly the older core that surrounds the central business district has begun to rot, and the fine

Proposed residence for married students, now under construction

NEW RESIDENCE
UNDER CONSTRUCTION

The Second Century Development Campaign now in progress has made possible the start of construction for a new married students' residence. This will bring an end to inadequate, substandard housing at C.T.S.

The new residence will be located on Woodlawn Avenue, across the street from the east end of the Seminary building. The first of two units will be a four-story structure accommodating 42 families in one or two-bedroom apartments.

An important part of the new building is a long-needed refectory. This will provide dining facilities where students can enjoy the special kind of fellowship and discussion which develops naturally around the dining table. It will provide, too, a place where students, faculty and staff can gather for special occasions.

C.T.S. students represent the finest of today's young men and women, a bright promise for the future. Here they receive the training which is a part of the leadership heritage of the Congregational Christian churches.

As many as 9 families have lived in these single family residences, sharing bathroom, kitchen, etc.

11

FIG. 3. Proposed Chicago Theological Seminary dormitory to replace the Robie house and photomontage of "blighted" housing stock of the kind used to accommodate married students. "New Residence under Construction," in "Annual Report Issue," special issue, *Chicago Theological Seminary Register* 48 (15 October 1958): 11. (Chicago Theological Seminary Archives)

FIG. 4. Proposed Chicago Theological Seminary dormitory, view looking from interior to the 1920s main building. "New Residence under Construction," in "Annual Report Issue," special issue, *Chicago Theological Seminary Register* 48 (15 October 1959): cover. (Chicago Theological Seminary Archives)

old homes and large apartments of the monied aristocracy have become misery mansions. Increasingly also that part of the population with economic mobility has taken flight to suburbia and has incorporated and built villages whose commuting population has no interest in the city except as a place to earn their living. The rot and blight at the core has spread quickly, assisted by a ruthless group of real estate speculators who make capital out of human wretchedness." Kimpton then pointed to the rise in crime, juvenile delinquency, and the vulnerability of university communities where faculty, students, and staff become victims of muggings, robbery, and rape. He insisted that the only remedy to these problems was to carve out "the blighted area within the zone of the university" and pursue demolition and rebuilding plans. He warned that city and university officials would need to be particularly tough in the face of the "enormous internal reverberations in the warfare between high principles and hard fact that convulse the university community" and the criticism of the urban renewal plan: "There are charges of discrimination of an economic and racial variety, and the university is cartooned as a cruel colossus more concerned with property values than human rights." But Kimpton encouraged officials to move ahead with the mission of salvaging both great American cities and their universities, which he viewed as the highest expression of urban culture: "The great city which is central to American life cannot be allowed to disintegrate and in the process crush the great educational institutions they created."[48]

Kimpton's message to urban colleges and universities was straightforward: support demolition and land clearance or be crushed by blight and deterioration. This perspective and the skepticism concerning voices raised against demolition provided a crucial context against which Robie house advocates struggled. Indeed, in May 1955 Kimpton had joined Mayor Richard J. Daley, Julian Levi, director of the South East Chicago Commission, and one thousand local residents in a torch-light procession through Hyde Park that ended with a rally in front of the partially demolished house at 5456 Blackstone Avenue, the first house being wrecked under the initial phase of the Hyde Park urban renewal program. Daley and Kimpton declared that "the battle of Hyde Park will be won." Kimpton pointed out, "When the University opened in 1892, Hyde Park was one of the city's most desirable residential sections, but the creeping deterioration spreading from the loop has threatened to destroy this attractiveness."[49] The first local urban renewal project covered 47 acres of land and involved the seizing of 169 parcels of land, the demolition of 191 buildings, and the relocation of more than 1,200 families and 123 businesses. The cost of clearing the land was over $10 million, with the federal government paying two-thirds of the charges and the City of Chicago paying the remaining third. Plans for redevelopment of this land envisioned two eight-story apartment buildings with 528 units total, 267 single-family row houses, and a 10-acre neighborhood shopping center.[50]

Hyde Park demolitions and their enthusiastic support by university and public officials did not provide the most promising or fertile ground for preserving the Robie house, and yet, in the end, crucial support for preservation actually came from *within* the Hyde Park urban renewal program. Despres fully supported the program. He had worked with the Hyde Park–Kenwood Community Conference as they surveyed over 880 buildings in the Robie house neighborhood that were slated for demolition. The conference identified 43 buildings worthy of being recorded with photographs and with help from the urban renewal agency salvaged interior and exterior ornaments from about 15 of the buildings. The conference even endorsed the removal of "good" buildings when they stood in the way of the broader urban renewals plans.[51] But Despres also had sponsored the January 1957 ordinance establishing the Commission on Chicago Landmarks and had quickly joined the campaign for the Robie house. That July Despres and a member of the landmarks commission wrote to Kimpton, placing the Robie house preservation within the context of urban renewal: "When the Robie House was built in the early 1900's, it shook world architecture as a great work of creative genius. . . . You know the world-wide interest in the structure, the world-wide concern over the threat of its demolition, and the present attractiveness of the structure for a wide variety of constructive purposes. We believe that neither the University nor the Chicago Theological Seminary can permit the loss of this great civic asset. What balance is there in urban reconstruction if such a priceless community asset is allowed to be destroyed? We submit that the responsibility is irrevocably on you to see to it that you do not, by permitting the Robie House to be destroyed, despoil our city of such a rich ornament."[52]

In urging "balance" Despres suggested that the urban renewal program could be cast in a better light if its demolition decisions seemed more discriminating and less arbitrary. The Robie house was not being targeted by the land clearance program, but both urban renewal and the seminary's proposed demolition had a shared logic: the old was being swept aside for the new, vestiges of the old were being eliminated to gain ground for institutional renewal. Still, in urging the preservation of the Robie house, Despres obviously hoped to shield urban renewal demolitions from community criticism of arbitrariness. The building's preservation could suggest balance in the program and show that the hand of urban destruction could, and would, be stayed for buildings of transcendent merit; other less worthy structures could be written off as collateral damage in the "battle of Hyde Park."

Like Despres, other interested observers supported urban renewal demolitions while vigorously opposing the seminary's plan to destroy the Robie house.[53] Hyde Park urban renewal and Robie house preservation converged in December 1957 when William Zeckendorf, a maverick New York real estate developer, offered to buy the Robie house for $125,000 from the seminary (fig. 5). In January 1957 Zeckendorf's firm, Webb & Knapp, had presented its plan to purchase and redevelop a primary parcel of the Hyde Park land being cleared by the Chicago Land Clearance Commission.[54] The sale of this land to Webb & Knapp was approved by the City Council six months later. Zeckendorf planned to use the Robie house as a headquarters for his project and subsequently donate the landmark to the National Trust or another historical organization. In Zeckendorf's view, Hyde Park could have preservation as well as demolition and urban renewal. His advertisement of the purchase put the issues succinctly: "Our Christmas Gift to Hyde Park, to Chicago, to Posterity: Robie House, Hyde Park's World Famous Monument. The Heritage of the Past. The headquarters of the Future. Acting as Guardian of Great Architecture Webb & Knapp is purchasing Robie House to be used for their headquarters during the development of Hyde Park A and B."[55]

FIG. 5. William Zeckendorf (right) handing Robie house deed to University of Chicago president, with Mayor Richard Daley and planning director Ira Bach (left) observing, February 1963. *Chicago Tribune* (5 February 1963): 23. (*Chicago Tribune*)

In 1956 Zeckendorf and Wright had struck up a friendship when they met on a television debate. Wright visited Zeckendorf when he was in New York supervising construction on the Guggenheim Museum and in fact was hopeful that Zeckendorf would commission him to design some of the architect's more visionary projects, including the Golden Beacon office and apartment tower for Chicago (1930) and the Mile-High Skyscraper.[56] Zeckendorf's purchase of the Robie house also demonstrated no small measure of business savvy. He helped solve a political and institutional crisis among people with whom he needed to work closely to promote his firm's Hyde Park redevelopment program. He purchased the first parcel of cleared land in Hyde Park, but there would be more parcels soon available. Zeckendorf's acquisition solved a problem with which Mayor Daley had been personally involved in searching for a solution. Zeckendorf needed to convince hundreds of middle-class homebuyers and renters of the viability of Hyde Park as a place to live. Having a "world famous monument" stand as part of the neighborhood landscape undoubtedly helped with that pitch. Zeckendorf also stood to benefit from associating his firm with high-caliber architecture. He had placed the design of his Hyde Park buildings in the hands of noted modernists I. M. Pei and Harry Weese.

Just a month after announcing the plan to purchase the Robie house, Webb & Knapp officials were unveiling their latest designs for new houses to potential purchasers, who likely carried in their minds Zeckendorf's stewardship of the dwelling.[57] Zeckendorf also worked closely on his plans with Kimpton and the South East Chicago Commission. The commission's executive director Julian Levi helped engineer the Robie house purchase. Zeckendorf had been the keynote speaker at the commission's annual meeting in June 1957. On 20 November Levi and Wright attended a party at Zeckendorf's home in New York. Zeckendorf first announced his decision to purchase the Robie house in a letter to Levi that was read at the 3 December meeting of the commission's Executive Committee, presided over by Kimpton. Six days later, when the letter was presented to the commission's full board, the news was "enthusiastically received."[58] A week later an obviously relieved Kimpton wrote to a member of his faculty: "You will be interested to know that I think we have this Robie House problem solved."[59] Ira Bach, Chicago's director of city planning, had also traveled to New York, with the "blessing" of Kimpton and Levi, to ask that Zeckendorf purchase the Robie for his Hyde Park urban renewal headquarters.[60] The irony of this significant development in the Robie campaign was that Wright, who had done so much to mobilize the preservation effort, was apparently out of the loop when the Zeckendorf purchase was settled upon. It was not until 20 December 1957, when the public at large learned of the purchase, that Wright telegrammed Zeckendorf writing, "our country has good cause to thank you" for the preservation of the house.[61]

Zeckendorf's purchase of the Robie house moved the responsibility for the property into the private hands that were certainly more disposed toward stewardship than the Chicago Theological Seminary had been. But Zeckendorf's purchase was not the only action necessary to roll back the seminary's determination to build its dormitory on the site. Indeed a very different sort of community contributed to the preservation solution. When Wright attended the University of Wisconsin he belonged to the Phi Delta Theta fraternity. Through a stroke of fortune and coincidence the University of Chicago's Phi Delta Theta chapter maintained its house on Woodlawn Avenue three lots north of the Robie house. At first the fraternity offered to trade its chapter house for the Robie house, promising to recondition the house and open a small museum devoted to Wright's architecture. The Zeta Beta Tau fraternity, with its chapter house standing two lots north of the Robie house, agreed to trade its house for another neighboring house that the seminary owned. The seminary already owned the Hunter-Goodman house, on the first lot north of the Robie house. Consolidating these three parcels provided a building site for the dormitory that was nearly as accessible to the main seminary building as the Robie house lot.[62] So Wright's extended fraternal community proved nearly as essential to resolving the preservation crisis as Zeckendorf's initiative. Phi Delta Theta did not end up with the Robie

FIG. 6. View of Chicago Theological seminary in early stages of construction, with north elevation of the Robie house in background. Photograph 1959. (Chicago Theological Seminary Archives)

house, but Zeckendorf's purchase gave the seminary the funds necessary to acquire the fraternity's property as a key part of the site for its new dormitory (fig. 6).

In transferring the Robie house to Zeckendorf, the seminary threw down the gauntlet to the preservation community that had challenged and disrupted its dormitory project for over a year. The transfer of the building permitted Webb & Knapp to use it as an office until 1966 in connection with its rehabilitation of Hyde Park and adjoining parts of Chicago. During this time Webb & Knapp was required by deed covenant to open the house to the public "subject to reasonable and customary restrictions . . . at reasonable and customary hours." After Webb & Knapp's office use ended, the house would have to be "held, used and maintained as an architectural library, an architectural school, or an architectural exhibit or monument, or . . . for any other purpose approved in writing" by the seminary.[63] If these conditions were not fulfilled, the property would revert automatically to the seminary. After the bruising battle with preservationists, members of the seminary board believed, and perhaps even hoped, that preservationists would not be able to afford the ongoing maintenance of the house or to establish a viable institution in it and that the property would then revert to the seminary.[64]

But in 1963 Zeckendorf donated the Robie house to the University of Chicago; as a condition of accepting the gift the university required that the seminary waive its restrictions on the use of the house. The seminary agreed. Nevertheless, the university did set out to maintain the house as an architectural monument and worked with an outside committee to launch a $250,000 fund-raising campaign for its restoration. The committee chair was Ira Bach, and the coordinating committee was dominated by leading Chicago architects, including Ludwig Mies van der Rohe, Alfred Shaw, Charles F. Murphy Sr., William Holabird, Philip Will Jr., Harry Weese, Jerrold Loebl, and Bertram Goldberg. The American Foundation and the Edgar J. Kaufmann Charitable Trust both made $10,000 contributions to the campaign. The restoration committee was especially hopeful in April 1964 when Secretary of the Interior Stewart L. Udall traveled to Chicago to present Mayor Daley and university officials with the plaque marking the designation of the Robie house a national historic landmark.[65] Udall praised the significance of the building: "It is not an overstatement to assert that no house built in America during the past century matches the importance of the Robie House. . . . It introduced so many new concepts in planning and construction that its influence cannot be measured. Without the concepts demonstrated here, modern architecture might have followed a different course."[66] The fundraising campaign moved slowly, and after two years just over $54,000 had been contributed for the restoration.[67] In 2002 the Frank Lloyd Wright Preservation Trust continued the earlier conservation and preservation efforts, undertaking an exterior and interior restoration of the Robie house that has cost nearly $8 million.

More than half a century after the campaign to preserve the Robie house the need for private stewardship and responsibility for architectural heritage has endured. The Robie house preservation effort provided a heady road map for what community preservation activism and public pressure could do to turn private parties away from destruction and toward proper care for historic buildings. The success of the campaign made the disappointments of subsequent Chicago preservation failures all the more bitter. Many of the same people who stood for the Robie house organized in 1960 to try and save Adler & Sullivan's Garrick Theater in downtown Chicago.[68] They failed, unable to persuade Daley, who had supported the Robie effort, to intervene for preservation of the Garrick. Samuel A. Lichtman, the chair of the Commission on Chicago Landmarks, declared that "the work of the commission has been an exercise in futility," failing to protect key buildings considered central to Chicago's heritage.[69] That reality changed in 1968 when the city council authorized the landmarks commission to regulate the exterior appearance of landmarks. Architectural changes proposed to be made to listed properties required approval of the commission, which also had the authority to deny demolition permits. This new regulatory power over landmark buildings could be implemented even over owner objections.[70] Chicago followed by three years the granting of similar powers to the New York City Landmarks Preservation Commission. Had these powers been in place in 1957, the commission most certainly would have barred the seminary from demolishing the Robie house. At the same time, the new powers left somewhat ambiguous who was actually responsible for stewarding heritage. The implication was that owners were responsible and that public power would intervene if necessary. Filbey's insistence that "responsibility [for preservation] rests upon the public rather than upon a single individual or upon a single institution" was wrong.[71] The new powers granted to the landmarks commission in 1968 still left responsibility for architectural stewardship in the hands of individual and institutional owners; however, now the public assumed the responsibility of both regulating and guiding stewardship. The memory of how close the Robie house came to being demolished provided a crucial frame and context for the granting of new powers to the Chicago landmarks commission.

In 1957 the German-born architect E. Walter Burkhardt, chair of the department of architecture at Alabama Polytechnic Institute (now Auburn University), suggested to Kimpton another possible route toward the Robie house's preservation: "It seems to me there should be some way to incorporate this structure as part of the apartment house intended on the site for married Seminary students. Being familiar with the plan, it should make a splendid social building in connection with a campus development project."[72] George Watkins, a vice president of the University of Chicago, appreciated the suggestion and sent a note to his colleague Filbey as he passed Burkhardt's letter to him for a response: "At least he's willing to put the thing to some good use instead of simply 'monumentalizing' it."[73] Burkhardt's suggestion amounted to a proposal for adaptive use of the Robie house, and it most certainly could have worked as the seminary could have completed its project by acquiring one less lot on Woodlawn Avenue. The program for the new dormitory included a dining hall and social lounges to encourage community among residents and space to accommodate special visitors during convocations. The Robie house had already served the seminary in similar capacities. At one point in the campaign, Wright offered to design the new dormitory, free of charge, for the seminary, as long as it was located on an alternative site. But even Wright did not suggest that the Robie house could be incorporated as part of the dormitory project. In 1957 the vast majority of Robie advocates could not imagine the house connected to a new structure. In their view the building needed isolation—detachment from its context—which Wright had rendered so definitively, so deceptively, in the Wasmuth Portfolio. In the mid-twentieth century, adaptive use was seldom marshaled into the service of the preservation movement, and Wright was committed to embracing a traditional house-museum scenario with his proposal to rescue one of his masterworks.

Mount Vernon is noted for its architecture, but its historical and patriotic associations with George Washington have always been more important than its architectural significance. One of the lasting legacies for the Robie house campaign was that it promoted iconic architectural design as the gold standard of the new preservation movement. As the artfulness of architecture ascended among the rationales for preservation, the movement narrowed, pushing aside the diversity represented by places like Mount Vernon where a broader swath of historical meaning and experience had previously dominated preservation ideals. In saving the Robie house, the preservation movement accomplished something important, but this was accompanied by an unfortunate loss and narrowing of the ways in which society conceives of national heritage. It is only relatively recently that preservationists have begun to seriously redress the imbalance that the Robie house campaign exemplified. Moreover, because of the timing of the creation of historic preservation regulations, preservation, in many communities, came to increasingly subject all preserved properties to levels of scrutiny and stewardship that might only be appropriate for buildings comparable to the Robie house.

Preservation by its very nature is about the material realities embodied in buildings, landscapes, and objects. But at the same time preservation needs to be about something greater; it needs to be about the role of heritage in cultivating a capacity for critical thinking about society and politics, about seeing the past in ways that can inform acts of citizenship devoted to shaping the future.[74] To accomplish this, preservation needs to move beyond the narrow curatorial focus on connoisseurship and iconic buildings that came with the success of the 1957 campaign to preserve the Robie house.

NOTES

1. Chicago Theological Seminary (hereafter CTS), Minutes of the Board of Directors, 6 June 1957, box 257, Chicago Theological Seminary Archives (hereafter CTSA).

2. Kathryn Smith, "How The Robie House Was Saved," *Frank Lloyd Wright Quarterly* 19 (Fall 2008): 4–19.

3. CTS, Minutes, 6 June 1957, box 257, CTSA.

4. Leon M. Despres to Frank Lloyd Wright, Leon M. Despres Papers, box 40, Research Center, Chicago History Museum.

5. "Wright Defends His Robie House," *Chicago Daily News,* 18 March 1957.

6. "Wright Defends His Robie House"; "Move Robie House? No! Roars Wright," *Chicago Daily News,* 15 April 1957.

7. Frank Lloyd Wright to Richard Howland, 27 October 1958, in Robie House Vertical File, box 28, National Trust for Historic Preservation Archives, University of Maryland, College Park.

8. "The Value of Used Architecture," *Architectural Forum* 106 (April 1957): 108.

9. Lydia Mattice Brandt, *First in the Homes of His Countrymen: George Washington's Mount Vernon in the American Imagination* (Charlottesville: University of Virginia Press, 2016).

10. Julius Lewis to Lawrence A. Kimpton, 4 March 1957; University of Chicago. Office of the President, Kimpton Administration Records, box 218, Special Collections Research Center, University of Chicago Library (hereafter KAR).

11. Allen P. Golden to Lawrence A. Kimpton, 6 May 1957, KAR.

12. Riesman quoted in Nancy Penkava, "Faculty Comments on Robie," *Chicago Maroon,* 15 November 1957.

13. John M. Shlien to Lawrence A. Kimpton, 6 December 1957, KAR.

14. John M. Shlien to Editors of the [Chicago] *Maroon,* 3 December 1957, KAR.

15. Cook County Deed Book 10192, pp. 368–69, 8 April 1908.

16. "Seminary Planning New Building," *Chicago Theological Seminary Register* 47 (February 1957): 1.

17. Albert R. Hauser, "Letter to the Editor," *Hyde Park Herald,* 22 May 1957. Hauser is not listed in the *American Institute of Architects Directory* for 1956 and 1962.

18. Lawrence A. Kimpton to Leon M. Despres and Barnet Hodes, 12 July 1957, KAR.

19. Emery T. Filbey to Peter Selz et al., 10 May 1957, KAR.

20. Emery T. Filbey to Arthur Rissman, 9 May 1957, KAR.

21. Emery T. Filbey to Robert G. Neiley, 10 May 1957, KAR.

22. Emery T. Filbey to E. L. Pattullo, 26 April 1957, KAR.

23. Abner J. Mikva to Leon M. Despres, 27 May 1957, Leon M. Despres Papers, box 40, Research Center, Chicago History Museum.

24. John H. Sprinkle Jr., "'Exceptional Importance': The Origins of the 'Fifty-Year Rule,' in Historic Preservation," *Public Historian* 29 (Spring 2007): 88–89, 93–94.

25. Leopold Arnaud to Lawrence A. Kimpton, 6 March 1957, KAR.

26. John H. Mackin to Arthur C. McGiffert Jr., 15 March 1957, KAR.

27. Allen S. Weller to Lawrence A. Kimpton, 24 April 1957, KAR.

28. Peter Selz et al. to Lawrence A. Kimpton, 3 May 1957, KAR.

29. Robert F. Bishop to Lawrence A. Kimpton, 9 May 1957, KAR.

30. Quoted in "Plans to Demolish Robie House Draw Criticism from Professors," *Harvard Crimson,* 17 April 1957.

31. Quoted in "Faculty Members Speak on Proposed Robie Razing," *Chicago Maroon,* 15 November 1957.

32. Quoted in "Faculty Members Speak."

33. Quoted in Ruth Moore, "Sandburg Recites a Solution for S. Side Problem," *Chicago Sun-Times,* 22 August 1957.

34. David Zack to John L. McCaffrey 8 May 1957, KAR.

35. Quoted in "Plans to Demolish Robie House."

36. Arthur Cushman McGiffert Jr. to Barnet Hodes, 17 July 1957, KAR.

37. "Save Robie House," *Chicago Sun-Times,* 22 March 1957.

38. "Move Robie House?"

39. "Seminary Planning New Building," 1.

40. Emery T. Filbey to Percival Goodman, 1 March 1957, KAR.

41. Emery T. Filbey to George Doyle, 3 May 1957, KAR.

42. Emery T. Filbey to Julius Lewis, 10 May 1957, KAR.

43. Quoted in David Zack, "Destroying Robie House?" *Chicago Maroon,* 1 March 1957. The house did require repairs, but Houghland's characterizations of its physical conditions were more hyperbolic than based on fact.

44. Chesly Manly, "U. of Chicago Opens Critical Fight for Life," *Chicago Tribune,* 1 August 1954.

45. Mitchell Duneier, *Ghetto: The Invention of a Place, The History of an Idea* (New York: Farrar, Straus and Giroux, 2016); Arnold R. Hirsch, *Making the Second Ghetto: Race and Housing in Chicago, 1940–1960* (Cambridge: Cambridge University Press, 1983).

46. "New Residence under Construction," *Chicago Theological Seminary Register* 48 (15 October 1958): 11.

47. "Building a Second Century," *Chicago Theological Seminary Register* 48 (15 October 1958): 7.

48. Lawrence A. Kimpton, "Education and Demolition," manuscript, 5 September 1957, KAR, box 232.

49. "Partial Demolition of Building Initiates Work on Hyde Park Redevelopment Plan," *Chicago Maroon,* 13 May 1955.

50. "Daley, Kimpton See Hyde Park Blight Defeated," *Chicago Sun-Times,* 4 June 1955; Harry Swegle, "Hyde Park Relocation Job Ending," *Chicago Daily News,* 14 November 1957. See also Daniel Bluestone, *Buildings, Landscapes and Memory: Case Studies in Historic Preservation* (New York: W.W. Norton, 2011), 158–83.

51. Hyde Park-Kenwood Community Conference, "Questions and Suggestions on Kenwood Block Groups on Urban Renewal Planning," February 1956, Housing and Home Finance Agency Records, Urban Renewal Demonstration Case Files, Record Group 207, box 17, National Archives and Record Center, College Park, Maryland.

52. Leon M. Despres and Barnet Hodes to Lawrence A. Kimpton, 8 July 1957, KAR.

53. Golden to Kimpton, 6 May 1957.

54. Sara Stevens, *Developing Expertise: Architecture and Real Estate in Metropolitan America* (New Haven: Yale University Press, 2016): 166, 167, 189–191.

55. Advertisement, *Hyde Park Herald,* 25 December 1957.

56. Smith, "How the Robie House Was Saved."

57. "Webb & Knapp Show Plans to Co-Op Homes Tomorrow," *Hyde Park Herald,* 29 January 1958.

58. South East Chicago Commission, Executive Committee Meeting Minutes, 3 December 1957; South East Chicago Commission, Board of Directors Meeting Minutes, 9 December 1957, KAR.

59. Lawrence A. Kimpton to John M. Shlien, 17 December 1957, KAR.

60. See Florence A. Hammet, "Robie House: The New Alumni House," *University of Chicago Magazine,* 73 (Winter 1981): 13.

61. Smith, "How The Robie House Was Saved," 4–19.

62. "Perspectives," *Architectural Record* 121 (April 1957): 7; "Wright Visits Robie House," *Hyde Park Herald,* 20 March 1957; Ernest Fuller, "Fraternity Acts to Save Home Wright Designed," *Chicago Tribune,* 12 March 1957, A8.

63. Cook County Deeds, Book 56542, p. 397.

64. Arthur Cushman McGiffert Jr., *No Ivory Tower: The Story of the Chicago Theological Seminary* (Chicago: Chicago Theological Seminary, 1965), 284.

65. Leon M. Despres to Stewart Udall, 27 March 1964; Leon Despres Papers, box 40, Research Center, Chicago History Museum.

66. Quoted in "The Robie House Received National Landmark Status," *Inland Architect* 7 (April 1964): 22.

67. "Robie House Fund Raising Campaign," *Inland Architect,* 8 (January 1965): 2; "James Arkin, "The Robie House: Prospects for Restoration," *Inland Architect,* 6 (January 1963): 14–16.

68. On preservation effort and demolition of the Garrick, see Daniel Bluestone, "'Desecration of the Highest Magnitude': Demolishing the Garrick, 1960–1961," in John Vinci, Tim Samuelson, Eric Nordstrom, and Chris Ware, eds., *Reconstructing the Garrick: Adler & Sullivan's Lost Masterpiece* (Chicago: Alphawood Foundation; Minneapolis: University of Minnesota Press, 2021): 114–89. See also Theodore W. Hild, "The Demolition of the Garrick Theater and the Birth of the Preservation Movement in Chicago," *Illinois Historical Journal* 88 (Summer 1995): 79–100; and Richard Cahan, *They All Fall Down: Richard Nickel's Struggle to Save America's Architecture* (Washington, D.C.: Preservation Press, 1994), 92–133.

69. Quoted in "Daley Seeks Law to Save Landmarks," *Chicago Tribune,* 16 November 1967, 2.

70. "Daley Seeks Law to Save Landmarks"; "Council Units to Study Law to Save Landmarks," *Chicago Tribune,* 4 June 1967; "Landmark Commission Reactivated," *Chicago Tribune,* 18 April 1968, E10; "Historical Site Unit Set to Act," *Chicago Tribune,* 19 May 1968, E1.

71. Emery T. Filbey to Arthur Rissman, 9 May 1957, KAR.

72. E. W. Burkhardt to Lawrence A. Kimpton, 14 May 1957, KAR.

73. George E. Watkins to Emery T. Filbey, May 1957 KAR.

74. See essays in Max Page and Marla Miller, eds., *Bending the Future: Fifty Ideas for the Next Fifty Years of Historic Preservation in the United States* (Amherst: University of Massachusetts Press, 2016). See also Daniel Bluestone, "Conservation's Curatorial Conundrum," *Change Over Time* 7 (Fall 2017): 234–51.

ALICE THOMINE-BERRADA

The Masieri Memorial Controversy in the Context of Venice's Cultural Heritage

Charmed by the architectural "magnificence" of Venice and alarmed by the damage that any "new construction" might inflict on the city, the French Romantic writer, politician, and public intellectual François René de Chateaubriand asked himself despairingly during his stay in Venice in 1833: "What could be built here [nowadays]?"[1] That question was still under debate 120 years later when Frank Lloyd Wright was commissioned in 1953 to design a new building situated at the turning point of the Grand Canal, between the Gothic Ca' Foscari and the late Renaissance–early Baroque Palazzo Balbi. The setting has long been celebrated since it forms the backdrop for one of the most important reviewing stands of the city's famous annual regatta (fig. 1).

The project was commissioned by the family of Angelo Masieri, a young Italian architect and admirer of Wright, who died tragically in 1952 during a journey to the United States to meet the American architect. The new building was to replace a small, modest house, dating from around the turn of the eighteenth century (fig. 2). Wright's Masieri Memorial was to house a foundation devoted to young architects in tribute to Angelo. The program followed the example of the Cini Foundation, created in 1951 by Vittorio Cini with the aim of restoring the island of San Giorgio Maggiore and making it a place of cultural activity in memory of his son. The Masieri program had been closely developed in collaboration with the School of Architecture of Venice where Masieri had studied. Since the arrival of the architect Guiseppe Samonà as director in 1945, the school was looking to become a place of innovation and international exchange.[2] Most of the professors believed that Wright's architecture afforded one of the most promising bases for bringing new life to Italian architecture in the postwar years. The individual most committed to this agenda was Bruno Zevi, the professor of history of architecture, who had discovered Wright's work during his self-imposed exile in

FIG. I. Grand Canal, Venice, showing Casa Masieri (center), Palazzo Balbi (right), and Ca' Foscari (left). (Author's photograph)

the United States in 1940–43. After his return to Italy, Zevi championed an architecture inspired by Wright through the creation of the Association for Organic Architecture in 1945, the publication of *Towards an Organic Architecture* that same year, and the review *Metron*, begun in 1945.[3]

Wright's Masieri project was a relatively simple, four-story edifice, clad in marble, with a belvedere and balconies (fig. 3). The volume and design recalled some of his work of the 1920s, such as the Millard house in Pasadena, California (1923–24). Its vertical lines accentuated the building's height, which exceeded that of the existing house by little more than two feet.[4] The project was ultimately rejected by municipal authorities during the autumn of 1955. Beginning with its first presentation to the public at the American Academy of Arts and Letters in New York in May 1953, the scheme aroused considerable debate, bringing into conflict architects, historians, critics of art and architecture, as well as admirers of Venice such as Ernest Hemingway. These exchanges involved the local, national, and international press. Although the project was a favorite of Wright's, who kept a drawing of it over his desk following its official rejection, it was undervalued in studies devoted to the architect until reconsiderations of the last twenty years by Neil Levine, Maristella Casciato, and Troy Michael Ainsworth. Ainsworth,

ALICE THOMINE-BERRADA

FIG. 2. Casa Masieri. (Private collection)

who analyzed the debates around the project, demonstrated that the reviews, from an architectural perspective, were not of much interest since few critics looked closely at the project.[5] Circumstances made the design difficult to evaluate since its publication was delayed for a long time. The Masieri family did not wish to publicize it because the initial presentation in New York, rather than Venice, caused consternation among the Venetian public and authorities alike.[6] In addition, the poor quality of the reproduction of Wright's drawing gave only an imperfect idea of the architecture, to the point that one Italian critic characterized the five-story building as a skyscraper.[7]

In fact, discussions mainly centered on the question raised by Chateaubriand; that is, on heritage. Because of the reputation of its architect and the significance of its location, the project continued to fuel debate well after its rejection. Coverage was given in numerous publications devoted to Venetian heritage, including *Save Venice,* the cultural heritage study published by UNESCO in 1971 following the dramatic flood of 1966, and *Venise au fil du temps: Atlas historique d'urbanisme et d'architecture* by Egle Renata Trincanato and Umberto Franzoi.[8] These publications, which considered

the project as a missed opportunity for Modern architecture, contributed to making the Masieri Memorial a benchmark in the evolving relationship between Modern architecture and historic settings, where unrealized efforts often take on as much importance as those that are built.

VENICE AND THE DEVELOPMENT OF HERITAGE CONSCIOUSNESS

Among places home to famous controversies over the proper approach to conservation and restoration, Venice became a premier example of a new view toward heritage beginning in the mid-nineteenth century with the writings of John Ruskin.[9] Contrary to the vision of restoration that Eugène-Emmanuel Viollet-le-Duc was beginning to establish in France, which centered on the notion of the monument, the English critic highlighted the cultural importance of domestic architecture and the urban fabric, where the monument counts for less than the urban whole of which it is a part. Becoming a component of the spirit of Venice, the famous *venezianità,* the importance given to the urban fabric permeated the nineteenth century in most of the numerous tourist guides and specialized writings devoted to heritage.[10] At the same time, the campaign for modernizing Venice, following the example of other important nineteenth-century European cities, made it clear that the special character of Venice would disappear with any massive demolition of buildings and infilling of canals. This point was emphasized in 1887 in the elaborate pamphlet, "Delendae Venetiae," by the historian Pompeo Molmenti.[11]

The unique character of Venice's urban fabric also played an important role in the development of planning theory. In *City Planning According to Artistic Principles* (1889), the Viennese architect Camillo Sitte highlighted the picturesque beauty of historic cities and their organization centered on open squares. The Piazza San Marco was one of his most important examples (fig. 4). For Sitte, Venice offered a new basis for rethinking the modern city aesthetically. From an opposite point of view, Le Corbusier, who was very antagonistic toward what he considered the backward-looking spirit of Sitte's thought, nonetheless considered Venice as an ideal example in his famous theoretical book of 1925, *Urbanisme* (fig. 5).[12] Venice also drew the attention of the most important American urbanists. Lewis Mumford, for example, acknowledged in *The Culture of Cities* (1938) the role of Ruskin's interpretation of Venice in perceiving the city as a social body. Twenty-five years later, in *The City in History,* Mumford formulated the notion of the "Venetian order," in which the Piazza San Marco became a basic module for the city, the canals a transportation network, and the Lagoon a greenbelt.[13]

All these writings examining Venice as a model for contemporary city planning contributed to the transformation of Venice into a veritable museum. If Mumford and Le Corbusier used the organicist metaphor, neither

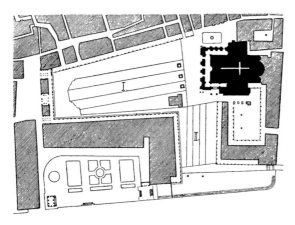

FIG. 4. Plan of Piazza San Marco from Camillo Sitte, *Der Städtebau nach seinen künstlerischen Grundsätzen,* 1909.

FIG. 5. Aerial view of Piazza San Marco from Le Corbusier, *Urbanisme,* 1925.

was thinking of a body capable of continuing to grow, to live, and thus to accept the architecture of the twentieth century. In fact, for them the history of Venice had stopped with the fall of the Republic in 1797, an idea propagated in most scholarly and popular historical writings about the city. Venice was portrayed as static, finished. In 1962, Le Corbusier advised the mayor to "declare Venice a sacred city."[14]

This point of view influenced the first preservation plan of Venice (1939).[15] Based on national legislation devoted to that city, it was drafted in 1937 by the engineer and city planner Eugenio Miozzi, director of urban planning of the city from 1931 and still in charge during the Masieri debate.[16] The plan protected the Piazza San Marco as an isolated masterpiece. In refusing to recognize the importance of the vernacular fabric of the surrounding districts, the plan also opposed the historic city to contemporary needs. Widely criticized after its issuance, the plan was deemed out-of-date by the end of World War II but was not replaced by new legislation until 1956 and supplemented by a new preservation plan in 1962.[17]

While the fate of Wright's Masieri Memorial was under debate between May 1953 and November 1956, the urban regulations concerning heritage were thus unformulated and vague. Bearing witness to this conundrum, the official examination of the project underwent long administrative delays and was shuffled from one department to another, including the Commissione Igienico-Edilizia (Sanitary Building Commission) and the Commissione di Edilizia ed Ornato (Decorative Building Commission), as well as the city council.[18] Miozzi's other projects allow us to understand the spirit of urban planning during his directorate as one based on the isolation of historic monuments and the practice of historicizing infill. His most famous work is the Ponte della Libertà (1931–33), an enormous bridge that was the first (and remains the only) automobile connection between Venice and the mainland (fig. 6). Here modern materials are masked by stone facing imitating the adjacent nineteenth-century railroad bridge, the Ponte delle Lagune, testifying to the historicizing spirit in which the modernization of Venice was then undertaken. But the vagueness of Venetian preservation policy also explains the contradictory nature of buildings contemporary with Wright's project. The 1949 addition to the Bauer Hotel by Marino Meo, for example, was rendered in a strong rectilinear fashion somewhat in the manner of Auguste Perret's work, breaking with the neighboring baroque facade of the church of San Moïse (fig. 7). The Palazzo Tito by Angelo Scattolin (1949–54) followed a nineteenth-century eclectic spirit, its facade festooned with balconies composed in a manner suggesting a simplified version of the older palaces along the Grand Canal.

If archival documents do not enlighten us about the precise role played by Miozzi throughout the evolution of the Masieri affair, they testify that

FIG. 6. Ponte della Liberta, Venice, postcard. (Private collection)

FIG. 7. Marino Meo, Bauer Hotel addition, Venice, 1949. (Author's photograph)

he was the person who gave the final recommendation of refusal to the mayor on the grounds that the rear of the proposed building exceeded the statutory height limit. The archives also reveal the arbitrary character of this decision, since a letter offering the possibility of modifying the plans to adhere to the height limit accompanied the building permit application.[19] The legal rationale was thus unjustified. The real reason lay perhaps in the fact that Wright was one of the first to propose a different way of dealing with the heritage of Venice in new construction. His approach was predicated on addressing two challenges: inserting Modern architecture into a historically significant place and justifying the destruction of an existing historic building.

THE WRIGHT HERITAGE ANSWER FOR VENICE

Wright defended his project in a series of writings intended to convince local authorities of its virtues. These texts can help us understand the ways in which he thought about the relationship between contemporary architecture and historic context. In part to appeal to the authorities, Wright wrote respectfully of the idea of genius loci, as he did earlier for the Imperial Hotel

ALICE THOMINE-BERRADA

in Tokyo.[20] Since the Masieri Memorial was intended to be an integral part of a historically significant place, Wright stated that his design was sensitive to its environs. He described the project as a "tribute to Venice. In every sense Venice lived in it anew."[21] Wright was aware that his previous buildings could raise fears that he was insensitive to the historic character of Venice, so he emphasized to the mayor the strength of his attachment to the city's beauty: "Loving Venice and being just as jealous of its beauty as a Venetian himself, alive or dead, I have tried to put this feeling into this small marble structure."[22]

In support of Wright, architects and art historian sympathetic to the proposal sought to emphasize his love for a certain category of historic architecture and thus mitigate his well-known criticism of the Renaissance.[23] These arguments were linked to Zevi's idea that organicism was not a specific moment in time but a universal way of conceiving architectural space in a "socially useful, dynamic, lived" kind of way.[24] Giuseppe Samonà spoke of "an enormous Wrightian world of new medievalism," while Zevi acknowledged Wright's disinterest in classical architecture.[25] But the most important development of this idea was made by the well-known historian of Byzantine art, Sergio Bettini, who wrote an important essay in 1953 devoted to Venice, in which he gave an organic interpretation of its urban development as a palimpsest of inseparable historical layers.[26] Bettini noted in his text, published in the *Metron* issue devoted to the defense of Wright's Masieri Memorial, the architect's aversion to Michelangelo and, more broadly, explained that Wright's organic architecture fit perfectly with the organic development of Venice, a skillful way to enhance the historical dimension of the design.[27]

Wright himself insisted on the universal and timeless character of organic architecture, which, he stated, "is not a style but is style and not only that but able to revivify genuine traditions in Architecture no matter what their nationality—preserving them alive."[28] In a long letter addressed to the mayor of Venice titled "This Venice Affair," Wright underscored the fact that the relationship with nature, so important in his work, was also an important point for Venice, a city historically surrounded by water: "Venice does not float upon the water like a gondola but rests upon the silt at the bottom of the sea. In the little building I have designed slender marble shafts firmly fixed upon concrete piles (two to each) in the silt rise from the water as do reeds or rice or any water plants."[29]

One other important point developed by Wright was the absence of a break between the past and the present: "True modern architecture, like classical architecture, has no age. It is a continuation of all the architecture that has gone before, not a break with it. A modernist does not destroy that culture that has been, nor set up a roadblock to the future. He belongs to the past, to the present, and offers a prophesy of the future."[30] This position was clearly opposed to the concept of the museum-city implemented by Miozzi and espoused by Le Corbusier.

The Masieri project was also more broadly considered by Wright as a symbol of his opposition to modern urban planning. In an article published in the London *Times* in November 1953, he explicitly set this project against the "massacre" recently perpetrated on the Marseilles waterfront, which he described as a "terrible offence."[31] This could be read as a general critique of the rebuilding of French cities after World War II, where only the more important monuments were preserved while most of the old urban fabric was destroyed.[32] Refusing the break and militating for an "organic" and lively continuity between past and present, Wright also repeatedly rejected the path of historicism: "Not imitation but interpretation of Venice" were the most important words he used to describe his project. He believed it defined a new kind of relationship with the historic city, freed from historical references yet respectful of the spirit of the urban architecture by its scale and use of traditional materials and of its site dominated by the presence of water.

It is clear that Wright was not immediately understood. The famous Renaissance art historian Bernard Berenson ironically compared the project to a "table ornament," while the modernist English critic James Maude Richards likened it to a "small art nouveau mouse, hardly fierce enough to justify the storm it had created there."[33] Such observations presumed the autonomous character of Wright's architecture, whereas the building had been designed to fit precisely into its setting along the Grand Canal. This misinterpretation of the design allows us to understand why Zevi, as well as Trincanato, could perceive the failure of the project as a devastating blow to the future of organic architecture in Italy.[34]

Nevertheless, Wright's project had an important afterlife in helping make acceptable a new kind of modern architectural intervention in historic contexts. Following his architect and journalist friends, who insisted on the insignificant character of the house that was to be replaced, Wright was also very conscious of the necessity of justifying the destruction of the existing building.[35] In "This Venice Affair" he offered a guideline for the conservation of the city's fabric at a time when there were no regulations governing the subject.[36] His program was based on the idea of culling: "Architecture should keep alive what is most worth preserving in Venice and that means to cut away what is already unfit to live if Venice is to live as herself. In this salvage, better building from the bottom up is needed. But there is no need to lose or damage her native beauty."[37]

This was an answer to those who thought that it was not acceptable to per-

ALICE THOMINE-BERRADA

mit the destruction of the existing house. The journalist Antonio Cederna, who was one of the more virulent defenders of historic centers in Italy, fought for the conservation of the existing house as an "irreplaceable environmental accompaniment to the Palazzo Balbi."[38] This raised the question of "minor" architecture, which was at that time the object of innovative thinking in Venice. Based in the continuity of nineteenth-century interest in the issue, this new way of considering the urban fabric emphasized its architectural qualities more than its cultural importance. The most significant writing in this regard is doubtless *Venezia Minore* by Trincanato, an architect close to Samonà and one of the pillars of the architecture school of Venice.[39] Following this book, Trincanato became the defender of a new heritage policy, advocating for a nuanced, precise, and accurate city plan that would project how "to appraise street by street, house by house" what can be eliminated and what has to be kept, a way of thinking similar to Wright's.[40]

During the 1953–54 academic year, the very time of the Masieri debate, Venice's architecture school organized a new curriculum. Samonà, who was willing since the end of World War II to cooperate with the municipal authorities, announced in his opening speech of the year the creation of a workshop devoted to Venice's urban planning.[41] The course had high ambitions: participating students were to undertake studies of the vernacular districts such as the Canareggio as a way to apply the survey approach recommended by Trincanato. Documents do not reveal if these initiatives were directly inspired by Wright's project, nor do they tell us if these initiatives would have considered the existing Masieri house as important, a relevant issue since the solution finally adopted in the 1980s was to restore the house while adding some chimneys, a very typical vernacular element of Venice.[42] But even if this interest was simply an aspect of the times, it is possible to think that Wright's idea helped feed these initiatives.

On a broader architectural level, Carlo Scarpa's work benefited greatly from Wright's Masieri project. His first personal encounter with the architect dated to 1951 when Wright visited Venice to receive an honorary degree.[43] It "swept me away like a wave," Scarpa said.[44] From 1940 to 1946, he was Masieri's teacher at the School of Architecture of Venice. With Samonà and his colleagues from the school, he helped Savina Masieri in her memorial project. Although Scarpa remained silent during the public controversy, he no doubt had a detailed knowledge of the project as well as of the substance of the discussions surrounding it.

At the same time, this period constituted a turning point in Scarpa's career, described by Francesco Dal Co as "devising increasingly complex spatial layouts, transforming the dialogue with the old existing elements into a process of abstraction."[45] Before the Masieri project, Scarpa's interventions in historic buildings in Venice were limited to their interiors and made no allusions to the buildings' historic forms. His first involvement with a historic building was a 1936 reworking of the Aula Baratto, a classroom in the Gothic Ca' Foscari. The scheme was inspired by Le Corbusier and based on modernist forms. By contrast, when Scarpa was asked to transform this same space into a lecture hall in 1956, following the defeat of the Masieri project, he proposed a structure in wood and glass whose design was a modern and simplified interpretation of the structural principles of Gothic architecture. This intervention in a historic context, like the one he undertook at the same time at the Museo Civico of Castelvecchio (1956), was not a restoration, as Ellen Soroka has explained, but rather a new creation following the example of Wright's Masieri Memorial.[46]

The Olivetti store of 1957, located on the Piazza San Marco, most reflects the influence of Wright's Masieri design (fig. 8). On the exterior Scarpa preserved the traditional proportions of the boutiques around the square and employed materials that established continuity with the surrounding stone and wood constructions, yet without formally imitating the older architecture. "The art of . . . the *caesura*" respectful of the continuity of the urban fabric and grounded in the formal abstraction of historic references invented by Scarpa in these years surely owes much to Wright, as Manfredo Tafuri has noted.[47] The Olivetti store can be considered the most important

FIG. 8. Carlo Scarpa, Olivetti store, Venice, 1957. (Photograph courtesy of George X. Lin)

ALICE THOMINE-BERRADA

heir to Wright's attitude toward architectural heritage, although its nearly hidden location saved it from the same kind of controversy. It is therefore not surprising that in 1968 Savina Masieri turned to Scarpa to revive the memorial project, this time limiting it to a reconfiguration of the interior of the existing house.[48]

Over time, the Masieri project helped raise the discussion of Venetian architecture and its heritage to an international level. Within the framework of the implementation of its new city planning scheme, the municipality organized in October 1962 an international colloquium titled "The Problem of Venice." This was the first step leading to the famous Venice Charter of 1964 and the invitation to numerous foreign architects, such as Le Corbusier, Richard Neutra, and Albert Laprade, to participate. The last was facing the same problem in France in implementing, in Paris's historic Marais district, the legislation regarding "conservation areas" launched by André Malraux in 1962.[49] During this meeting, the defeat of the Wright project was publicly lamented. Had it been built, it would have, according to Agostino Zanon dal Bo, the city councilor in charge of urbanism and private construction, established a firm basis for the introduction of Modern architecture in the city center of Venice.[50]

Two years later, Le Corbusier was invited to plan a new hospital, and six years subsequently, Louis Kahn was asked to design a new convention center (1968–72). These projects did not see the light of day, but the way was opened for Modern architecture to enter the city. In 1985, Aldo Rossi organized the Venice Architecture Biennale around the idea of a completely open international competition devoted to the modernization of Venice. And recently signature works by Santiago Calatrava, Tadao Ando, and Rem Koolhaas introduced an international aura of high modernism to Venice.[51] By contrast, Wright's project aimed to show how Modern architecture could also resonate with the vernacular; that is to say, belong to a place and respect its local traditions.

NOTES

This text owes a great deal to Neil Levine, who shared with me the documentary research he collected on this project in the early 1990s. I thank him for his confidence and the intellectual exchanges that allowed this text to mature.

1. [François-René] de Chateaubriand, *Mémoires d'outre-tombe,* ed. Edmond Biré (Paris: Garnier Frères, 1898–99), 6:233 (entry of 10 September 1833).
2. Giovanni Marras and Marco Pogacnik, eds., *Giuseppe Samonà e la scuola di architettura a Venezia: Archivio progetti* (Padua: Il Poligrafo, 2006); Franco Man-

cuso, ed., *Io IUAV di Giuseppe Samonà e l'insegnamento dell'architettura* (Rome: Fondazione Bruno Zevi, 2007), esp. Donatella Calabi, "La nascità dello IUAV et l'impronta di Giuseppe Samonà," 15–35.

3. For more on Zevi, see Jean-Louis Cohen's essay in this volume.

4. Elio Zorzi, "Ingiustificato allarme a Venezia per la nuova casa sul Canal Grande progettata dal famoso architetto Wright," *Metron* 8, no. 48 (1953): 64.

5. Bruce Brooks Pfeiffer, *Treasures of Taliesin: Seventy-Six Unbuilt Designs* (London: Thames & Hudson, 1985), 118; Neil Levine, *The Architecture of Frank Lloyd Wright* (Princeton: Princeton University Press, 1996), 374–83; Maristella Casciato, "Wright and Italy: The Promise of Organic Architecture," in Anthony Alofsin, ed., *Frank Lloyd Wright: Europe and Beyond* (Berkeley: University of California Press, 1999), 76–86; Troy Michaël Ainsworth, "Modernism Contested: Frank Lloyd Wright in Venice and the Masieri Memorial Debate" (Ph.D. diss., Texas Tech University, 2005).

6. Ainsworth, "Modernism Contested," 12, 114.

7. Roberto Papini, "Perchè sarebbe una stonatura il palazzotto di Wright sul Canalazzo—A parte l'inopportunità di turbare l'equilibrio scenografico in uno dei punti più belli della città; il progetto dell'architetto americano, riecheggianto lo stile 'liberty,' appare artisticamente molto debole," *Corriere della Sera* [Milan], 25 March 1954, 3.

8. UNESCO, *Sauver Venise* (Paris: Robert Laffont, 1971); Egle Renata Trincanato and Umberto Franzoi, *Venise au fil du temps: Atlas historique d'urbanisme et d'architecture* (Boulogne-Billancourt: Joël Cuenot,1971).

9. In particular, Ruskin's famous *The Stones of Venice,* originally published in 1851–53. A stunning sense of his perspective on Venice may be gleaned from Ken Jacobson and Jenny Jacobson, *Carrying Off the Palaces: John Ruskin's Daguerreotypes* (London: Bernard Quaritch, 2015).

10. See, for example, Margaret Plant, *Venice: Fragile City, 1797–1997* (New Haven: Yale University Press, 2002), 182–87, and the numerous writings of the architect and preservationist Camillo Boito, one of the major specialists of Venetian heritage.

11. Pompeo Molmenti, "Delendae Venetiae," *Nuova Antologia,* 1887, 414; see Giuseppe Pavanello, *L'enigma della modernità: Venezia nell'età di Pompeo Molmenti* (Venice: Istituto Veneto di Scienze Lettere ed Arti, 2006).

12. Marida Talamona, ed., *L'Italie de Le Corbusier* (Paris: Editions de La Villette, 2010), esp. 77–87; Stanislas von Moos, "A propos de Venise," 201–209; Antonio Foscari, "Le Corbusier à Venise en juillet 1934."

13. Lewis Mumford, *The City in History: Its Origins, Its Transformation, and Its Prospects* (New York: Harcourt Brace Jovanovich, 1961), 321–28.

14. Le Corbusier to the Syndic of Venice, 3 October 1962, I2-20-70-001, Fondation Le Corbusier, Paris.

15. Trincanato and Franzoi, *Venise au fil du temps,* 34.

16. For Miozzi, see Valeria Farinati, *Eugenio Miozzi: 1889–1979: Iinventario analitico dell'archivio* (Venice: Istituto Universitario di Architettura di Venezia, 1997).

17. Trincanato and Franzoi,*Venise au fil du temps,* 46.

18. Ainsworth, "Modernism Contested," 254–83.

19. The building permit application, as reproduced in Ainsworth, "Modernism Contested," 279, states: "The preliminary project attached here is only for the purpose of obtaining a preliminary approval of the plans and volumes, before proceeding

to the final design of the building. For the plans, two different solutions are presented: the first one meets the actual perimeter on the Grand Canal, while the second foresees extension over the Canal with occupation of public space. The party concerned [the applicants] would prefer this second solution. Plans, elevations, [and perspectives] respect the City's maximum building height requirements, and that the plan follows within the specified perimeter."

20. See the brilliant explanation of this building in Levine, *The Architecture of Frank Lloyd Wright,* 374–83.

21. Quoted in "A New Debate in Old Venice—Frank Lloyd Wright's Design for a 'Different' Building Divides a City That Cherishes Tradition," *New York Times Magazine,* 21 March 1954, 8.

22. Wright to the Syndic of Venice, 28 December 1953, Frank Lloyd Wright Foundation Archives, Avery Architectural & Fine Arts Library, Columbia University, and Museum of Modern Art, New York (hereafter FLWFA).

    The expression "as a Venetian himself" was a response to the argument by Venetian art critics such as Roberto Papini, who opposed Wight on the grounds of his being a foreigner: "No foreigner who has gone to Venice to design buildings, or paint, or sculpt, has ever been able to take root, not because he lacked genius, but because Venice must be lived and must be felt in the flesh and adored." ("Perche sarbbe una stonatura il palazzo di Wright sul Canalazzo," *Corriere della Sera* [Milan], 25 March 1954, 3.) The role played in the rejection of the project by opposition to the postwar American political interventionism in Italy, which was particularly important in the very independent and proud city of Venice, has been well highlighted in Casciato, "Wright and Italy," and Ainsworth, "Modernism Contested," 120–60.

23. In its decision against the Masieri project, made on 24 March 1954, for instance, the Decorative Building Commission remarked on Wright's reservations regarding Renaissance architecture in general and "Michelangelo's dome" [of St. Peter's] in particular. Masieri Memorial folder, Comune di Venezia Archivio Storico, Venice.

24. See, for example, Bruno Zevi, "Architecture organique," *Encyclopedia Universalis,* https://www.universalis.fr/encyclopedie/architecture-organique/.

25. Giuseppe Samonà, "Sull architettura di Frank Lloyd Wright," *Metron,* nos. 41–42 (1951), 12; Zevi, "Wright and Italy: A Recollection," in Alofsin, *Frank Lloyd Wright,* 70–71.

26. Sergio Bettini, *Venezia* (Novara: Instituto Geografico de Agostini, 1953.

27. Sergio Bettini, "Venezia e Wright," *Metron,* nos. 49–50 (1954): 14–25.

28. Wright to Savina Masieri, 11 March 1953, FLWFA.

29. Wright, "This Venice Affair," 24 March 1954, 2, MS 2401.561A, FLWFA.

30. Wright, "This Venice Affair."

31. "Architect's Reply to Critics," *Times* [London], 15 November 1953.

32. In this volume, by contrast, Jean-Louis Cohen interprets the article, as Bruce Pfeiffer did, as a critique of Le Corbusier's Unité d'Habitation, despite the fact that the building is nowhere near the waterfront.

33. "A New Debate in Old Venice," 7; J[ames] M[aude] Richards, "Venice Preserv'd," *Journal of the Royal Architectural Institute of Canada* 31 (August 1954): 282.

34. Zevi, "Wright and Italy," 69.

35. For example, Roberto Pane, "La laguna 'organica,'" *Il Mondo* [Rome], 2 February 1954, 11, called it "an old house without any artistic importance."

36. Wright, "This Venice Affair."
37. Wright, "This Venice Affair."
38. Antonio Cederna, "L'operazione Wright—la laguna 'organica'," *Il Mondo,* 9 February 1954, 11. Cederna was unusual in this regard, cf. note 35.
39. See Maddalena Scimemi and Anna Tonicello, eds., *Egle Renata Trincanato 1910–1998* (Venice: Marsilio; IUAV, 2008), esp. 11–24 (M. Scimemi, "Riscrivere l'architettura: Venezia minore e il volto delle città").
40. On Trincanato's methodology, see Guido Piovene, *Viaggio in Italia* (Milan: Mondadori, 1914), 56.
41. "Uno studio de Venezia per la pianificazione urbanistica delle sue esigenze moderna," *Annuario di Istituto universitario di architettura di Venezia,* 1954, 34.
42. The work was done under the direction of Scarpa. See Francesco Dal Co and Giuseppe Mazzariol, eds., *Carlo Scarpa: The Complete Works* (New York: Electa/Rizzoli, 1985), 134.
43. Zevi, "Wright and Italy," 70–71.
44. "Interview with Carlo Scarpa," Martin Dominguez, in Dal Co and Mazzariol, *Carlo Scarpa,* 29.
45. Francesco Dal Co, "Genie ist Fleiss: L'architecture de Carlo Scarpa," in Dal Co and Mazzariol, *Carlo Scarpa,* 58.
46. Ellen Soroka, "Restauro in Venezia," *Journal of Architectural Education* 47 (May 1994): 224–41.
47. Manfredo Tafuri, "Carlo Scarpa and Italian Architecture," in Dal Co and Mazzariol, *Carlo Scarpa,* 89.
48. For a discussion of the Olivetti store and the remodeling of the Masieri palace, see Robert McCarter, *Carlo Scarpa* (London: Phaidon, 2013), 114–29 and 190–97, respectively.
49. The phrase is *secteurs sauvegardés* in French.
50. Agostino Zanon dal Bo, "Il piano regolatore di Venezia: realtà, prospettive, problemi," in *Atti del Convegno internazionale: Il problema di Venezia, 4–7 ottobre 1962* (Venice: Commune di Venezia, Fondazione GiorgioCini, 1964), 31.
51. Calatrava built the Ponte della Costituzione in 2008; Ando the Punta della Dogana in 2008–9; and Koolhaas the Fondaco dei Tedeschi in 2016.

BARRY BERGDOLL

Afterword

A decade after a single year studying architecture at Columbia University, Art Garfunkel was still intoning the name of Frank Lloyd Wright. His and Paul Simon's lyrical tribute, "So Long, Frank Lloyd Wright," was, and remains, probably the only popular song recorded in the United States devoted to an architect. Wright, of course, died the year before Garfunkel enrolled in 1960 in the architecture program, dropping out after a year only to reenroll in the university a few years later and graduate in 1965 as an art history major. Wright's spirit still pervaded the studios even after the master's death, no doubt enhanced after Edgar Kaufmann jr. joined the faculty in 1963. And the headlines—and lines—as Wright's Guggenheim Museum at long last opened its doors in late October 1959, a few months after the master's death, no doubt turned more than one adolescent onto architecture.

It would be more than a half century later that the Frank Lloyd Wright Foundation Archives—thousands of drawings, letters, and other documents transferred from Wright's Taliesin West—came to be housed in the lower reaches of the Avery Architectural and Fine Arts Library, a few floors below—then as now—the design studios in the upper reaches of McKim, Mead & White's 1912 Avery Hall. In the early 1960s Wright's name, it seems, wafted in the air and helped keep inspiration flowing while the lights shone from those studio windows until dawn. Or was it the nights that the old friends Paul Simon and Art Garfunkel stole away to compose, strut, and sing? As fans of Simon & Garfunkel know, the song "So Long, Frank Lloyd Wright" on their final album, *Bridge over Troubled Water,* was also a type of elegy for a singing partnership about to break up. The multiple shades of meaning and ambiguities of the song, which built on the mellifluous rhythm of the architect's partially invented name "Frank Lloyd Wright," seem almost a metaphor today for the dichotomous relationship between Wright's public and professional reputations.

Already in his own lifetime Wright's name had become a synonym for architecture itself, and this for a broad swath of the American public. This can be gauged still on YouTube by watching the clip of Wright's appearance on the popular game show *What's My Line?*, where his identity is guessed inadvertently by one of the panelists who asks if the mystery guest might be in some field "like architecture or design, such as Frank Lloyd Wright." In the 1950s the octogenarian was still grabbing headlines and to be seen almost as frequently on TV shows as in the magazines and daily press. Then, even as now—although there is no way to get a scientific read on this perception—he was very likely to be the first, and maybe the only, architect that most people outside an architectural school or office would think of if asked to name an architect. Yet inside an architectural office today surely another name— maybe Frank Gehry—would be more likely to come rapidly to the interlocutor's lips. And if the office library still has volumes on the shelves on which to draw inspiration, it is more likely to be volumes on Aalto, Le Corbusier, or Mies than Wright, or on the most influential of today's practitioners such as Alvaro Siza, Rem Koolhaas, or Herzog & De Meuron.

In his introduction to this book Neil Levine invokes this very dichotomy today whereby Wright's fame seems never to wane among the general public, even as he continues to be a designer who most architects know they should respect but often profess to have no personal artistic connection to his approach to design. And this despite the fact that Wright worked on more building programs than perhaps any of the other revered masters of twentieth-century architecture. Certainly the addition of eight Wright buildings to the UNESCO World Heritage List in 2019 will boost even further tourism to these architectural masterworks, even if it will probably have little effect on changing the meaning of Wright's work to contemporary architectural education and practice. But short of collecting college and university syllabi, this is more an impression than a documented fact to serve as the point of departure here for a reflection on just why Wright's reputation seems to diverge so sharply between popular appeal and professional inspiration. It would be interesting to study the regional differences in Wright's degree of presence or absence from the course work of architecture students. And to discover where abroad his flag is still flying.

I consider the transfer of the Frank Lloyd Wright Foundation Archives to the joint stewardship of Columbia University's Avery Architectural and Fine Arts Library and the Museum of Modern Art to be the most significant long-term accomplishment of the decade I spent at MoMA. The new accessibility of the archives is borne out in the huge spike of outside research requests for archival and rare materials at the Avery Library, and this activity generated as much by outside researchers to the country's most important architectural library as by the use among Columbia students and faculty. In historical studies the impact at Columbia is profound. Wright's work has figured for decades in the curriculum of the undergraduate required course known popularly as Art Humanities or officially—despite much soul-searching of its being out of sync with globalism and cultural inclusiveness in the curriculum—as Masterpieces of Western Art. But now with the presence of the drawings related to the buildings, every single Columbia undergraduate's exposure to Wright is greatly amplified by a visit to the drawings in the Avery Archives as part of the course. No less are the undergraduate and graduate courses in both the Department of Art History and in the Ph.D. program of the Graduate School of Architecture, Planning & Preservation inflected to take advantage of the presence of Wright's archive a short walk from the classrooms. The Buell Center for the Study of American Architecture, under the leadership of Professor Reinhold Martin, organized a multi-year research project, "Living in America: Frank Lloyd Wright, Harlem, and Modern Housing," juxtaposing Wright's work on multifamily urban and suburban housing schemes in relationship to the larger issues of public and private engagement with housing in America, replete with its often explicit, and sometimes even implicit, reinforcement of racial exclusion.

The hope that Wright might become relevant to the issues that connect the history of architecture and the built environment to the ongoing politics of spatial practices by forces from design studios to zoning to financial instruments was confirmed by this provocative and highly original insertion of Wright into the larger project of tracing new contours for American architectural history in the twentieth century and beyond. And with it was suggested that the reverence so often enforced for architects' attitudes toward Wright might in part be at the root of his diminished influence. Mies, Le Corbusier, and the Bauhaus have all gained new life by reevaluation, revisionism, and even critical reconsideration. Indeed, it was very much the larger aim of taking on the huge conservation responsibility of the Wright archives that their presence in a major research university—in a library largely open to outside scholars—would be the trampoline for a rebounding of study of Wright's career outside the steady beat of monographic studies. From the first the discussions of MoMA curators and Avery staff to the Frank Lloyd Wright Foundation centered on the multifarious ways in which the settings of a research university library and a premier collection of modernist art and architecture could help reintegrate Wright's achievements in the never-ending work of interpreting afresh the historical significance and indeed resonance of experimental architecture in the twentieth century.

That was precisely the ambitious agenda of the research project that culminated in the exhibition "Unpacking the Archive: Frank Lloyd Wright at 150," staged from 12 June to 1 October 2017 to mark both the 150th birthday of the architect and the fifth anniversary of the transfer of the drawings, papers, photographs, films, models, and certain building fragments—and a single drafting table—from the storehouses of the two Taliesins to New York. The catalog introduction explains in detail the philosophy behind this display, whose main objectives were multifold and experimental. The aim was to encourage a group of, mostly, younger scholars whose research did not focus on or even include Wright's work to engage in that subject and pose fresh questions or approaches to existing ones from a relevant, if not monographically internal, perspective. The show was intended to open up new lines of thinking and research, but also to invite new voices and new perspectives, and to advertise, in a way, that much remains to be done to see Wright's work from today's perspective.

Future historians will no doubt see that many of today's preoccupations, both within and outside the academy, were high on the agenda, including issues of race and identity (Wright's work on schools for African American children for the Rosenwald Foundation or his relationship to Native American cultures), of landscape and infrastructure, of building systems, or of the role of architecture in the modern culture of publicity and the politics of fame, and were all brought to the fore, if by no means exhausted. And other issues were merely suggested such as the role of women designers in the Taliesin Fellowship, clearly evident in some of the film footage that was cleaned and restored from the uncataloged boxes that came with the transfer. In addition to the catalog, the videos recording the discovery process of the guest curators are viewable on YouTube, under MoMA, "How to See."

But the aim was not merely historical, for at a moment when biodiversity, climate change, renewable materials, and affordability of housing are all pressing concerns, as is the relationship of new materials and technologies to the generation of new forms of ornament, we hoped to suggest that Wright had worked on precisely these same issues. We hoped to show that the history of architecture is not a catalog of solutions but a catalyst to joining a conversation on the relationship of previous masterful designs to ongoing challenges of the way we make buildings and landscapes that change the world around us even as they put a roof over our heads.

The jury is out on the impact of the transfer of the archive and on the longer-term effect of an ephemeral display. Many possibilities for the use of the archive by scholars and curators were suggested, and to judge from demand for the collection results are in the offing in terms of architectural history and criticism. But the key outstanding question—since I am confident that a renewal of scholarly interest is already on the horizon—is, Will contemporary architects engage once again with Wright's protean body of work and complex legacy?

For decades after Wright's death the Taliesin Fellowship curated not only the archive but the meaning of what it meant to be engaged with Wright. The fellowship, of course, was founded to keep Wright's notions of "organic architecture" alive and to assure its continued influence in the future. Paradoxically it might just have been counterproductive, since few viewed the work of Taliesin Associated Architects as upholding that dialogue between committed continuity of convictions and periodical renewal and unexpected new departures that makes the study of Wright's many decades of practice so breathtaking a pursuit. Instead Taliesin became a bit of a calcified brand, and Wright's ongoing influence in, say, the practice of those who took up the cause of organicism in Italy in the wake of Bruno Zevi's championing of Wright charted a much more innovative and unexpected course. Is it too late for any such renewed engagement? Is there a way in which Wright might come back into the studio to inspire, rather than our bidding him once again farewell as memories of the 2017 exhibition and the stimulating conference documented in these pages fade from memory.

It seems to me that regeneration will not come from building an unrealized design, such as the boathouse in Buffalo. Nor will the compelling need to rally all forces to protect the great diversity of Wright's work that can be experienced at first hand, which brings together in urgency and in extremis historians, preservationists, architects, and the public to rally for a threatened Wright building, help a renewed conversation of contemporary design. Rather it is by fostering a sense in which Wright was an exploratory designer who posed issues that are still meaningful, from attitudes toward nature to building affordably with innovative low energy-consuming materials, that Wright becomes a person to refer to rather than a venerated deity of an outdated era to be visited perhaps in leisure moments. The change, then, will occur when the question comes up in a design studio—be it a classroom or a professional office—of how to deal with a particular site, how to find a material that can be produced cheaply and perform a multitude of roles in construction, or how to combine an intimate interior with an expansive experience of a horizon, and when the answer is let's look again at how Wright grappled with that in such and such a design. Certainly, for instance, the demonstration that Michael Desmond gives of Wright's geometry in relationship to movement in his video from the 2017 exhibition is exemplary of how Wright's working method can be brought back to life for emerging designers, not as dogma but as exhilarating insight and challenge. At that point a renewal of historical and design engagement with the archive can chart further trajectories for what we tried to map in sketch form in "Unpacking the Archive"—a way in which Wright again becomes part of design culture and not simply a cherished heritage.

CONTRIBUTORS

BARRY BERGDOLL is the Meyer Schapiro Professor of Modern Architectural History at Columbia University and curator in the Department of Architecture and Design at the Museum of Modern Art, where from 2007 to 2013 he served as the Philip Johnson Chief Curator of Architecture and Design. At MoMA he organized, curated, and consulted on several major architecture exhibitions, including most recently (with Jennifer Gray), "Frank Lloyd Wright at 150: Unpacking the Archive" and, in 2014, "Frank Lloyd Wright and the City: Density vs. Dispersal." Bergdoll is author or editor of numerous publications. He served as president of the Society of Architectural Historians from 2006 to 2008, Slade Professor of Fine Art at Cambridge University in 2011, and in 2013 delivered the 62nd A.W. Mellon Lectures in the Fine Arts at the National Gallery of Art in Washington, D.C.

DANIEL BLUESTONE is Director of the Preservation Studies Program and Professor of the History of Art and Architecture at Boston University. His *Buildings, Landscapes, and Memory: Case Studies in Historic Preservation* received the Society of Architectural Historians' 2013 Antoinette Forrester Downing Book Award for "the most outstanding publication devoted to historical topics in the preservation field that enhances the understanding and protection of the built environment." The book surveys the changing history, nature, and politics of historic preservation in the United States between the early nineteenth century and the present. His *Constructing Chicago* (1991) was awarded the American Institute of Architects International Book Award and the National Historic Preservation book prize.

JEAN-LOUIS COHEN, who trained as an architect and a historian, has held a chair at New York University's Institute of Fine Arts since 1994. Twenty years later he was also appointed a guest professor at the Collège de France. His forty books include *Architecture in Uniform* (2011), *The Future of Archi-*

tecture since 1889 (2012), and *Le Corbusier: An Atlas of Modern Landscapes* (2013). He has curated numerous exhibitions, including "Building a New New World," at the Canadian Centre for Architecture (1995); "Interférences / Interferenzen—Architecture, Allemagne, France", at the Musées de Strasbourg (2013); and "L'Aventure Le Corbusier," at the Centre Pompidou" (1987).

NEIL LEVINE is Emmet Blakeney Gleason Emeritus Professor of History of Art and Architecture Emeritus at Harvard University. He has published numerous articles and essays on subjects dealing with eighteenth-, nineteenth-, and twentieth-century architecture in Europe and the United States. Much of Levine's work has focused on Frank Lloyd Wright, including *The Architecture of Frank Lloyd Wright* (1996) and *The Urbanism of Frank Lloyd Wright* (2016). His *Modern Architecture: Representation and Reality* (2008) was developed from his Slade Lectures on Fine Art at Cambridge University. A Fellow of the American Academy of Arts and Sciences, he has also devoted years of service to the Frank Lloyd Wright Building Conservancy.

RICHARD LONGSTRETH is Professor Emeritus of American Studies at George Washington University, where he taught architectural and urban history and directed the Graduate Program in Historic Preservation from 1983 to 2018. He has served as president of the Society of Architectural Historians and the Frank Lloyd Wright Building Conservancy. Longstreth has written extensively on a range of subjects from campus planning to retail architecture, urban renewal to tract housing. Four of his ten books have won six national awards. He has edited six volumes and has contributed chapters to twenty others. Since the early 1970s he has been involved in preservation initiatives at the national, state, and local levels, in both public and private sectors.

CAMMIE MCATEE is a Montreal-based historian and curator. She holds a doctorate in art and architectural history from Harvard University. She has curated many exhibitions and published widely in the field of postwar architecture and design. She is the coeditor of *The Politics of Furniture: Identity, Diplomacy and Persuasion in Post-War Interiors* (with Fredie Floré, 2017), editor of *Montreal's Geodesic Dreams: Jeffrey Lindsay and the Fuller Research Foundation Canadian Division* (2017), and lead researcher and editorial consultant for an exhibition and book on BBPR's Canada Pavilion at the Venice Biennale (National Gallery of Canada, 2018–20). She is currently working on a history of the international expansion of the modern furniture company Knoll.

DIETRICH NEUMANN is Professor of History of Art and Architecture and Director of Urban Studies at Brown University, where he has taught since 1991. Trained as an architect in Munich and at the Architectural Association in London, Neumann subsequently received his Ph.D. from Munich University. He writes on modern European and American architecture and has organized a number of traveling exhibitions. Among his books are volumes on the history of movie set design, architectural illumination, Richard Neutra's Windshield House for the Brown family, and a children's book about the Empire State Building. He is currently finishing a biography of Ludwig Mies van der Rohe. He is a past president of the Society of Architectural Historians.

JACK QUINAN is Distinguished Service Professor Emeritus at the State University of New York at Buffalo. He studied art history at Dartmouth College and Brown University. In 1975 he began a long-term involvement in Wright's Darwin D. Martin house, which led to the formation of the Frank Lloyd Wright Building Conservancy, the acquisition of the Wright-Martin Papers, and the restoration of the Martin house complex. He is the author of *Frank Lloyd Wright's Larkin Building: Myth and Fact* (1987), *Frank Lloyd Wright's Martin House: Architecture as Portraiture* (2004), *Frank Lloyd Wright's Buffalo Venture* (2012), and numerous articles and book chapters on Wright. He is currently working on a study of Wright and phenomenology.

TIMOTHY M. ROHAN is an Associate Professor in the Department of the History of Art and Architecture at the University of Massachusetts, Amherst. His research focuses on architecture and design from the mid-twentieth century to the present. He is the author of *The Architecture of Paul Rudolph* (2014) and also edited a volume of scholarly articles about the architect, *Reassessing Rudolph* (2017). Rohan has published chapters in edited volumes about subjects ranging from Brutalism to disco architecture, as well as articles in a number of periodicals, including the *Journal of the Society of Architectural Historians* and *Art in America*. He is working on a book about the interactions between lighting, furnishings, and media in late-twentieth-century Manhattan residential interiors.

ALICE THOMINE-BERRADA, who trained at the École des Chartes and the École du Patrimoine in Paris, followed by a postdoctoral fellowship at the Canadian Centre for Architecture, published the first of her books and catalogs in 2004 based on her Ph.D. dissertation on the important nineteenth-century French architect Emile Vaudremer. She was head of the programs for history of architecture at the Institut National d'Histoire de l'Art between

2000 and 2007. From 2008 to 2018, she was a curator at the Musée d'Orsay and now is director of the Museum of the École des Beaux-Arts. Between 2015 and 2018, she co-organized and taught a graduate seminar on Frank Lloyd Wright at the Université de Lorraine in Nancy, involving an ongoing lecture series at the Orsay museum devoted to Wright.

INDEX

Page references in italics refer to illustrations. Bolded page references refer to buildings.

Wright, Frank Lloyd (*continued*)

—, buildings: **Auldbrass plantation,** near Yemessee, S.C., 212n67; **Barnsdall house,** Los Angeles, 22, 31; **Barton house,** Buffalo, 10, 146–51, *147, 149, 150, 151,* 174n8, 174nn12–19; **Broadacre City** (project), 13, 66, 67, 72; **Coonley house,** Riverside, *22, 29,* 31, 36, 61; **Cooper house** (project), La Grange, Ill., 111n24; **Dana house,** Springfield, Ill., 22, 61; **Doheny Ranch** (project), Beverly Hills, 20, 22; **Ennis house,** Los Angeles, 101; **Fallingwater,** Kaufmann house, Mill Run, Pa., 2, 5, 10, 11, 57, 69, *70,* 72, 76, *77,* 95, *95,* 99, 113n40, 115n56, 121, 154–57, *155, 156,* 167, 175nn26–27, 185–87, *186,* 189; **Florida Southern College,** Lakeland, 9, 122; **Francis Apartments,** Chicago, 199; **Francisco Terrace,** Chicago, 199, *200,* 211n61; **Freeman house,** Los Angeles, 61, 101; **Gillin house,** Dallas, 141; **Golden Beacon** apartment and office tower (project), Chicago, 232; **Gordon Strong Automobile Objective** (project), Dickerson, Md., 19, 98; **Guggenheim Museum,** New York, 2, 5, 68, *68,* 72, 74, 83, *86,* 90, 91, *91,* 95, 98, *108,* 109, 115n51, 126, 135, 232, 257; **Hanna house,** Palo Alto, Cal., 57, 173n1; **Heurtley house,** Oak Park, Ill., 61; **Hoffman house,** Rye, N.Y., 204n7; **House on the Mesa** (project), 37–38, *38;* **Imperial Hotel,** Tokyo, 10, 11, 13, 22, 30, 31, 188, 190–93, *192,* 199, 248–49; **Jacobs house (I),** Madison, Wis., 13, 39; **Jacobs house (II),** Middletown, Wis., 13, 151; **Johnson Wax Building (S. C. Johnson Company Administration Building),** Racine, Wis., 2, 5, 39, 98, 99, 100, 101, 102–4, *104,* 114n50, 115n52, 115n54, 116n66, 117n69, 121, 136, 141, 180–81; **Kalita Humpgreys Theater,** Dallas, 10, 159–60, *159;* **Lake Geneva Hotel,** Lake Geneva, Wis., 200; **Lake Tahoe Resort** (project), Cal., 20, 22; **Larkin Company Administration Building,** Buffalo, 2, 9, 10, 17, 20, 21, 22, 27, *28,* 29, 31, 34, 47n52, 52, 56, 137, 141, 180, 181–83, *183,* 184, 203n3, 204n11; **Laurent house,** Rockford, Ill., 10, 151–53, *152, 153,* 163; **Little house,** Deephaven, Minn., 199–200; **Luxfer Prism building** (project), 31; **Marin County Civic Center,** San Rafael, Cal., 2, 13; **Martin house,** Buffalo, 9, 22, 27, *29,* 42, 47n52; **Masieri Memorial** (project), Venice, 12, 181, 241–42, 244, *244,* 246, 249, 250, 251, 253; **Mc-Cord house** (project), North Arlington, N.J., 100; **Midway Gardens,** Chicago, 31, 180;

Mile-High Skyscraper (project), 232; **Millard house,** Pasadena, Cal., 20, 22, 101, 242; **Moore house,** Oak Park, Ill., 180; **National Life Insurance Company building** (project), Chicago, 19; **New Theater** (project), Woodstock, N.Y., 158–60; **Park City Inn Hotel and City National Bank,** Mason City, Iowa, 200; **Pauson house,** Phoenix, 117n67; **Pew house,** Shorewood Hills, Wis., 154; **Pope-Leighey house,** Fairfax Co., Va., 10, 187–89, *189,* 208n41; Prairie houses, 52, 56, **60,** 61, 74, 146 (*see also* Prairie School); **Rayward house** (New Canaan, Conn.), 126; **Roberts house,** River Forest, Ill., 180; **Robie house,** Chicago, 10, 11, 18, 20, 22, 54, 61, 180, 181, *182,* 184, 187, 188, 189, 213–37, *227, 232, 234;* **Rosenbaum house,** Florence, Ala., 39, 121, *121,* 137; **"Small House with Lots of Room in It"** (project for *Ladies Home Journal*), 146–47; **Steel Cathedral** (project), 31; **St. Mark's-in-the-Bowerie Tower** (project), New York, 31; **Storer house,** Los Angeles, 10, 201, *201;* **Unitarian Meeting House (First Unitarian Society of Madison Meeting House),** Shorewood Hills, Wis., 95–96, 204n7; **Unity Temple,** Oak Park, Ill., 2, 17, 21, 22, 34, 49n84, 135; Usonian houses, 7, 40, 57, 67, 72, 74, 122, 132; **Walker house,** Carmel, Calif., 154; **Wingspread,** Racine, Wis., 57; **Williams house,** River Forest, Ill., 43n4; **Willits house,** Highland Park, Ill., 13, 21, 42; **Winslow house,** River Forest, Ill., 43n4, 44n7; **Wright house and studio,** Oak Park, Ill., 10, 180, 197–99, *198;* **David and Gladys Wright house,** Phoenix, 11, 98, 201, *201;* **Yahara Boat Club,** Madison, Wis. (project), 40, 41, *42,* 50n110. *See also* **Taliesin; Taliesin West**

—, exhibitions on, including, 2, 3, 5, 8, 12, 16, 31, 40, 57–59, *58,* 71, 72–73, 75, 101, 102–3, 104–5, *104, 105,* 106, 109n1, 110n3, 111n21, 113n40, 115n56, 115n66, 117n69, 117n72, 117n75, 130, 260, 261–62; "Form Givers at Mid-Century," 84–92, *84, 86, 91;* "Modern Architecture: International Exhibition," 31, 36, 37, 102

—, publication of work, writings, 20–25, *22, 23,* 27–28, 30–31, *30,* 32, 34, 39, 40–41, 44n26, 45n28, 49n84, 51, 52, 54–59, *59, 60,* 61, 62–63, 66, 68, 69–71, 101–2, 107, 138, 204n11; *The Future of Architecture,* 67, 93; *Genius and Mobocracy,* 93; *In the Nature of Materials,* 39; Wasmuth monographs on (1910, 1911), 7, 16, 17, 32, 40, 43n1, 43n4, 53, 60–61, 68

Wright, Henry, Jr. (New York), 96
Wright, Olgivannna, 64
Wurster, William (San Francisco), 87, 111n14

Yale University, 124, 137
Yamasaki, Minoru (Detroit), 111n14

Zeckendorf, William, 11, 184, 190, 231–35, *232*.
   See also Webb & Knapp

Zervos, Christian, 54
Zevaço, Jean-Francois (Casablanca), 7, 73
Zevi, Bruno, 7, 69–71, *71,* 72, 73, 76, 241–42, 249,
   261; *Towards an Organic Architecture,* 69,
   70, 242
Zimbacca, Dominique (Lyon), 7, 58, 74
Zodchii, 61
Zurich Federal Institute of Technology, 223